D0883917

IR

PUNISHER MAX FRANK

WRITER
JASON AARON

ARTIST
STEVE DILLON

COLORIST
MATT HOLLINGSWORTH

LETTERER
VC'S CORY PETIT

COVER ARTIST
DAVE JOHNSON

EDITOR
SEBASTIAN GIRNER

COLLECTION EDITOR JENNIFER GRÜNWALD
EDITORIAL ASSISTANTS JAMES EMMETT & JOE HOCHSTEIN
ASSISTANT EDITORS ALEX STARBUCK & NELSON RIBEIRO
EDITOR, SPECIAL PROJECTS MARK D. BEAZLEY
SENIOR EDITOR, SPECIAL PROJECTS JEFF YOUNGQUIST
SENIOR VICE PRESIDENT OF SALES DAVID GABRIEL
SVP OF BRAND PLANNING & COMMUNICATIONS MICHAEL PASCIULLO
BOOK DESIGN JEFF POWELL

EDITOR IN CHIEF AXEL ALONSO
CHIEF CREATIVE OFFICER JOE QUESADA
PUBLISHER DAN BUCKLEY
EXECUTIVE PRODUCER ALAN FINE

JNISHERMAX: FRANK. Contains material originally published
magazine form as PUNISHERMAX #12-16. First printing 2011.
ardcover ISBN# 978-0-7851-5208-8. Softcover ISBN# 978-0-7851-
209-5. Published by MARVEL WORLDWIDE, INC., a subsidiary of MARVEL
NTERTAINMENT, LLC. OFFICE OF PUBLICATION: 135 West 50th Street, New York,
√ 10020. Copyright © 2011 and 2012 Marvel Characters, Inc. All rights reserved.
ardcover: $24.99 per copy in the U.S. and $27.99 in Canada (GST #R127032852).
oftcover: $19.99 per copy in the U.S. and $21.99 in Canada (GST #R127032852). Canadian
greement #40668537. All characters featured in this issue and the distinctive names and
enesses thereof, and all related indicia are trademarks of Marvel Characters, Inc. No similarity
tween any of the names, characters, persons, and/or institutions in this magazine with those of
y living or dead person or institution is intended, and any such similarity which may exist is purely
incidental. **Printed in the U.S.A.** ALAN FINE, EVP - Office of the President, Marvel Worldwide, Inc.
d EVP & CMO Marvel Characters B.V.; DAN BUCKLEY, Publisher & President - Print, Animation &
gital Divisions; JOE QUESADA, Chief Creative Officer; JIM SOKOLOWSKI, Chief Operating Officer;
VID BOGART, SVP of Business Affairs & Talent Management; TOM BREVOORT, SVP of Publishing;
B. CEBULSKI, SVP of Creator & Content Development; DAVID GABRIEL, SVP of Publishing Sales
Circulation; MICHAEL PASCIULLO, SVP of Brand Planning & Communications; JIM O'KEEFE, VP
Operations & Logistics; DAN CARR, Executive Director of Publishing Technology; SUSAN CRESPI,
itorial Operations Manager; ALEX MORALES, Publishing Operations Manager; STAN LEE, Chairman
neritus. For information regarding advertising in Marvel Comics or on Marvel.com, please contact
hn Dokes, SVP Integrated Sales and Marketing, at jdokes@marvel.com. For Marvel subscription
quiries, please call 800-217-9158. **Manufactured between 8/29/2011 and 9/26/2011
ardcover), and 8/29/2011 and 3/26/2012 (softcover), by R.R. DONNELLEY, INC., SALEM, VA, USA.**
9 8 7 6 5 4 3 2 1

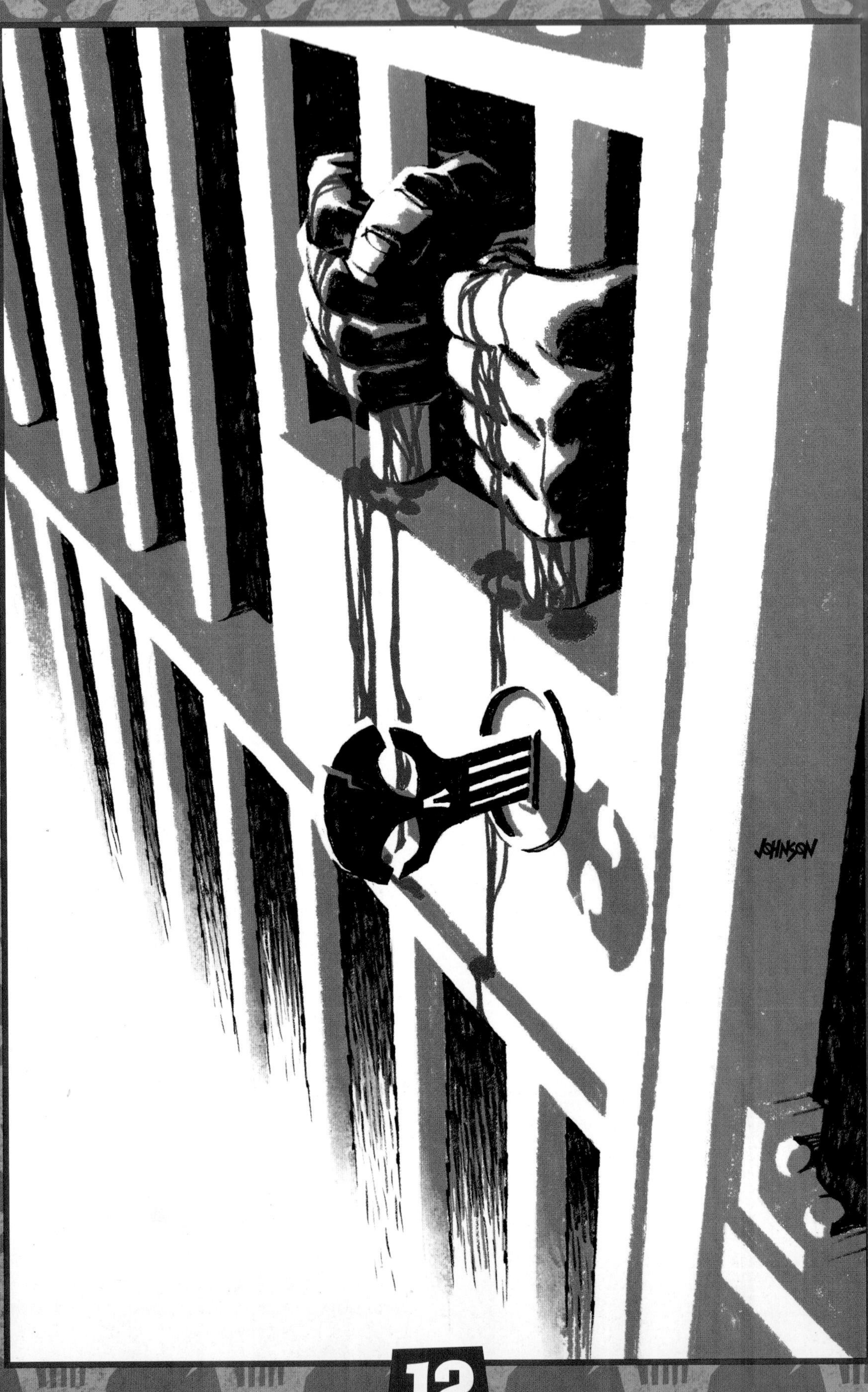
JOHNSON

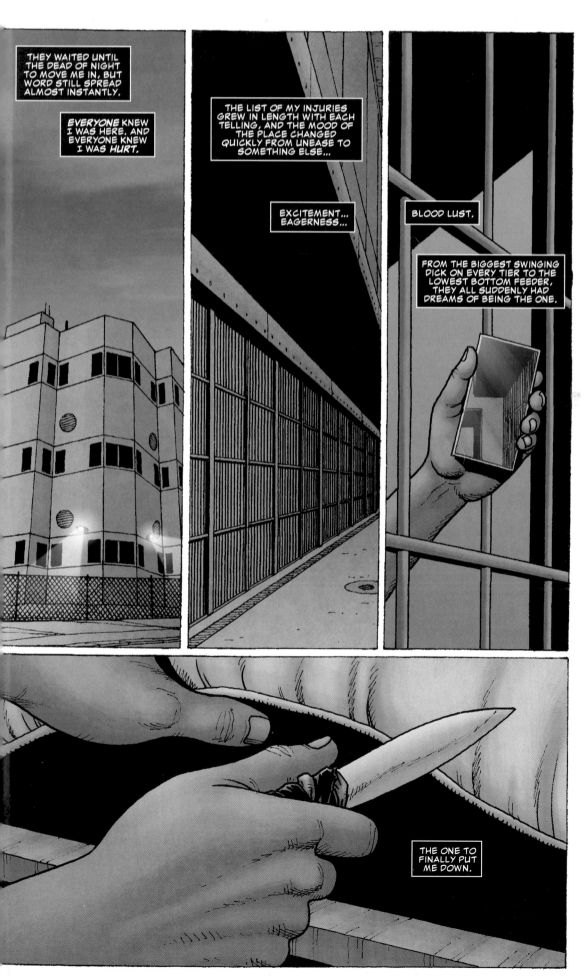

THEY WAITED UNTIL THE DEAD OF NIGHT TO MOVE ME IN, BUT WORD STILL SPREAD ALMOST INSTANTLY.

EVERYONE KNEW I WAS HERE. AND EVERYONE KNEW I WAS HURT.

THE LIST OF MY INJURIES GREW IN LENGTH WITH EACH TELLING, AND THE MOOD OF THE PLACE CHANGED QUICKLY FROM UNEASE TO SOMETHING ELSE...

EXCITEMENT... EAGERNESS...

BLOOD LUST.

FROM THE BIGGEST SWINGING DICK ON EVERY TIER TO THE LOWEST BOTTOM FEEDER, THEY ALL SUDDENLY HAD DREAMS OF BEING THE ONE.

THE ONE TO FINALLY PUT ME DOWN.

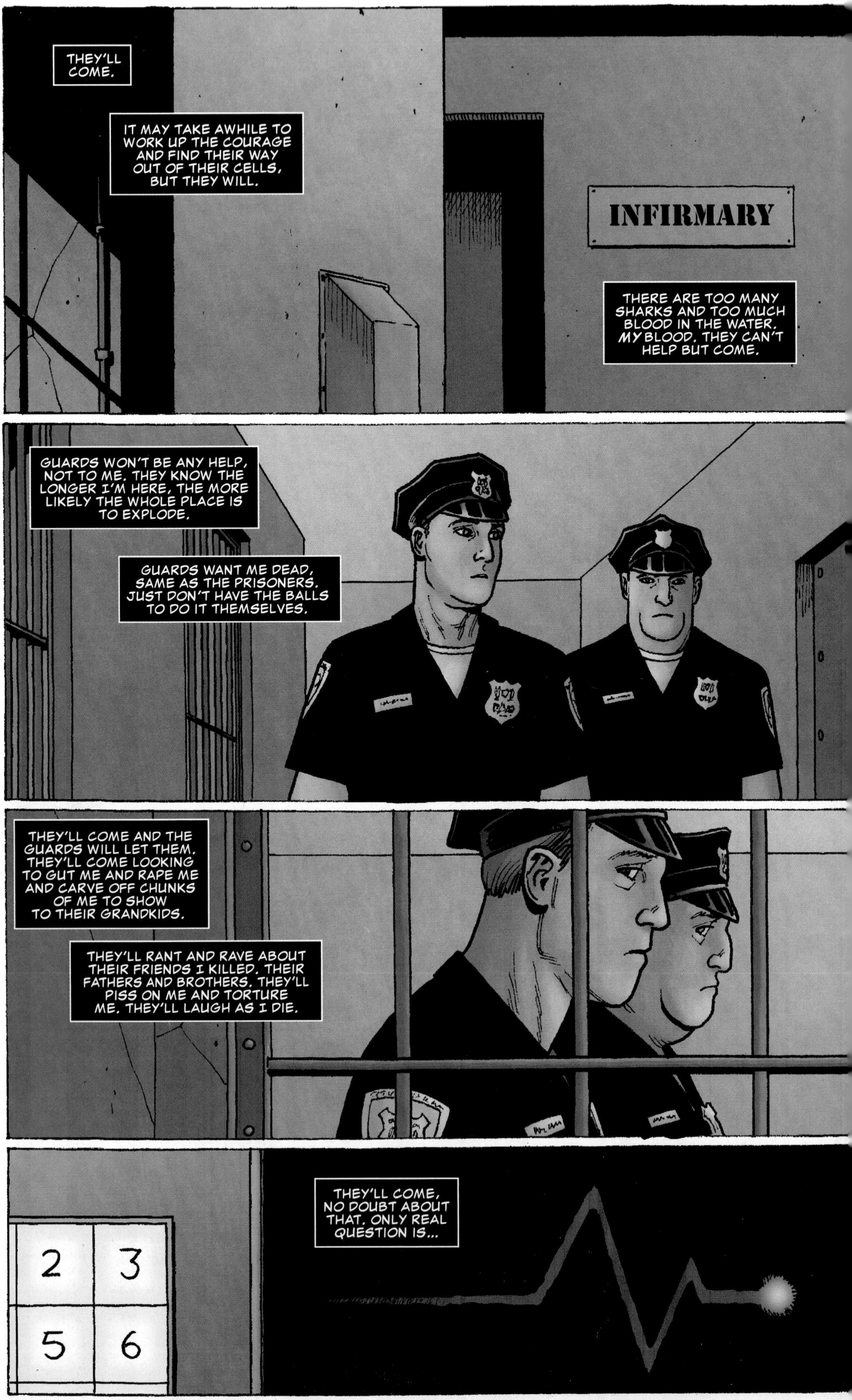

THEY'LL COME.
IT MAY TAKE AWHILE TO WORK UP THE COURAGE AND FIND THEIR WAY OUT OF THEIR CELLS, BUT THEY WILL.
INFIRMARY
THERE ARE TOO MANY SHARKS AND TOO MUCH BLOOD IN THE WATER. MY BLOOD. THEY CAN'T HELP BUT COME.
GUARDS WON'T BE ANY HELP, NOT TO ME. THEY KNOW THE LONGER I'M HERE, THE MORE LIKELY THE WHOLE PLACE IS TO EXPLODE.
GUARDS WANT ME DEAD, SAME AS THE PRISONERS. JUST DON'T HAVE THE BALLS TO DO IT THEMSELVES.
THEY'LL COME AND THE GUARDS WILL LET THEM. THEY'LL COME LOOKING TO GUT ME AND RAPE ME AND CARVE OFF CHUNKS OF ME TO SHOW TO THEIR GRANDKIDS.
THEY'LL RANT AND RAVE ABOUT THEIR FRIENDS I KILLED. THEIR FATHERS AND BROTHERS. THEY'LL PISS ON ME AND TORTURE ME. THEY'LL LAUGH AS I DIE.
THEY'LL COME, NO DOUBT ABOUT THAT. ONLY REAL QUESTION IS...
2 3
5 6

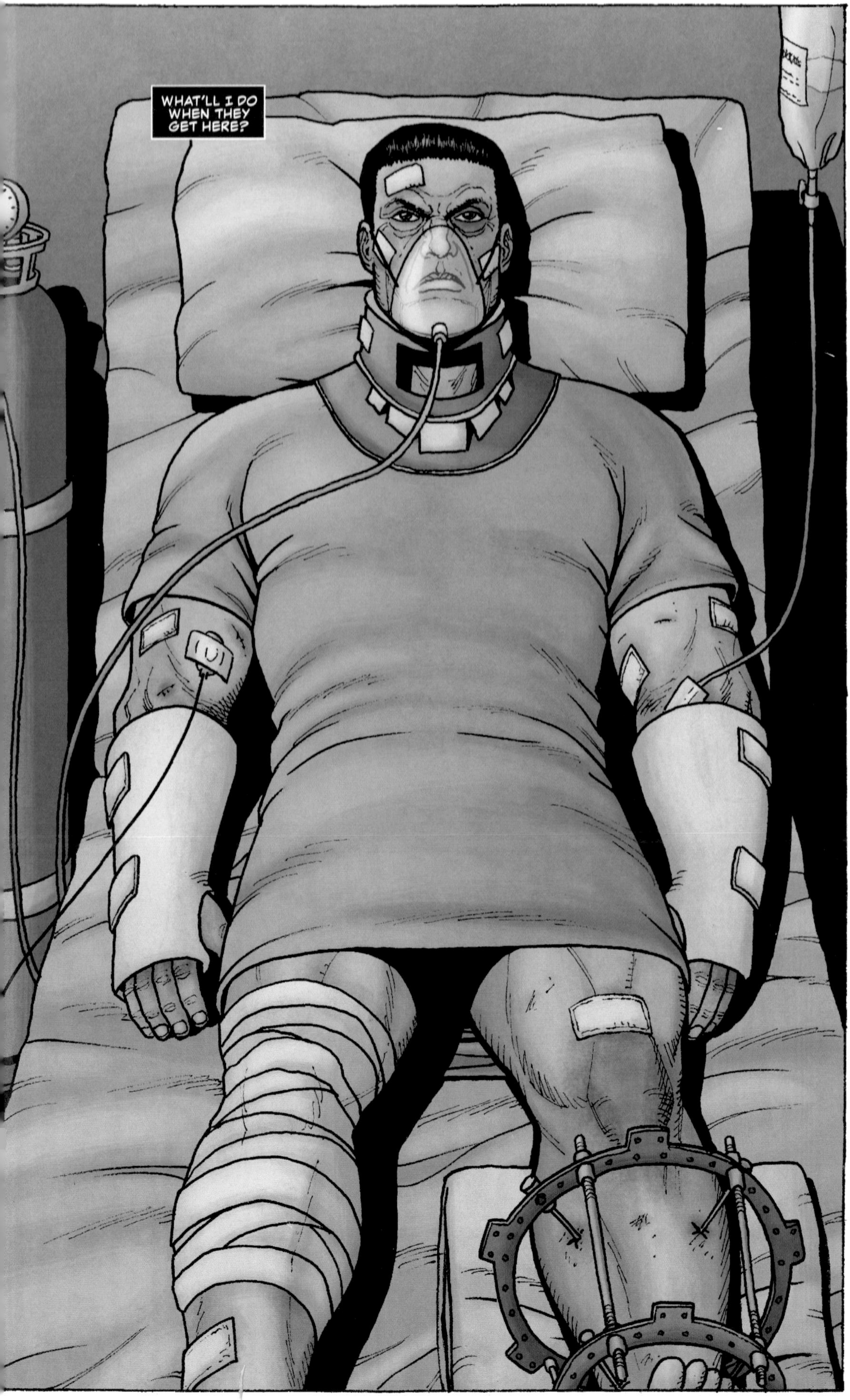
WHAT'LL I DO WHEN THEY GET HERE?

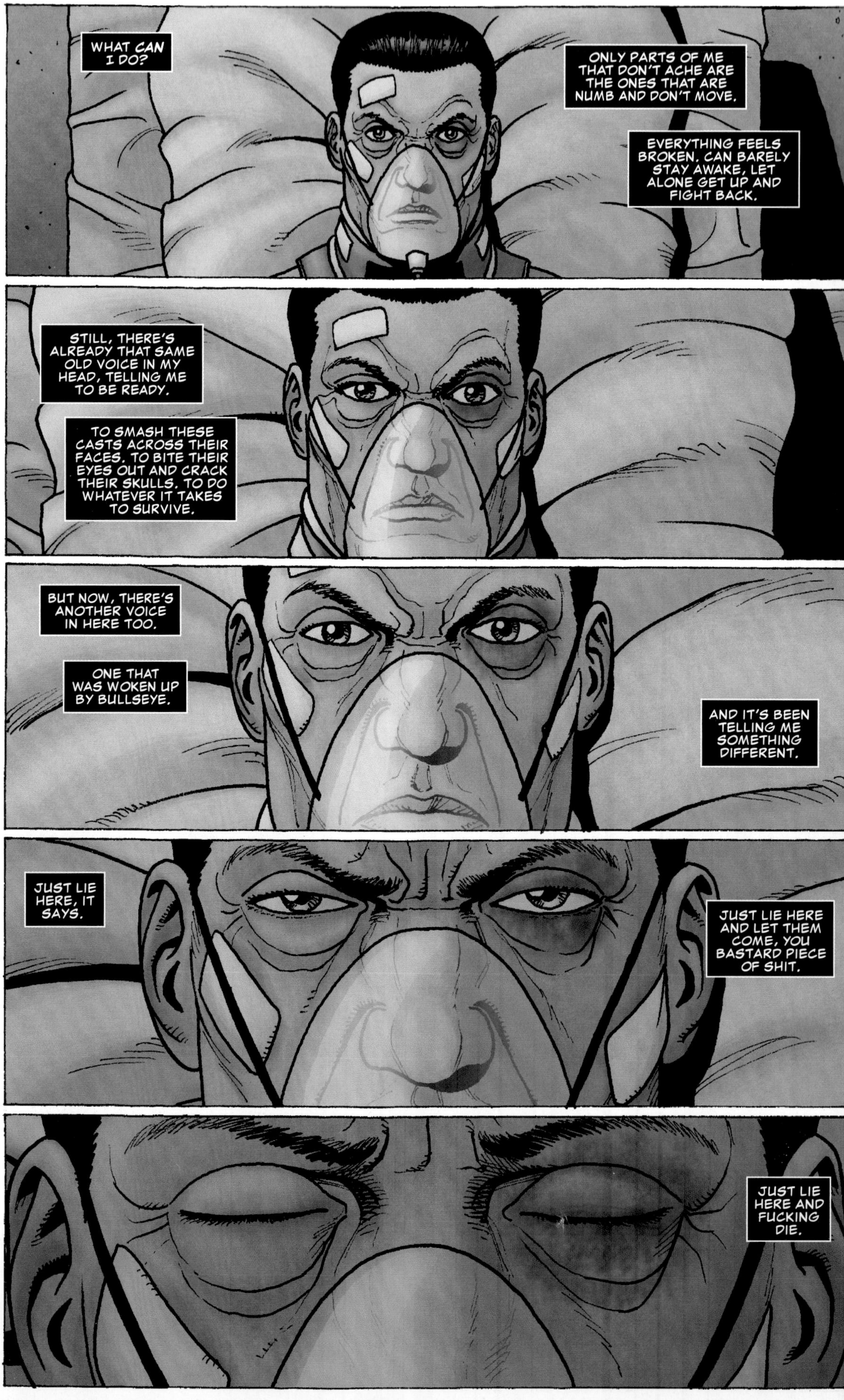

WHAT CAN I DO?
ONLY PARTS OF ME THAT DON'T ACHE ARE THE ONES THAT ARE NUMB AND DON'T MOVE.
EVERYTHING FEELS BROKEN. CAN BARELY STAY AWAKE, LET ALONE GET UP AND FIGHT BACK.
STILL, THERE'S ALREADY THAT SAME OLD VOICE IN MY HEAD, TELLING ME TO BE READY.
TO SMASH THESE CASTS ACROSS THEIR FACES. TO BITE THEIR EYES OUT AND CRACK THEIR SKULLS. TO DO WHATEVER IT TAKES TO SURVIVE.
BUT NOW, THERE'S ANOTHER VOICE IN HERE TOO.
ONE THAT WAS WOKEN UP BY BULLSEYE.
AND IT'S BEEN TELLING ME SOMETHING DIFFERENT.
JUST LIE HERE, IT SAYS.
JUST LIE HERE AND LET THEM COME, YOU BASTARD PIECE OF SHIT.
JUST LIE HERE AND FUCKING DIE.

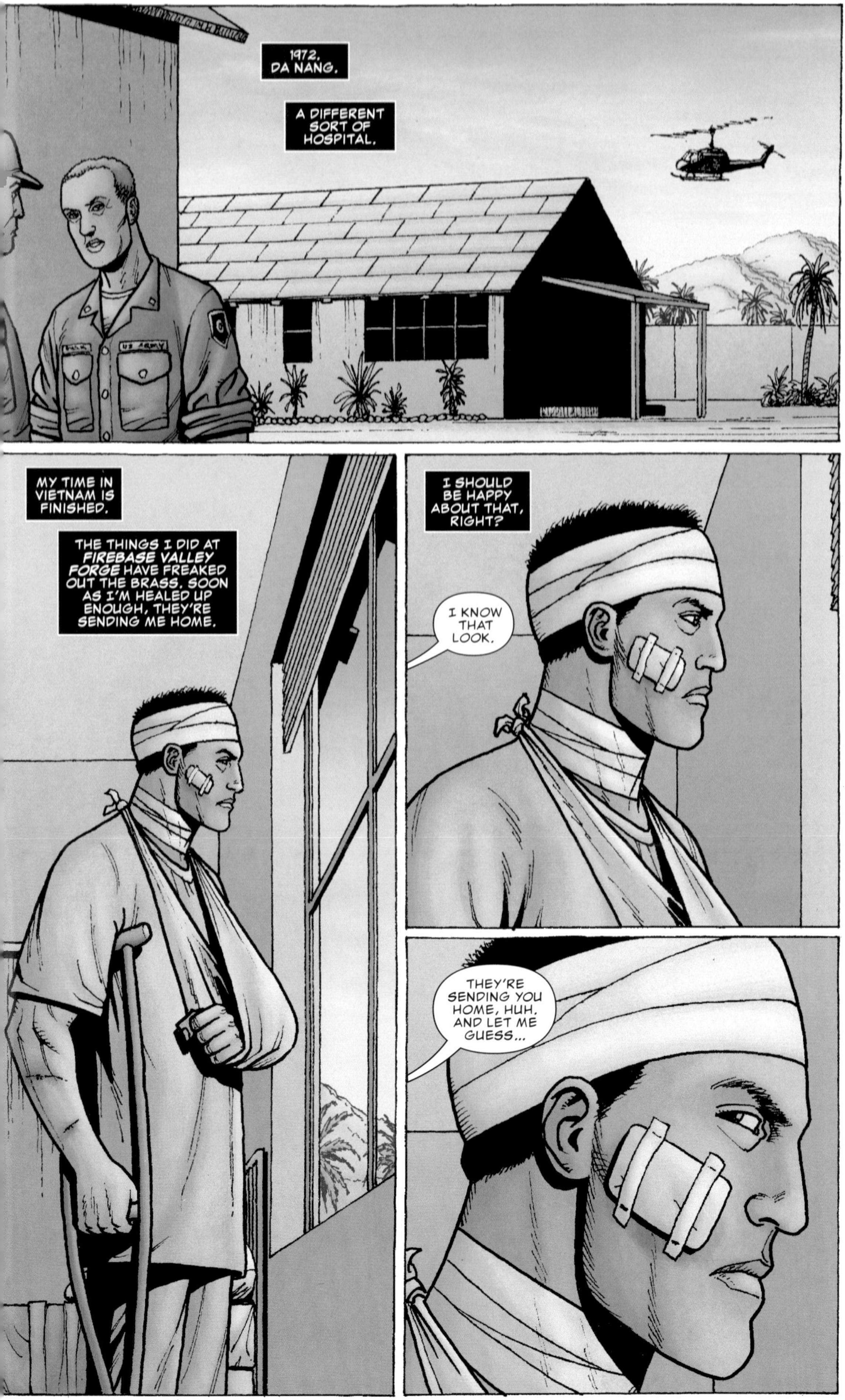
1972, DA NANG.
A DIFFERENT SORT OF HOSPITAL.
MY TIME IN VIETNAM IS FINISHED.
THE THINGS I DID AT FIREBASE VALLEY FORGE HAVE FREAKED OUT THE BRASS. SOON AS I'M HEALED UP ENOUGH, THEY'RE SENDING ME HOME.
I SHOULD BE HAPPY ABOUT THAT, RIGHT?
I KNOW THAT LOOK.
THEY'RE SENDING YOU HOME, HUH. AND LET ME GUESS...

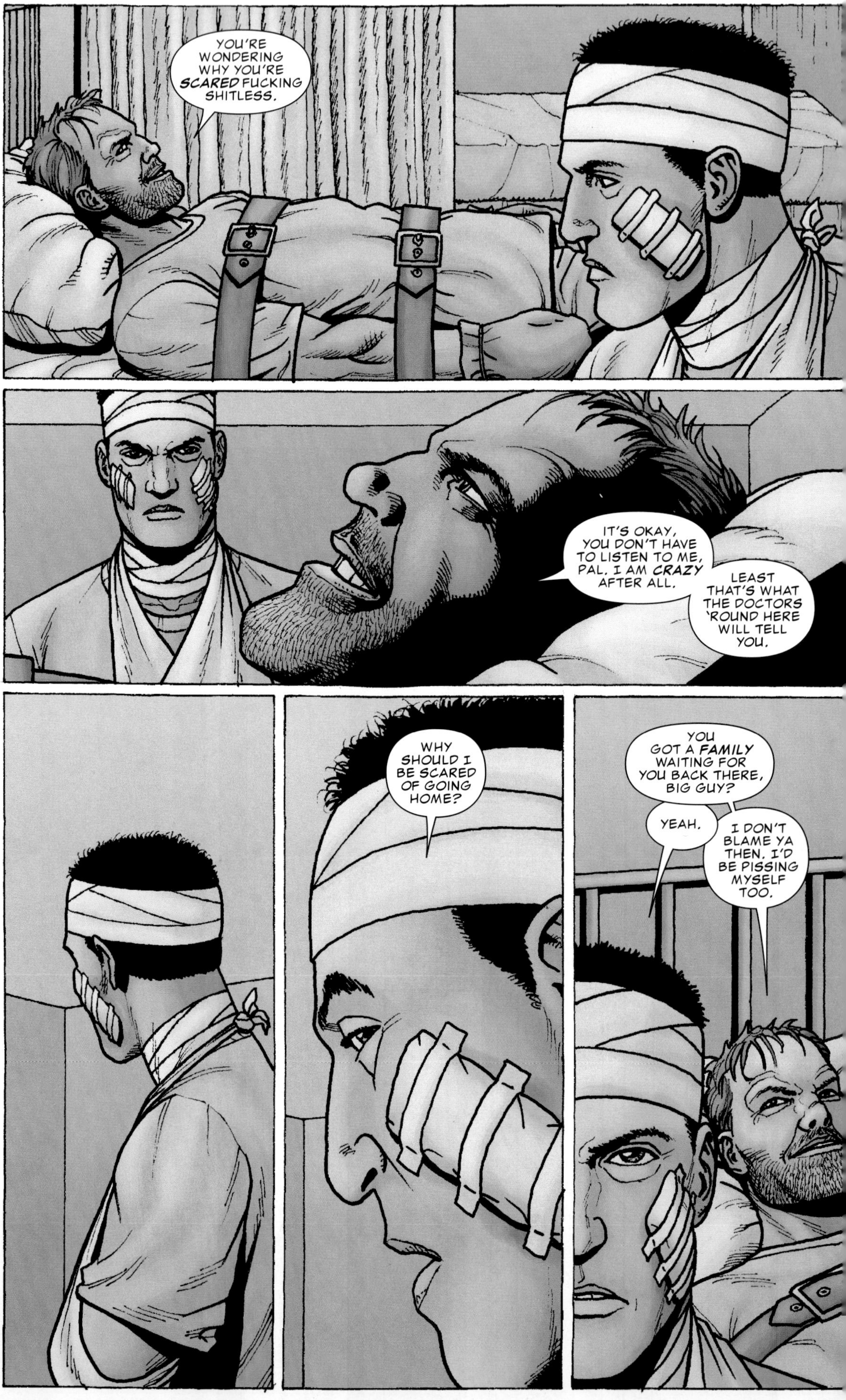
YOU'RE WONDERING WHY YOU'RE SCARED FUCKING SHITLESS.
IT'S OKAY, YOU DON'T HAVE TO LISTEN TO ME, PAL. I AM CRAZY AFTER ALL.
LEAST THAT'S WHAT THE DOCTORS 'ROUND HERE WILL TELL YOU.
WHY SHOULD I BE SCARED OF GOING HOME?
YOU GOT A FAMILY WAITING FOR YOU BACK THERE, BIG GUY?
YEAH.
I DON'T BLAME YA THEN. I'D BE PISSING MYSELF TOO.

FUCK YOU, YOU DON'T KNOW ME, ASSHOLE.

YOU'RE RIGHT, I DON'T. I DON'T KNOW WHERE YOU BEEN OR WHAT YOU DONE.

BUT I SURE AS HELL KNOW A *LIFER* WHEN I SEE ONE.

BET IF I ASKED YOU TO KILL A MAN WITH A KA-BAR, YOU COULD OFFER UP A LENGTHY ANSWER, DEMONSTRATING DOZENS OF DIFFERENT OPTIONS.

BUT WHAT IF I WAS TO ASK YOU HOW TO HOLD A BABY? OR HOW TO ROCK ONE TO SLEEP WHEN THEY'RE CRYING?

BET YOU CAN FIELD STRIP AN M-16 WITH YOUR EYES CLOSED, BUT WHAT DO YOU REMEMBER ABOUT PLEASURING A WOMAN?

NOT ONE OF THOSE WHORES DOWN ON DAC LOP STREET, BUT A REAL WOMAN. A WIFE. YOU THINK YOU'RE STILL CAPABLE OF TALKING TO HER, OF TELLING HER SWEET THINGS?

WHEN WAS THE LAST TIME YOU CARESSED SOMETHING THAT WASN'T A TRIGGER?

YOU'D BE LESS SCARED WALKING OUT INTO THE BUSH RIGHT NOW, KNEE-DEEP IN CHARLIES, AND YOU WITH NOTHING BUT YOUR DICK IN YOUR HAND, THAN YOU ARE ABOUT GOING HOME TO FACE THAT FAMILY OF YOURS, TELL ME I'M WRONG.

DYING? THAT DON'T MEAN SHIT TO YOU. NO...

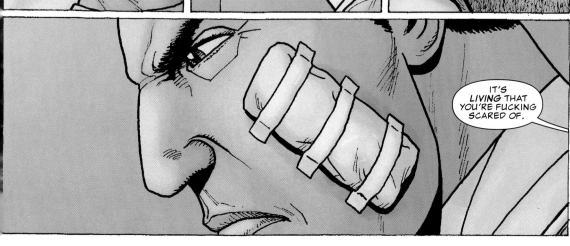

IT'S *LIVING* THAT YOU'RE FUCKING SCARED OF.

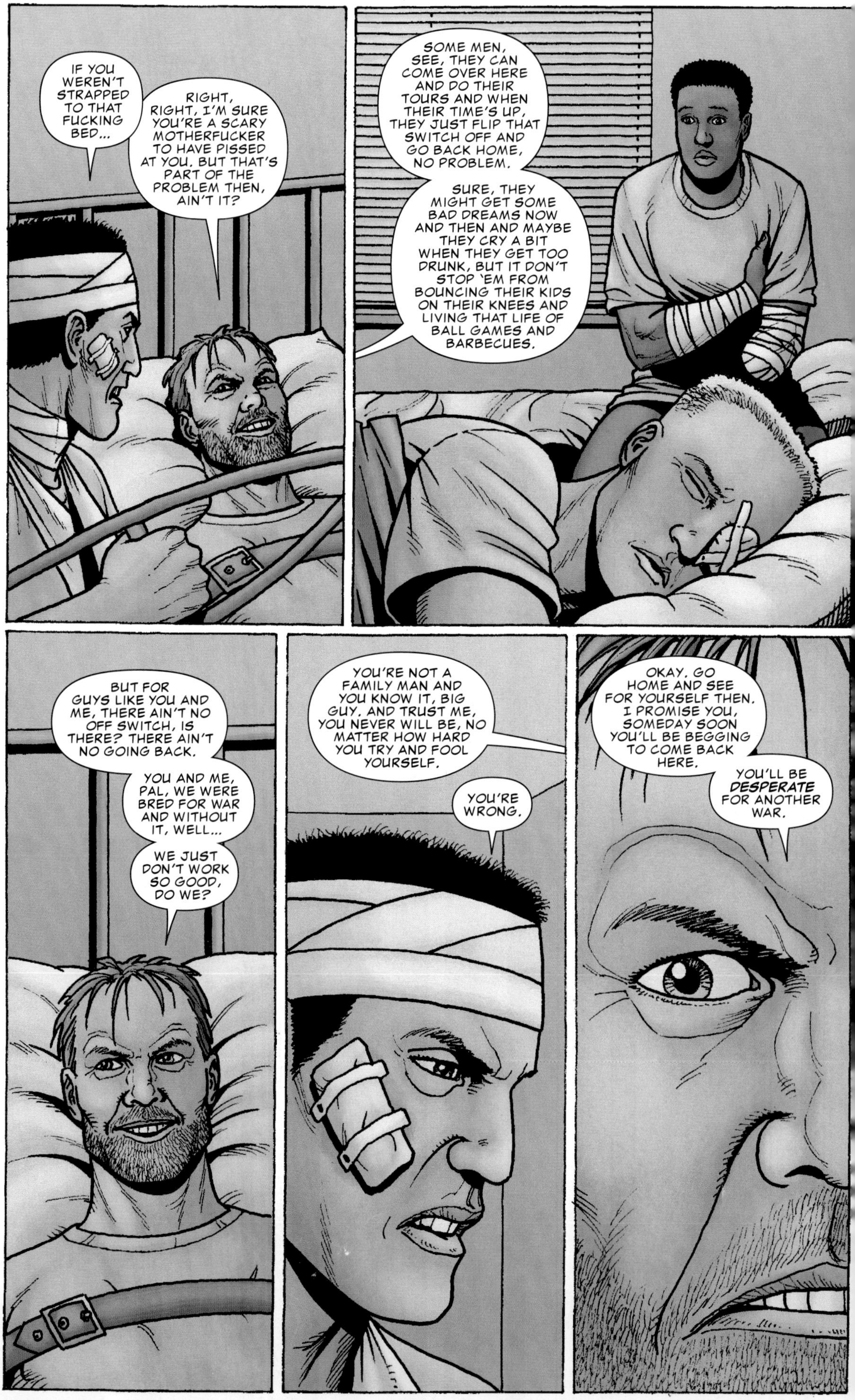
IF YOU WEREN'T STRAPPED TO THAT FUCKING BED...
RIGHT, RIGHT, I'M SURE YOU'RE A SCARY MOTHERFUCKER TO HAVE PISSED AT YOU. BUT THAT'S PART OF THE PROBLEM THEN, AIN'T IT?
SOME MEN, SEE, THEY CAN COME OVER HERE AND DO THEIR TOURS AND WHEN THEIR TIME'S UP, THEY JUST FLIP THAT SWITCH OFF AND GO BACK HOME, NO PROBLEM.
SURE, THEY MIGHT GET SOME BAD DREAMS NOW AND THEN AND MAYBE THEY CRY A BIT WHEN THEY GET TOO DRUNK, BUT IT DON'T STOP 'EM FROM BOUNCING THEIR KIDS ON THEIR KNEES AND LIVING THAT LIFE OF BALL GAMES AND BARBECUES.
BUT FOR GUYS LIKE YOU AND ME, THERE AIN'T NO OFF SWITCH, IS THERE? THERE AIN'T NO GOING BACK.
YOU AND ME, PAL, WE WERE BRED FOR WAR AND WITHOUT IT, WELL...
WE JUST DON'T WORK SO GOOD, DO WE?
YOU'RE NOT A FAMILY MAN AND YOU KNOW IT, BIG GUY. AND TRUST ME, YOU NEVER WILL BE, NO MATTER HOW HARD YOU TRY AND FOOL YOURSELF.
YOU'RE WRONG.
OKAY. GO HOME AND SEE FOR YOURSELF THEN. I PROMISE YOU, SOMEDAY SOON YOU'LL BE BEGGING TO COME BACK HERE.
YOU'LL BE *DESPERATE* FOR ANOTHER WAR.

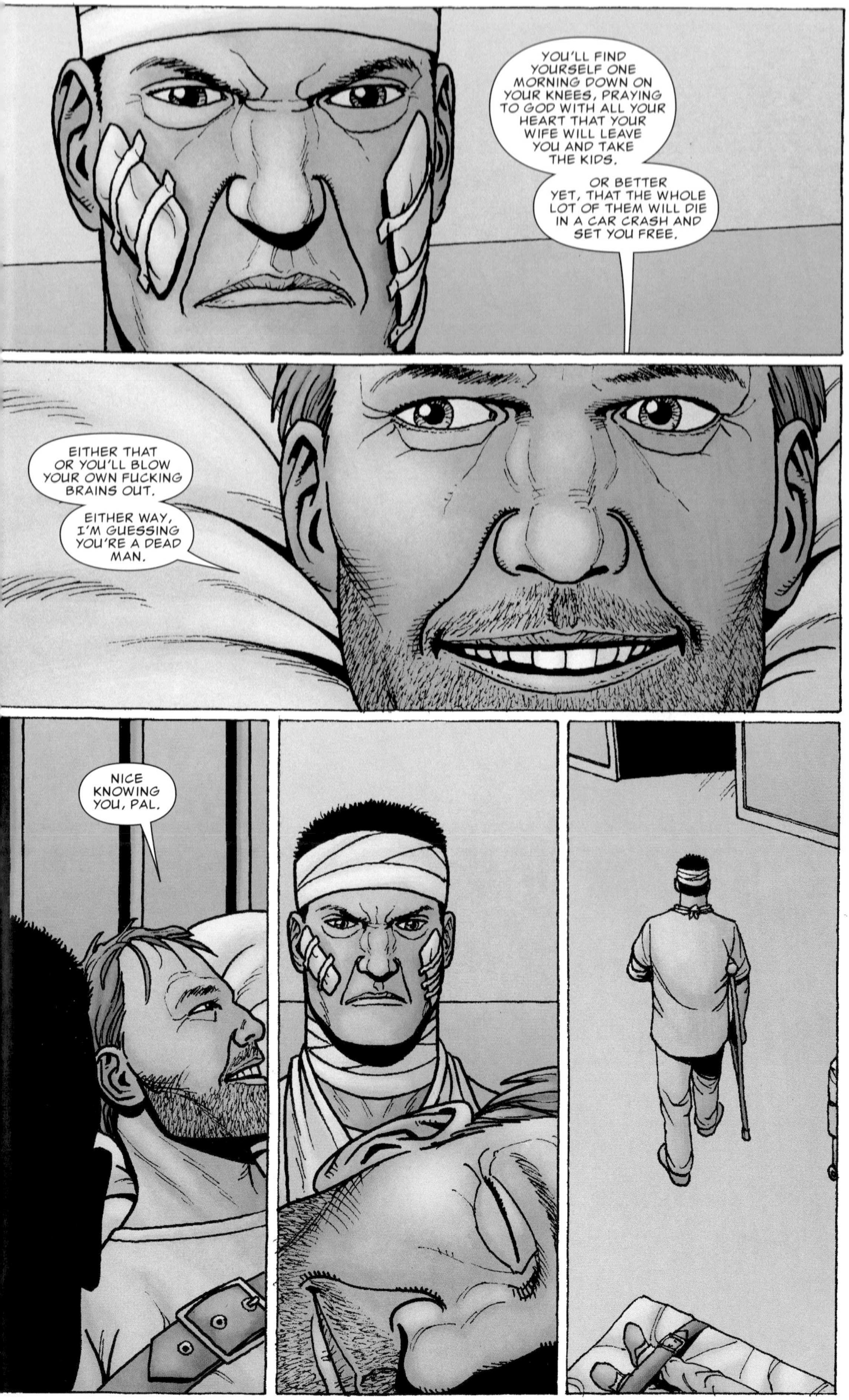
YOU'LL FIND YOURSELF ONE MORNING DOWN ON YOUR KNEES, PRAYING TO GOD WITH ALL YOUR HEART THAT YOUR WIFE WILL LEAVE YOU AND TAKE THE KIDS.
OR BETTER YET, THAT THE WHOLE LOT OF THEM WILL DIE IN A CAR CRASH AND SET YOU FREE.
EITHER THAT OR YOU'LL BLOW YOUR OWN FUCKING BRAINS OUT.
EITHER WAY, I'M GUESSING YOU'RE A DEAD MAN.
NICE KNOWING YOU, PAL.

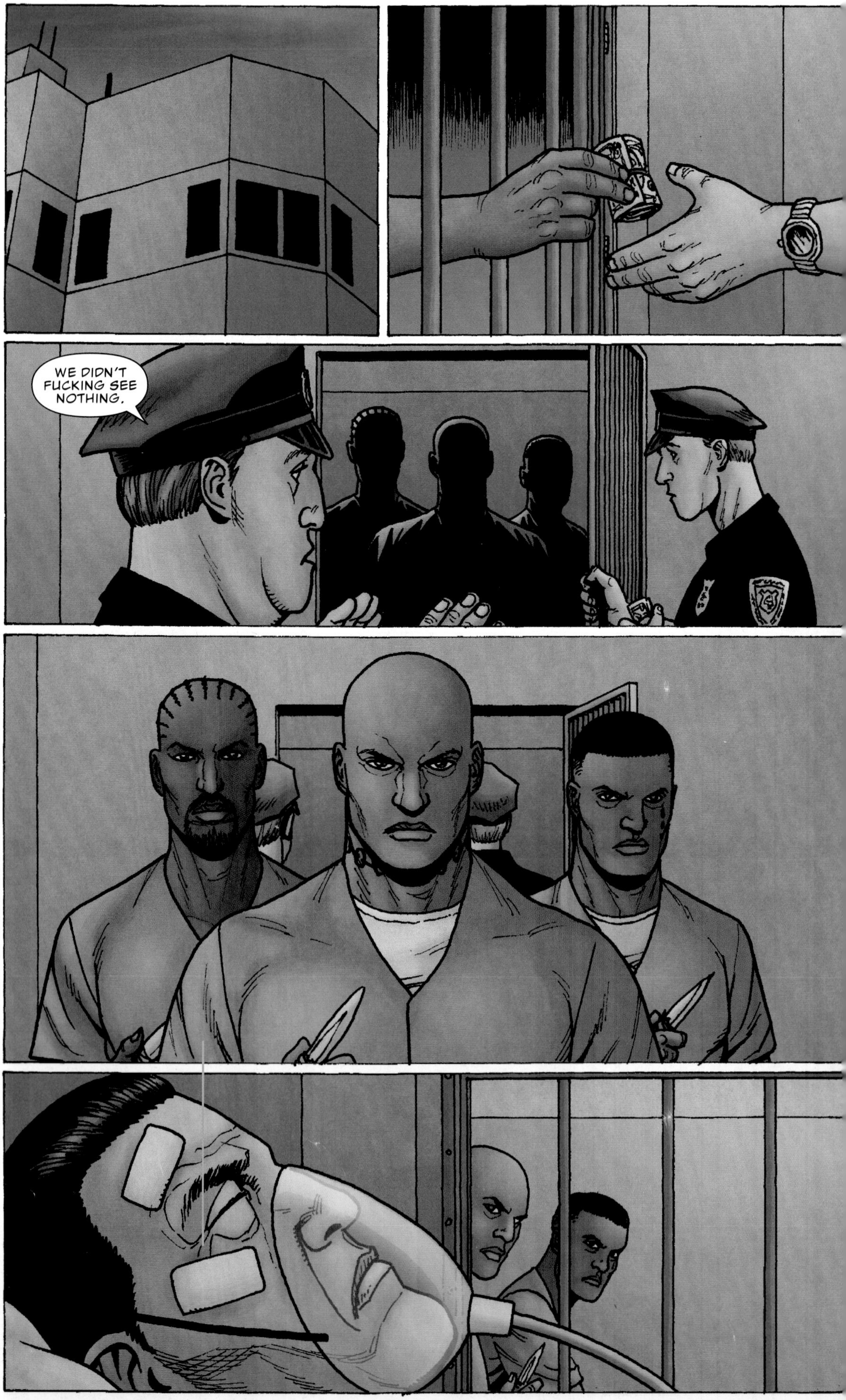
WE DIDN'T FUCKING SEE NOTHING.

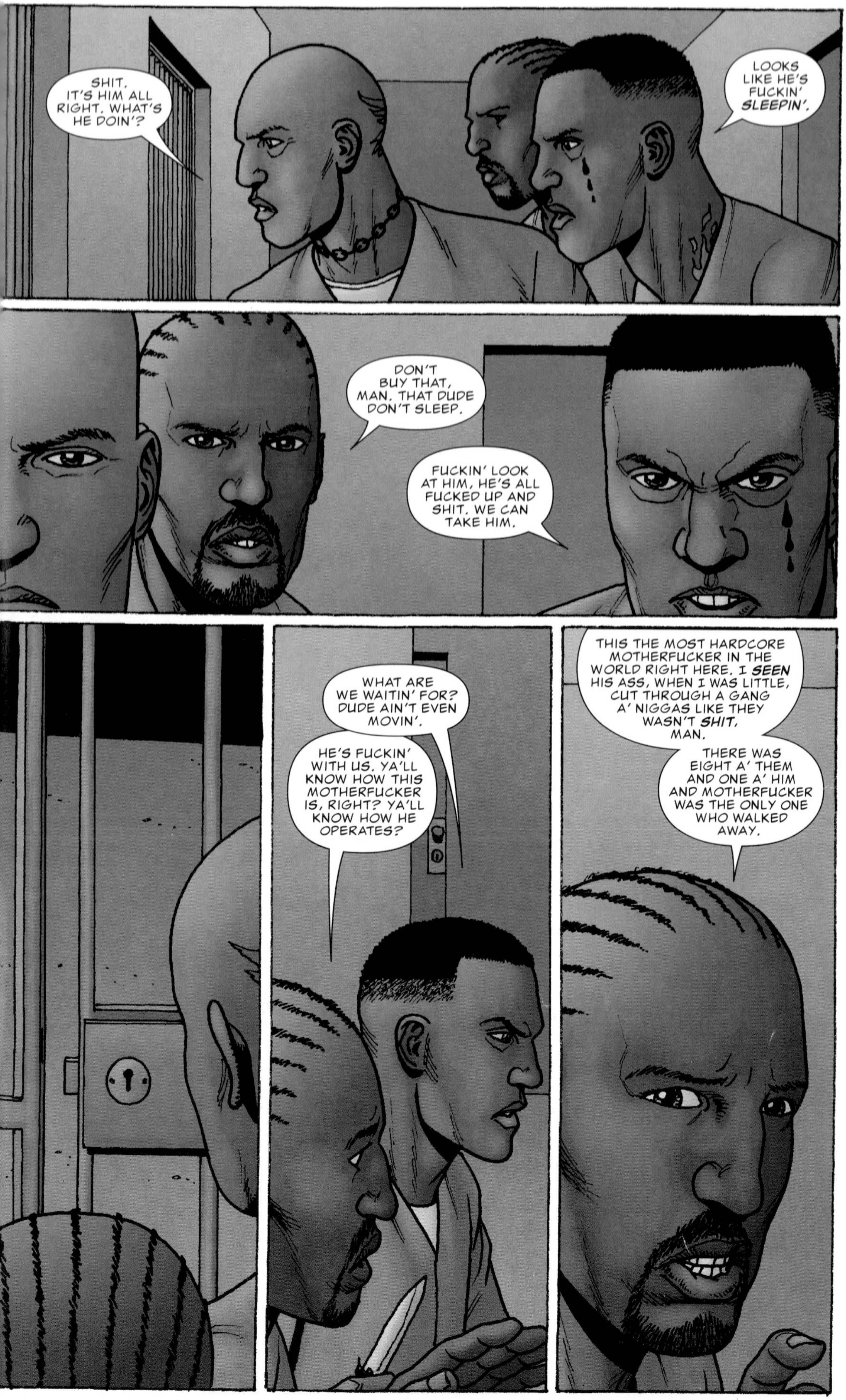
SHIT. IT'S HIM ALL RIGHT. WHAT'S HE DOIN'?
LOOKS LIKE HE'S FUCKIN' SLEEPIN'.
DON'T BUY THAT, MAN. THAT DUDE DON'T SLEEP.
FUCKIN' LOOK AT HIM, HE'S ALL FUCKED UP AND SHIT. WE CAN TAKE HIM.
WHAT ARE WE WAITIN' FOR? DUDE AIN'T EVEN MOVIN'.
HE'S FUCKIN' WITH US. YA'LL KNOW HOW THIS MOTHERFUCKER IS, RIGHT? YA'LL KNOW HOW HE OPERATES?
THIS THE MOST HARDCORE MOTHERFUCKER IN THE WORLD RIGHT HERE. I SEEN HIS ASS, WHEN I WAS LITTLE, CUT THROUGH A GANG A' NIGGAS LIKE THEY WASN'T SHIT, MAN.
THERE WAS EIGHT A' THEM AND ONE A' HIM AND MOTHERFUCKER WAS THE ONLY ONE WHO WALKED AWAY.

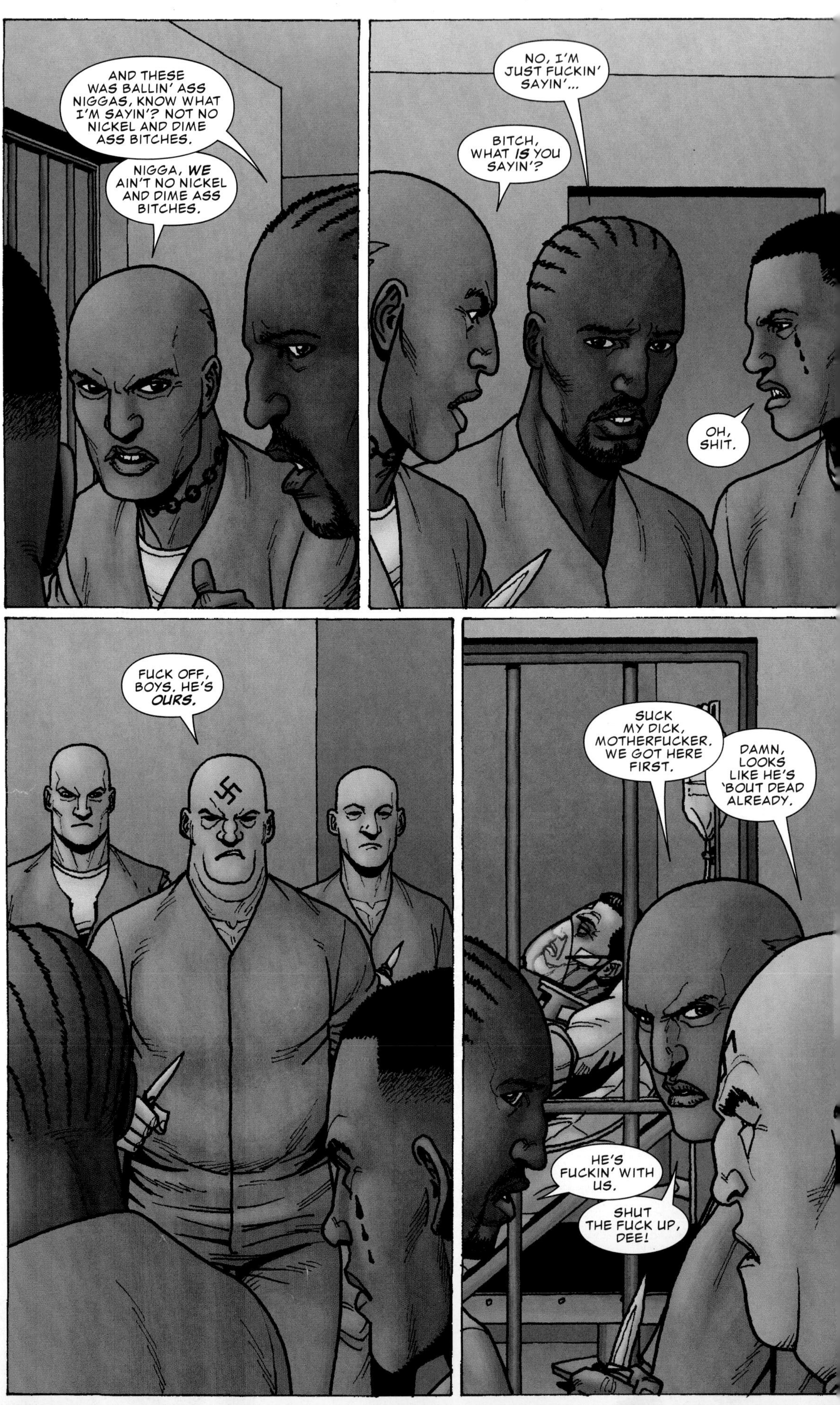
AND THESE WAS BALLIN' ASS NIGGAS, KNOW WHAT I'M SAYIN'? NOT NO NICKEL AND DIME ASS BITCHES.
NIGGA, WE AIN'T NO NICKEL AND DIME ASS BITCHES.
NO, I'M JUST FUCKIN' SAYIN'...
BITCH, WHAT IS YOU SAYIN'?
OH, SHIT.
FUCK OFF, BOYS. HE'S OURS.
SUCK MY DICK, MOTHERFUCKER. WE GOT HERE FIRST.
DAMN, LOOKS LIKE HE'S 'BOUT DEAD ALREADY.
HE'S FUCKIN' WITH US.
SHUT THE FUCK UP, DEE!

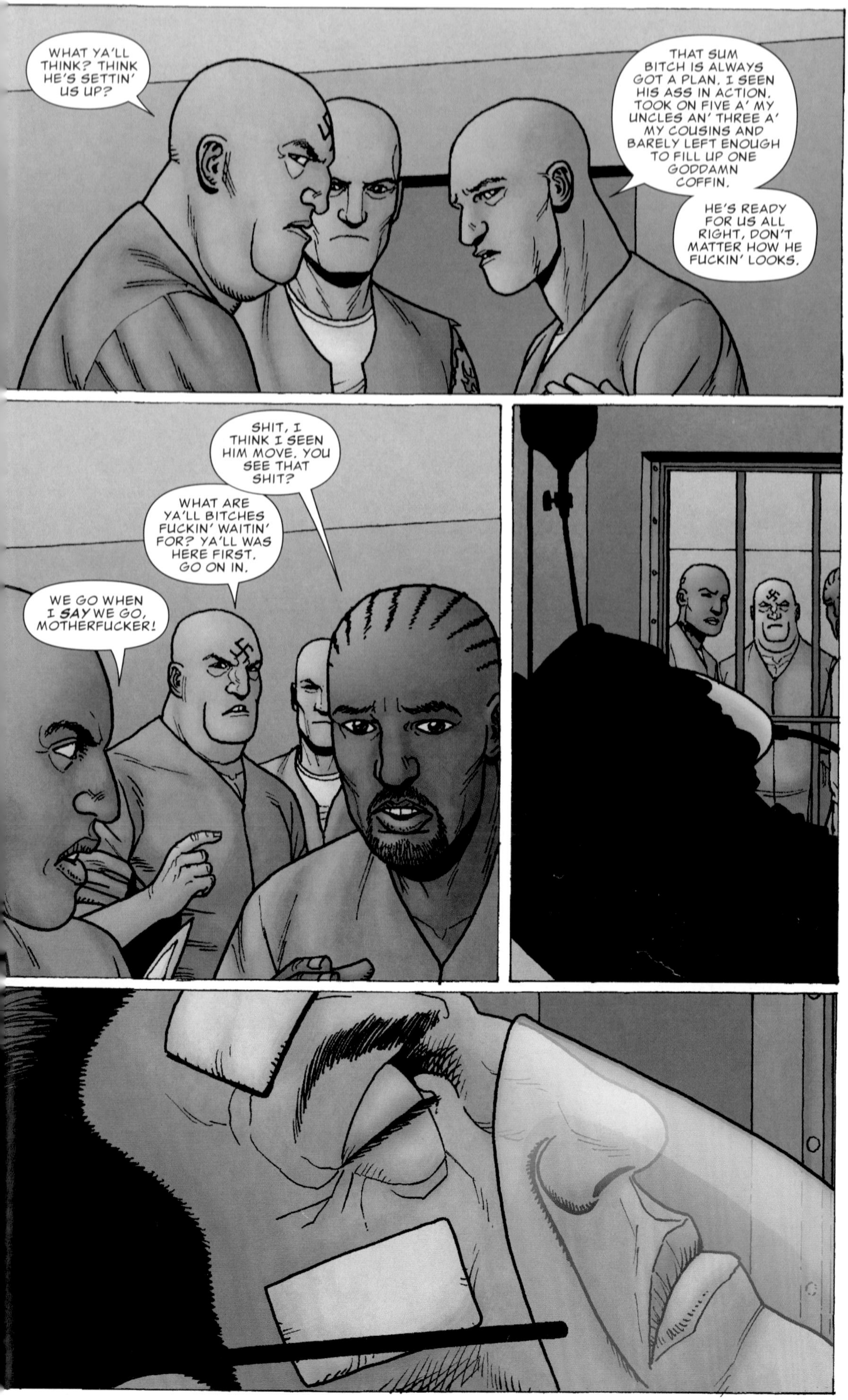
WHAT YA'LL THINK? THINK HE'S SETTIN' US UP?
THAT SUM BITCH IS ALWAYS GOT A PLAN. I SEEN HIS ASS IN ACTION. TOOK ON FIVE A' MY UNCLES AN' THREE A' MY COUSINS AND BARELY LEFT ENOUGH TO FILL UP ONE GODDAMN COFFIN.
HE'S READY FOR US ALL RIGHT, DON'T MATTER HOW HE FUCKIN' LOOKS.
SHIT, I THINK I SEEN HIM MOVE. YOU SEE THAT SHIT?
WHAT ARE YA'LL BITCHES FUCKIN' WAITIN' FOR? YA'LL WAS HERE FIRST. GO ON IN.
WE GO WHEN I *SAY* WE GO, MOTHERFUCKER!

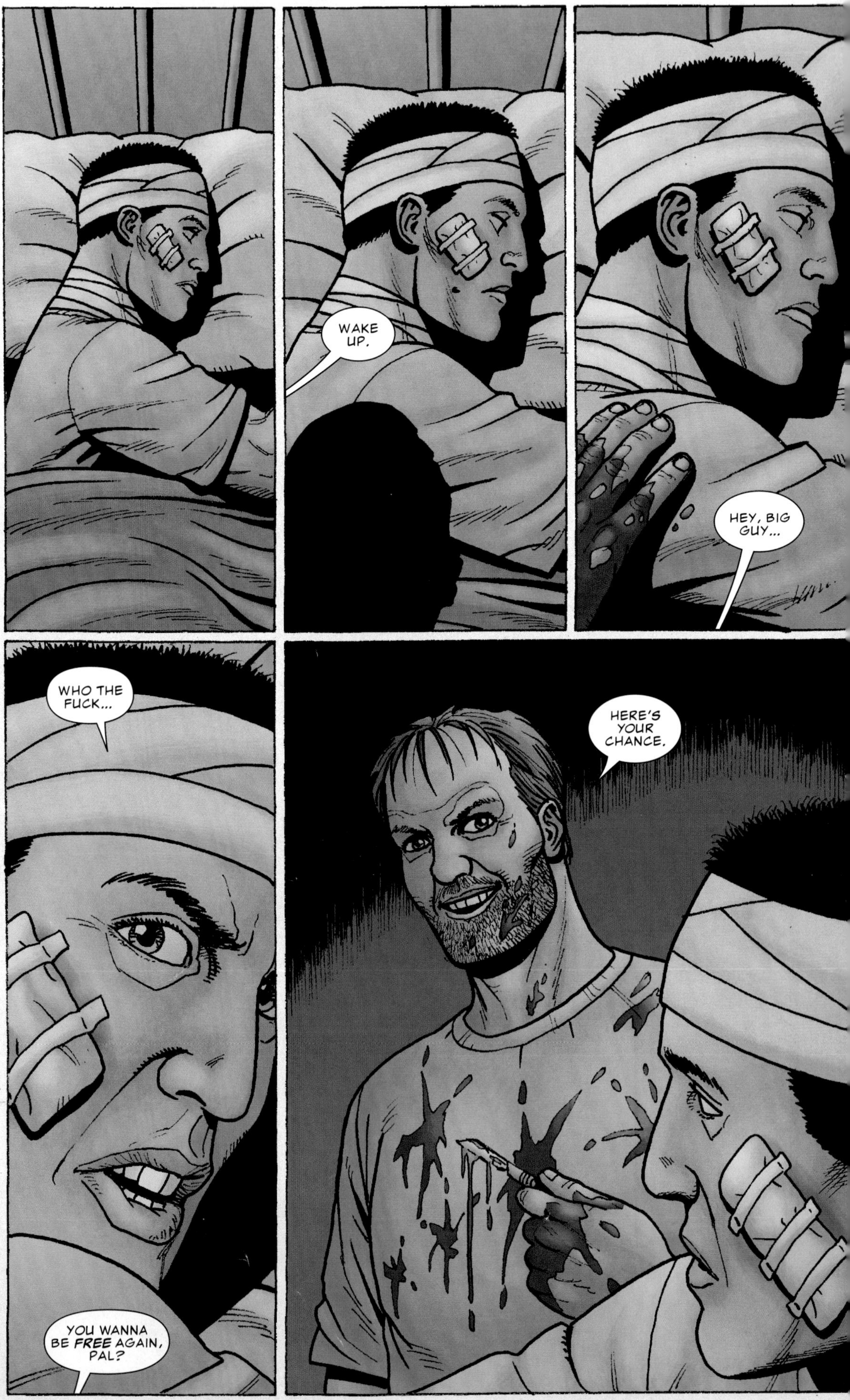
WAKE UP.
HEY, BIG GUY...
WHO THE FUCK...
HERE'S YOUR CHANCE.
YOU WANNA BE FREE AGAIN, PAL?

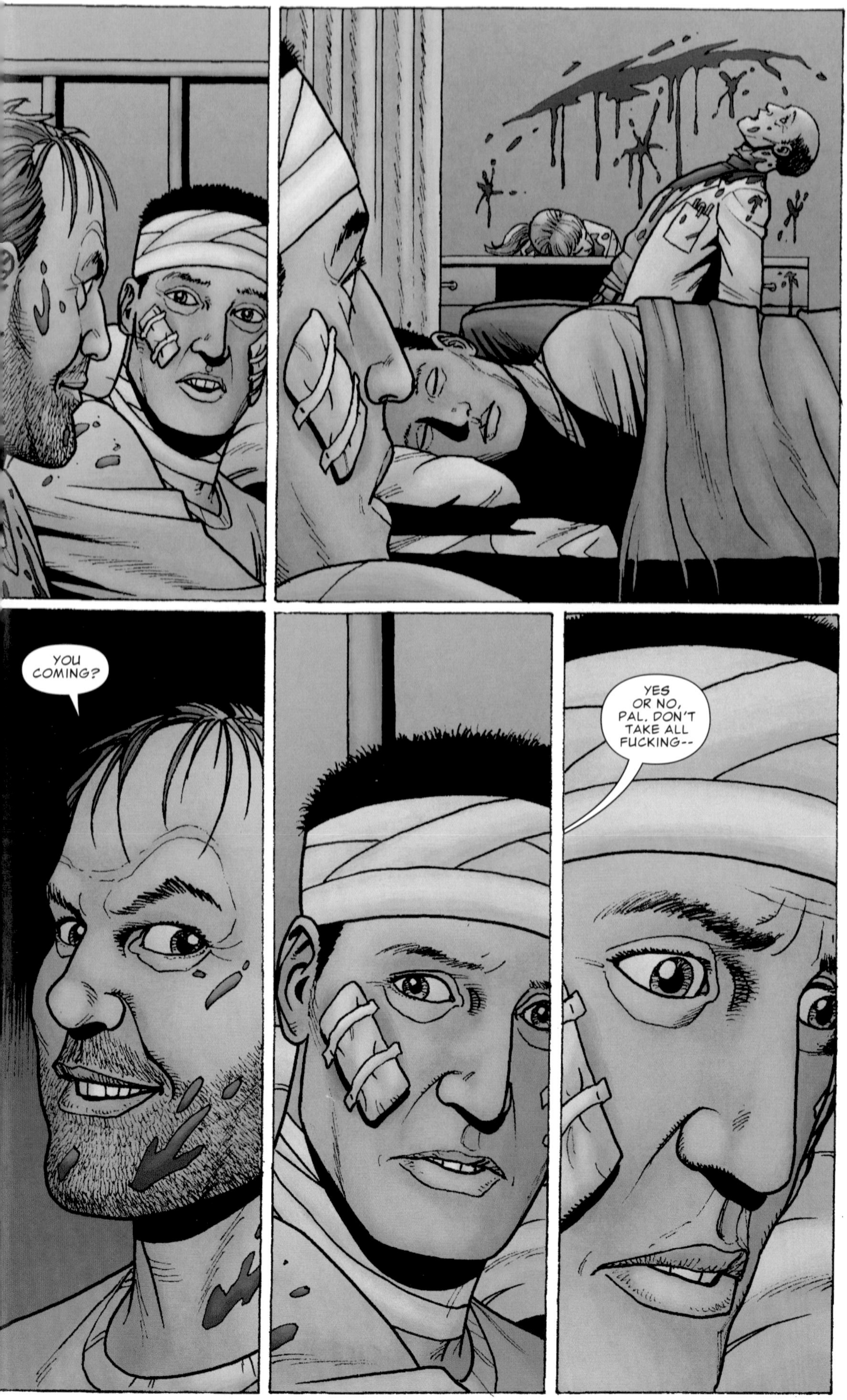
YOU COMING?
YES OR NO, PAL. DON'T TAKE ALL FUCKING--

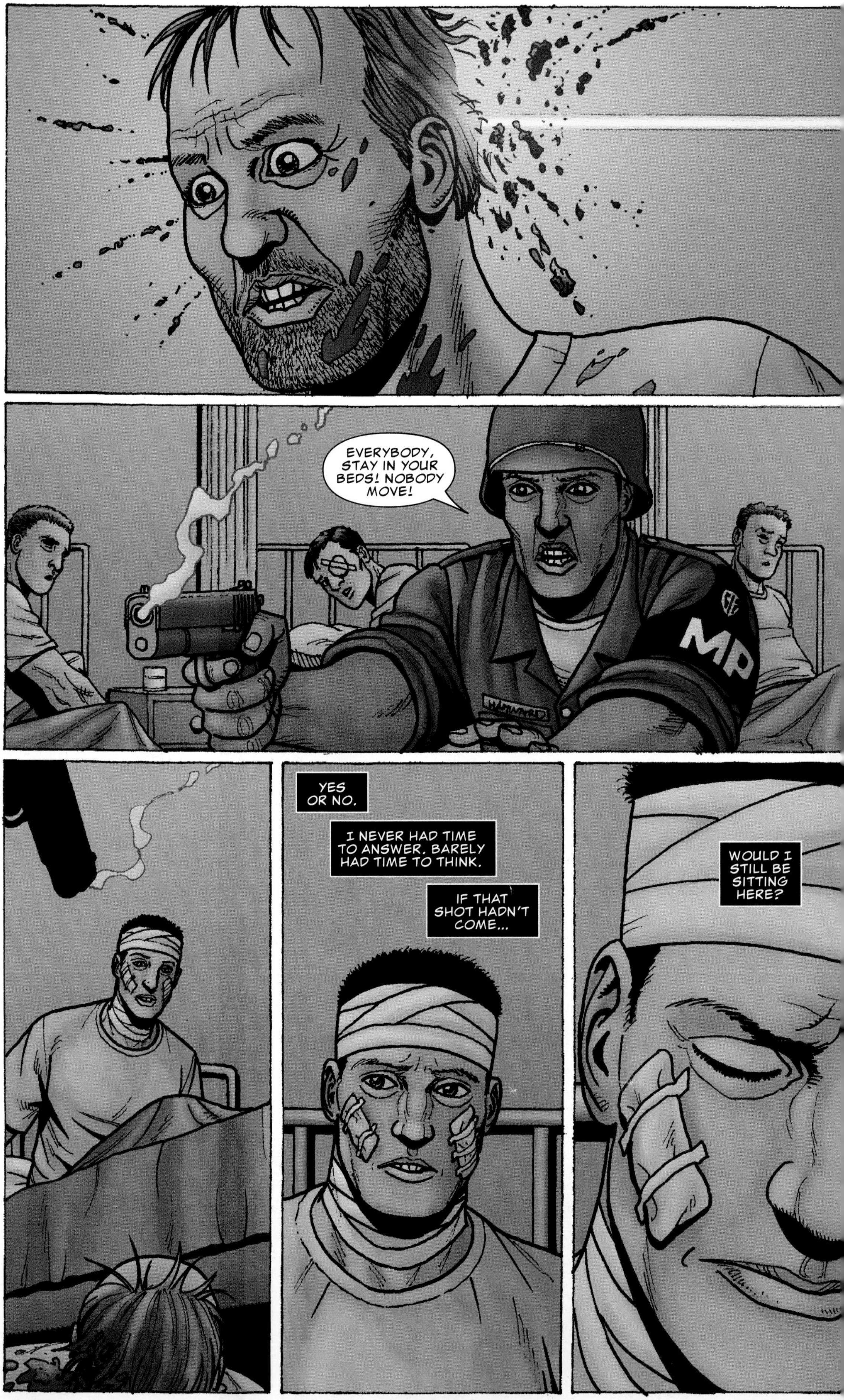
EVERYBODY, STAY IN YOUR BEDS! NOBODY MOVE!
MP
YES OR NO.
I NEVER HAD TIME TO ANSWER. BARELY HAD TIME TO THINK.
IF THAT SHOT HADN'T COME...
WOULD I STILL BE SITTING HERE?

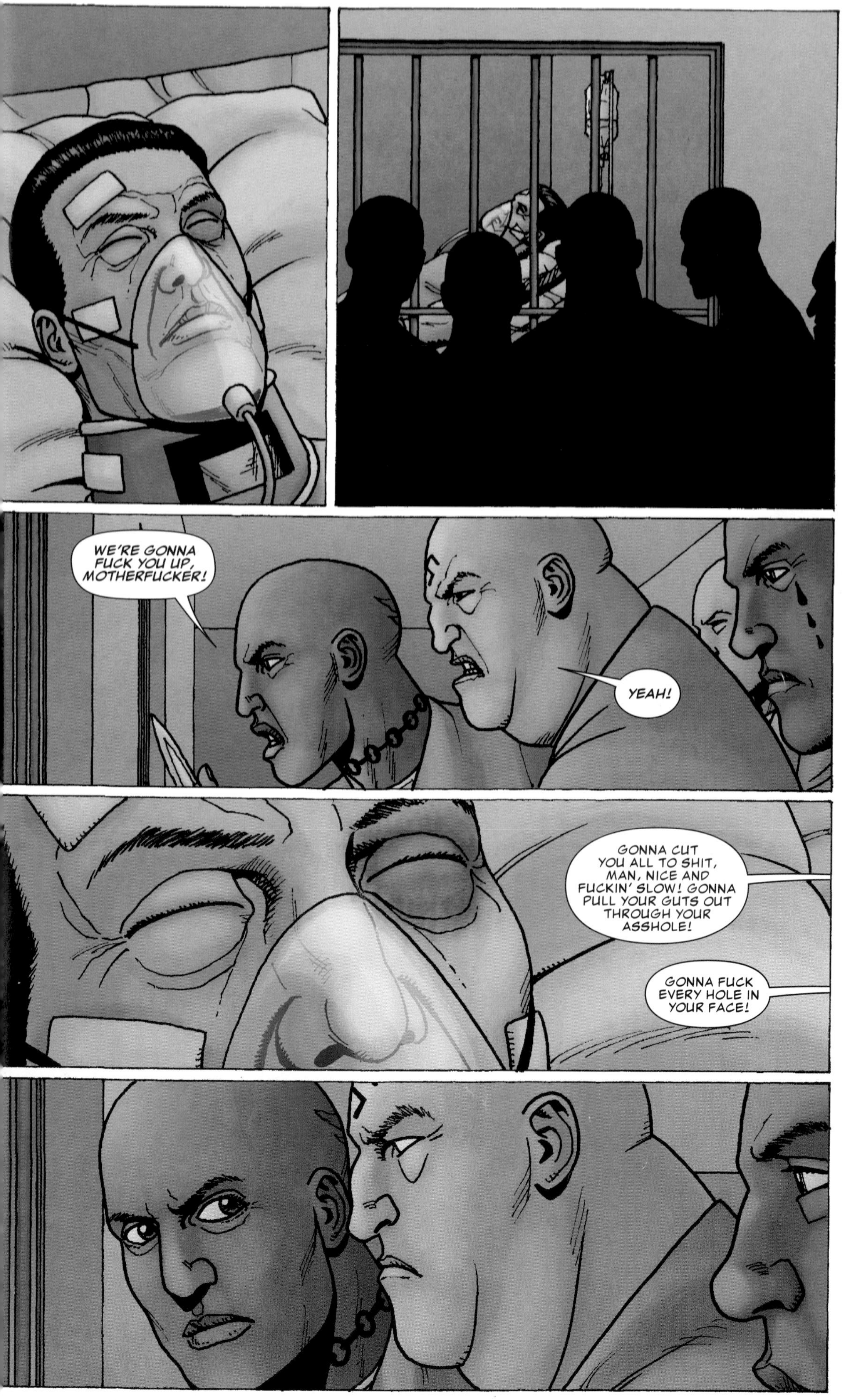
WE'RE GONNA FUCK YOU UP, MOTHERFUCKER!
YEAH!
GONNA CUT YOU ALL TO SHIT, MAN, NICE AND FUCKIN' SLOW! GONNA PULL YOUR GUTS OUT THROUGH YOUR ASSHOLE!
GONNA FUCK EVERY HOLE IN YOUR FACE!

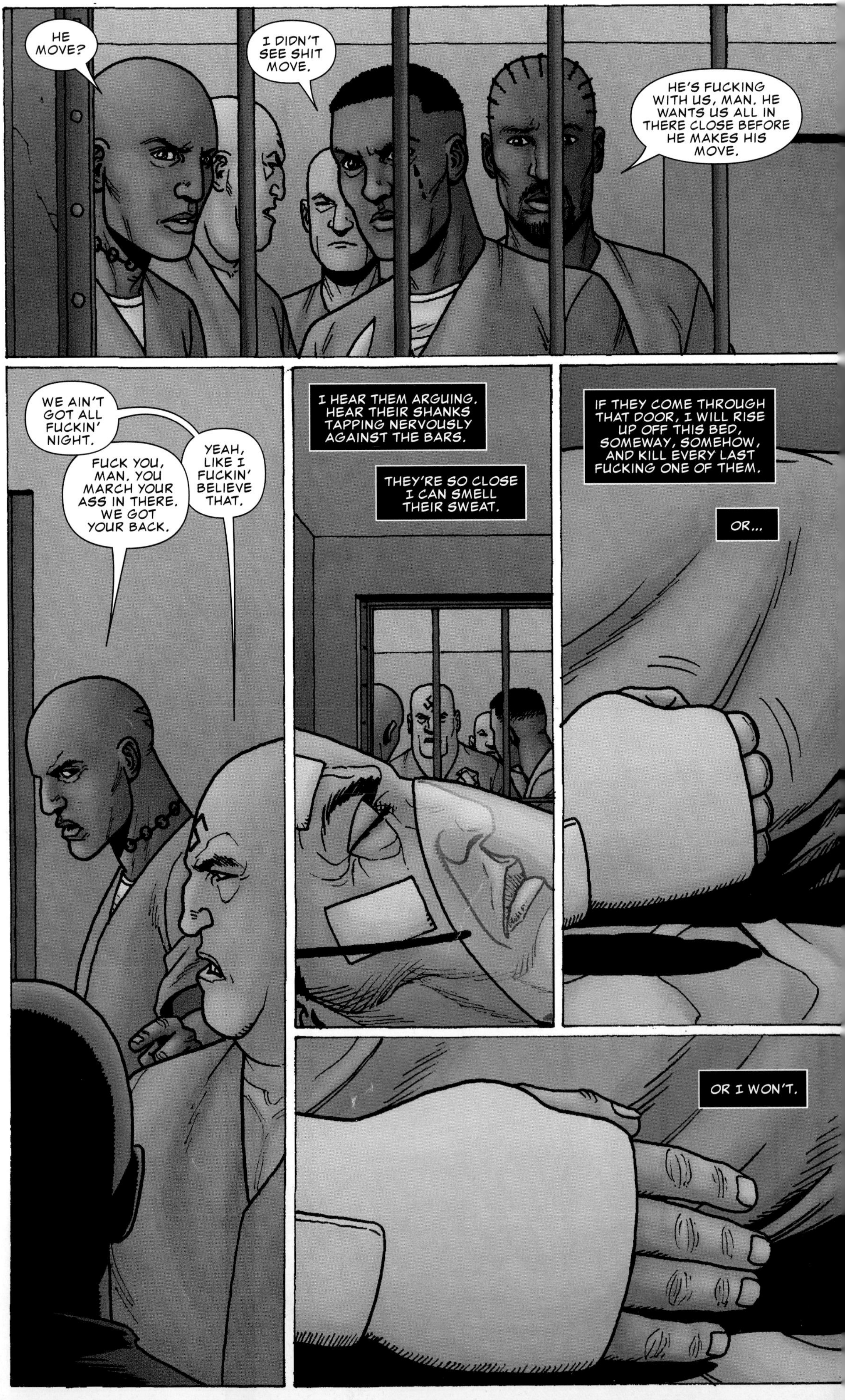
HE MOVE?
I DIDN'T SEE SHIT MOVE.
HE'S FUCKING WITH US, MAN. HE WANTS US ALL IN THERE CLOSE BEFORE HE MAKES HIS MOVE.
WE AIN'T GOT ALL FUCKIN' NIGHT.
FUCK YOU, MAN. YOU MARCH YOUR ASS IN THERE. WE GOT YOUR BACK.
YEAH, LIKE I FUCKIN' BELIEVE THAT.
I HEAR THEM ARGUING. HEAR THEIR SHANKS TAPPING NERVOUSLY AGAINST THE BARS.
THEY'RE SO CLOSE I CAN SMELL THEIR SWEAT.
IF THEY COME THROUGH THAT DOOR, I WILL RISE UP OFF THIS BED, SOMEWAY, SOMEHOW, AND KILL EVERY LAST FUCKING ONE OF THEM.
OR...
OR I WON'T.

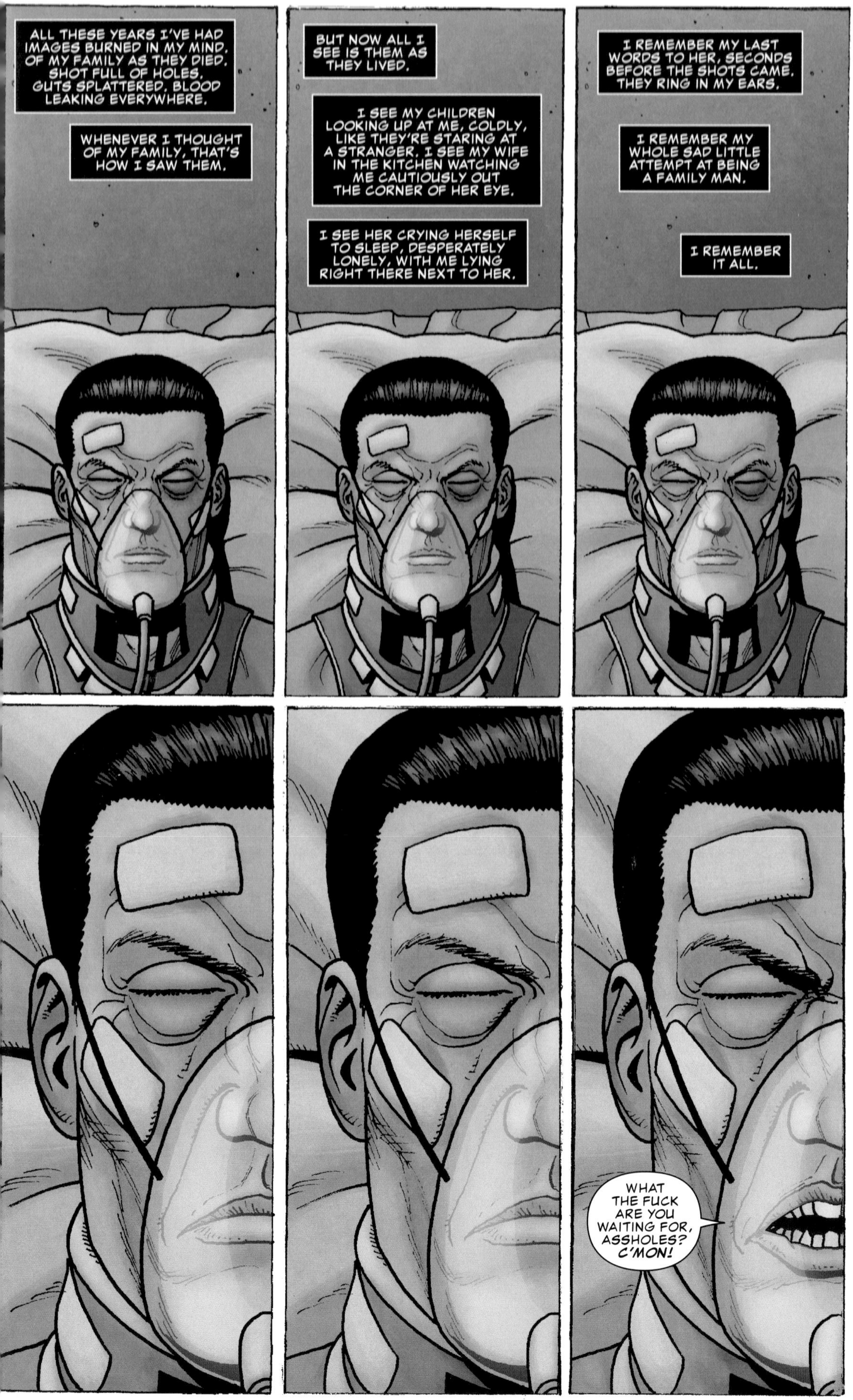
ALL THESE YEARS I'VE HAD IMAGES BURNED IN MY MIND, OF MY FAMILY AS THEY DIED. SHOT FULL OF HOLES. GUTS SPLATTERED. BLOOD LEAKING EVERYWHERE.
WHENEVER I THOUGHT OF MY FAMILY, THAT'S HOW I SAW THEM.
BUT NOW ALL I SEE IS THEM AS THEY LIVED.
I SEE MY CHILDREN LOOKING UP AT ME, COLDLY, LIKE THEY'RE STARING AT A STRANGER. I SEE MY WIFE IN THE KITCHEN WATCHING ME CAUTIOUSLY OUT THE CORNER OF HER EYE.
I SEE HER CRYING HERSELF TO SLEEP, DESPERATELY LONELY, WITH ME LYING RIGHT THERE NEXT TO HER.
I REMEMBER MY LAST WORDS TO HER, SECONDS BEFORE THE SHOTS CAME. THEY RING IN MY EARS.
I REMEMBER MY WHOLE SAD LITTLE ATTEMPT AT BEING A FAMILY MAN.
I REMEMBER IT ALL.
WHAT THE FUCK ARE YOU WAITING FOR, ASSHOLES? C'MON!

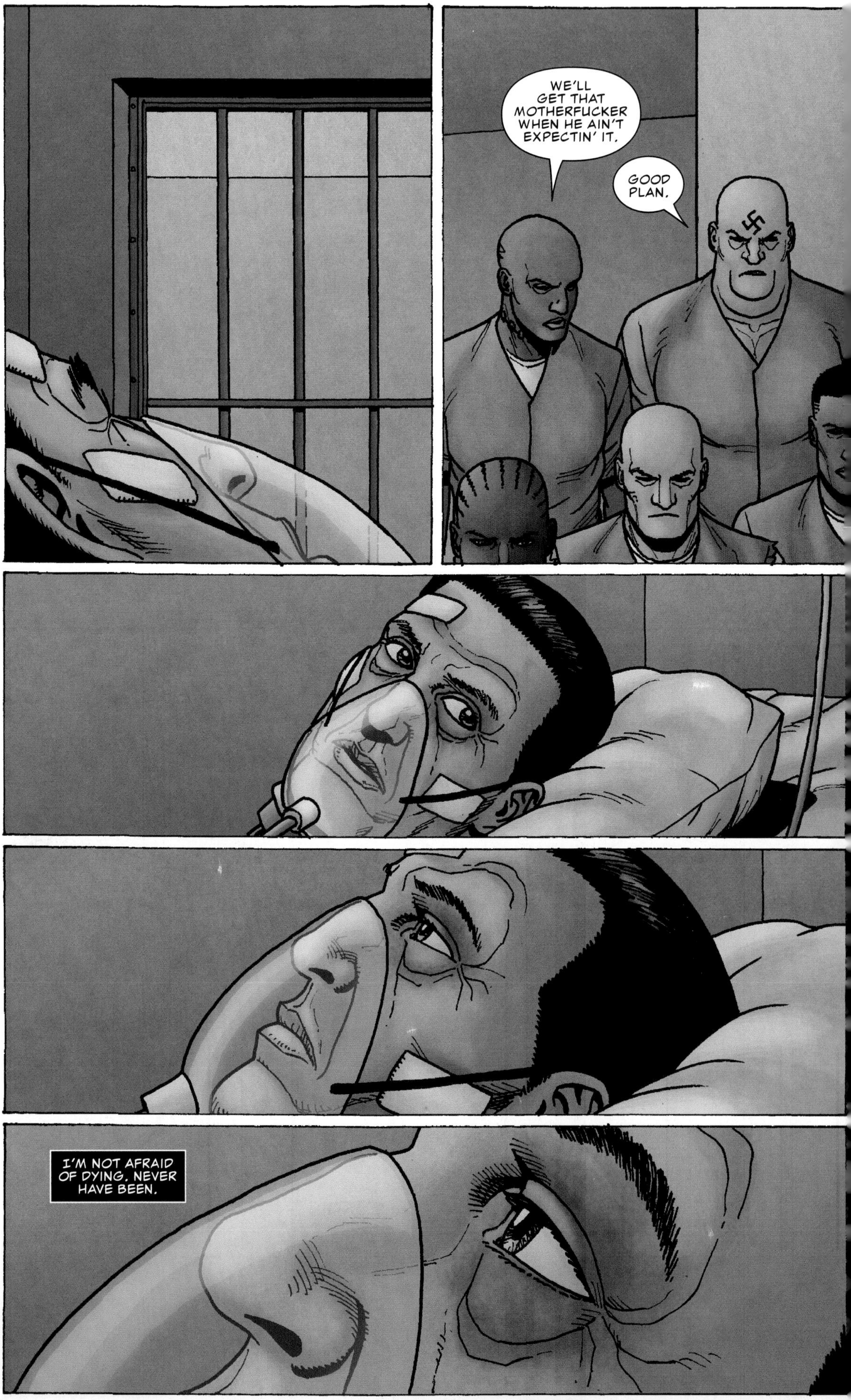
WE'LL GET THAT MOTHERFUCKER WHEN HE AIN'T EXPECTIN' IT.
GOOD PLAN.
I'M NOT AFRAID OF DYING. NEVER HAVE BEEN.

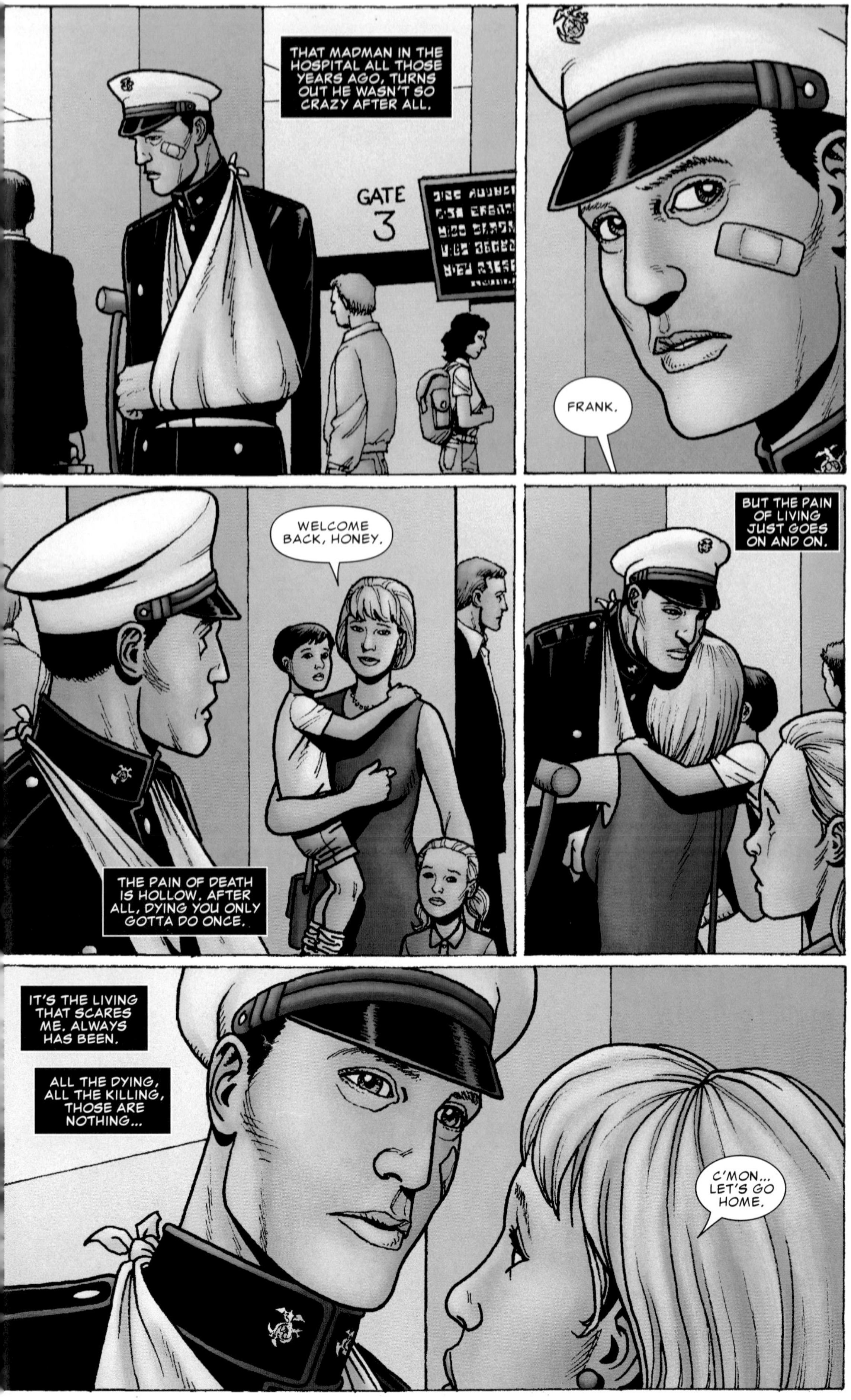
THAT MADMAN IN THE HOSPITAL ALL THOSE YEARS AGO, TURNS OUT HE WASN'T SO CRAZY AFTER ALL.
GATE 3
FRANK.
WELCOME BACK, HONEY.
THE PAIN OF DEATH IS HOLLOW. AFTER ALL, DYING YOU ONLY GOTTA DO ONCE.
BUT THE PAIN OF LIVING JUST GOES ON AND ON.
IT'S THE LIVING THAT SCARES ME. ALWAYS HAS BEEN.
ALL THE DYING, ALL THE KILLING, THOSE ARE NOTHING...
C'MON... LET'S GO HOME.

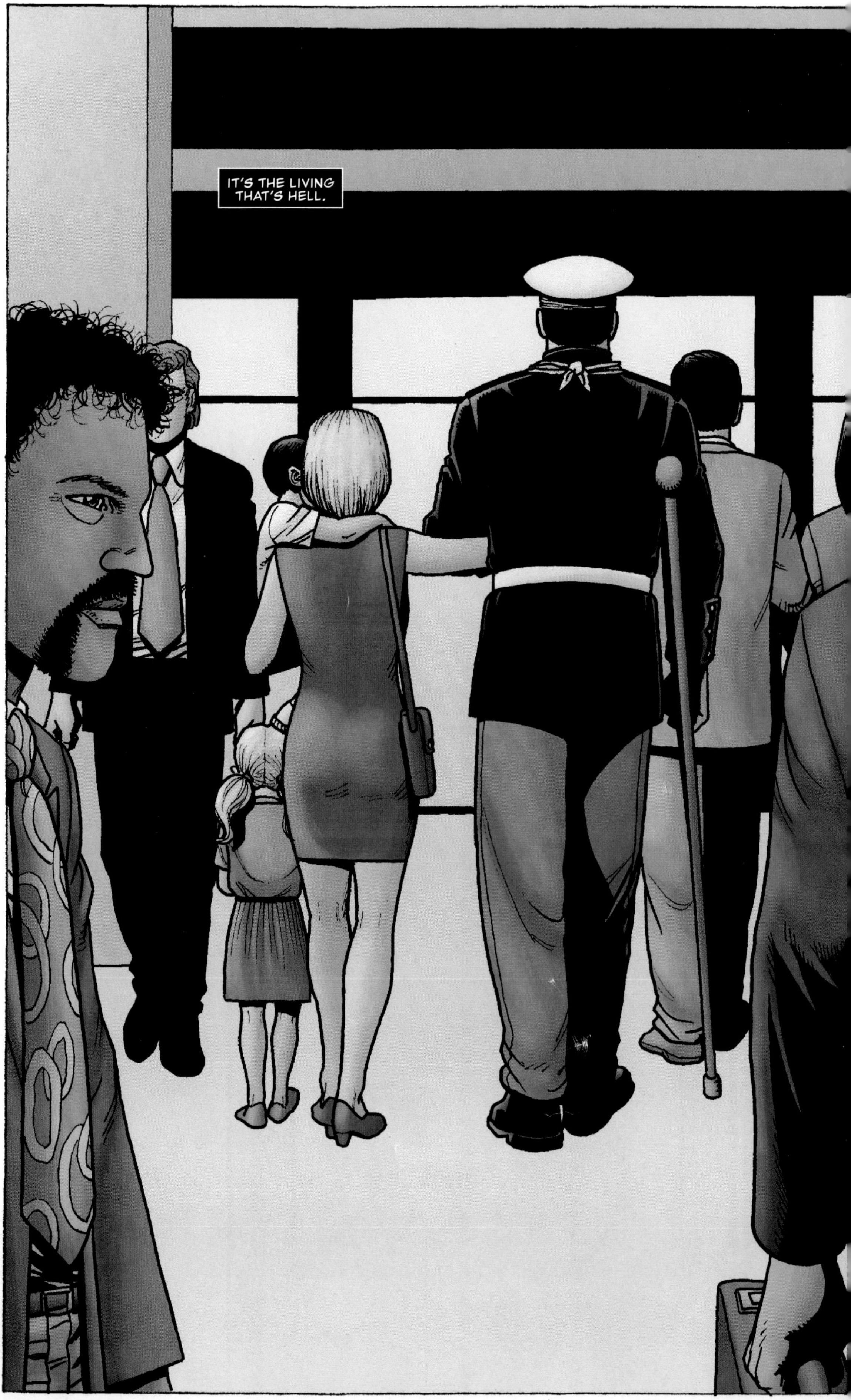
IT'S THE LIVING
THAT'S HELL.

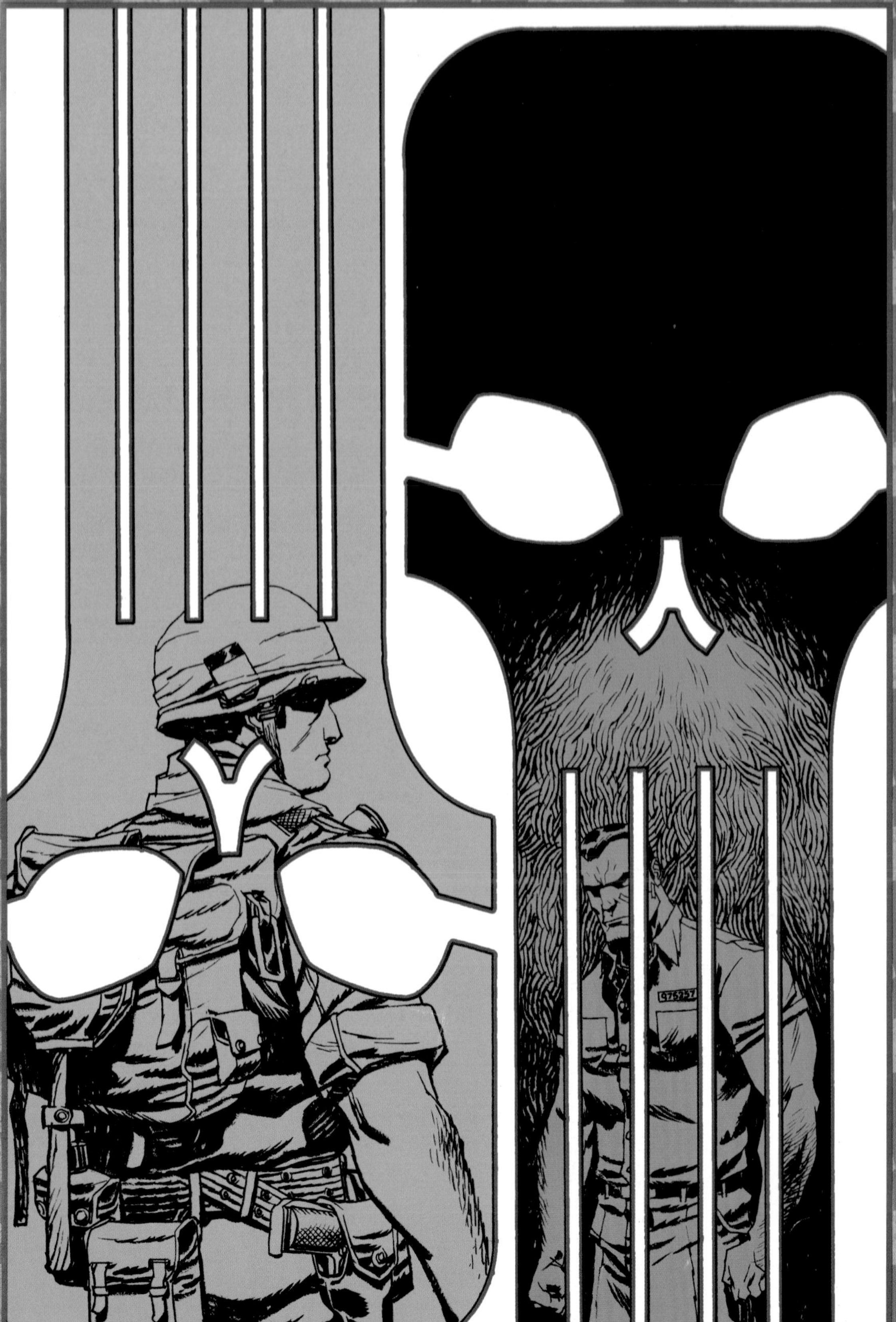

13

SOON AS I'M ABLE TO STAND, THEY MOVE ME OUT OF THE INFIRMARY.

NO COVER OF DARKNESS THIS TIME. GUARDS PARADE ME OUT BRIGHT AND EARLY. WHOLE PRISON AWAKE AND WATCHING.

NO ONE SPEAKS. BUT I FEEL THEM EYEING ME. EVERY SHITBIRD AND RATFUCK IN THE WHOLE DAMN BUILDING. ALL LOOKING FOR SIGNS OF WEAKNESS.

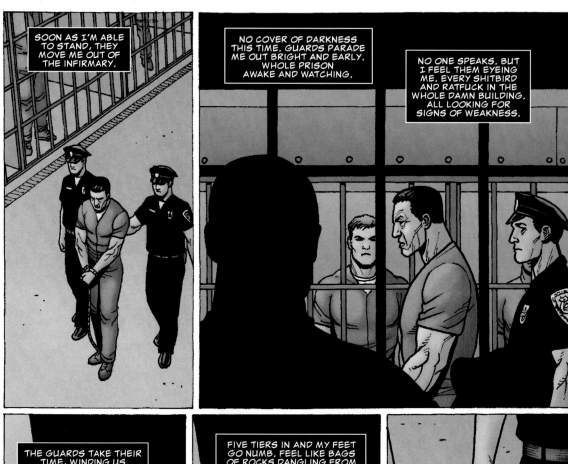

THE GUARDS TAKE THEIR TIME, WINDING US THROUGH THE TIERS. I REALIZE RIGHT AWAY WHAT THEY'RE DOING.

I THINK ABOUT TAKING A SHOT AT ONE OF THEM, TO TRY AND MOVE THINGS ALONG. BUT THAT'LL ONLY TAKE MORE OUT OF ME. ONLY MAKE ME LOOK DESPERATE.

NO, ALL I CAN DO IS KEEP WALKING.

FIVE TIERS IN AND MY FEET GO NUMB. FEEL LIKE BAGS OF ROCKS DANGLING FROM MY LEGS. MY KNEES START TO CREAK SO LOUD I SWEAR I CAN HEAR IT ECHOING.

I TRY TO IMAGINE I'M BACK IN I CORPS, HUMPING THE BOONIES UNDER A 20 POUND PACK, A KID AGAIN, AN UNSTOPPABLE WAD OF GRISTLE AND BILE.

BUT SOMEWHERE IN CELL BLOCK D...

UGH.

REALITY CATCHES UP TO ME.

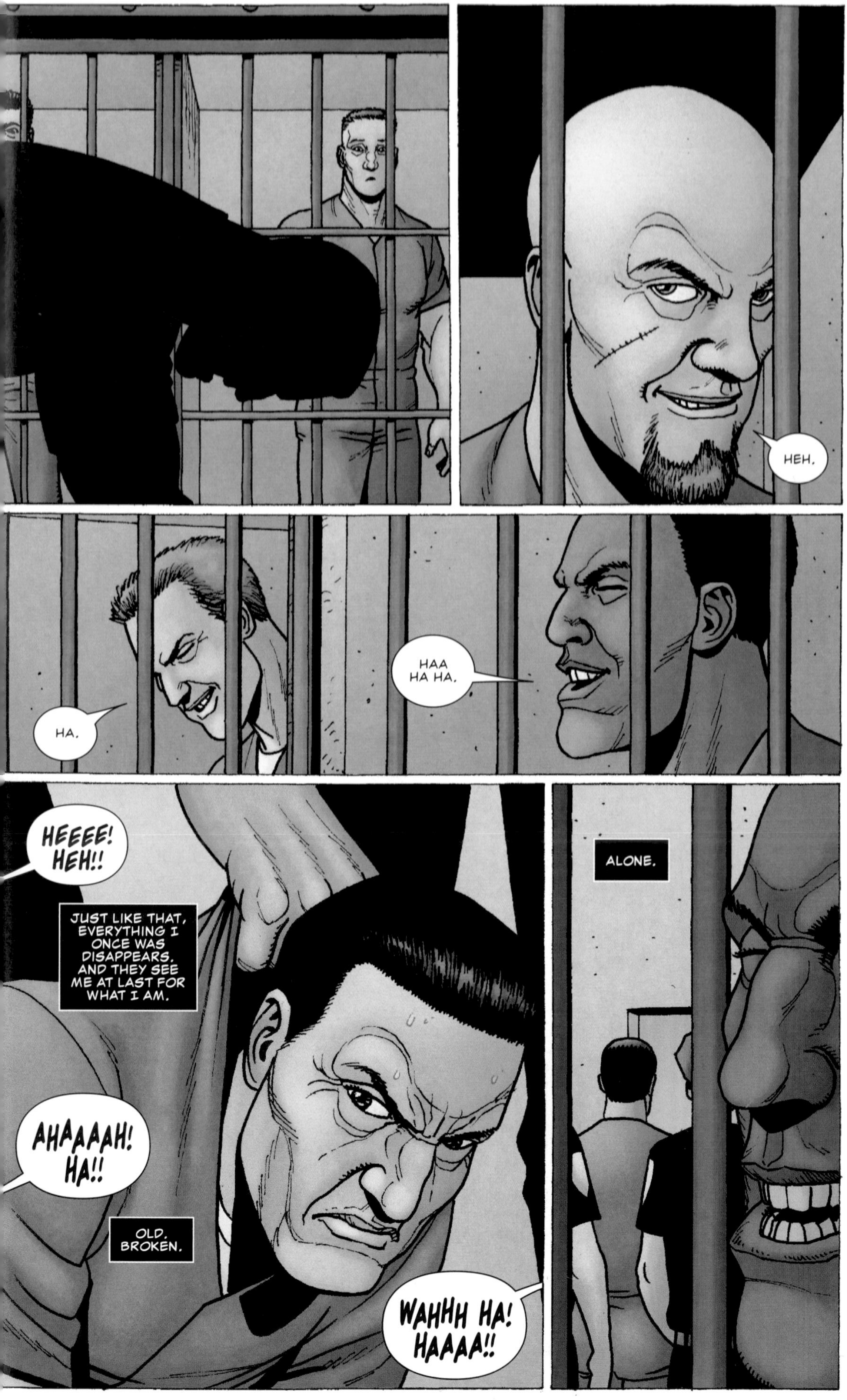

HEH.
HA.
HAA HA HA.
HEEEE! HEH!!
JUST LIKE THAT, EVERYTHING I ONCE WAS DISAPPEARS, AND THEY SEE ME AT LAST FOR WHAT I AM.
AHAAAAH! HA!!
OLD. BROKEN.
WAHHH HA! HAAAA!!
ALONE.

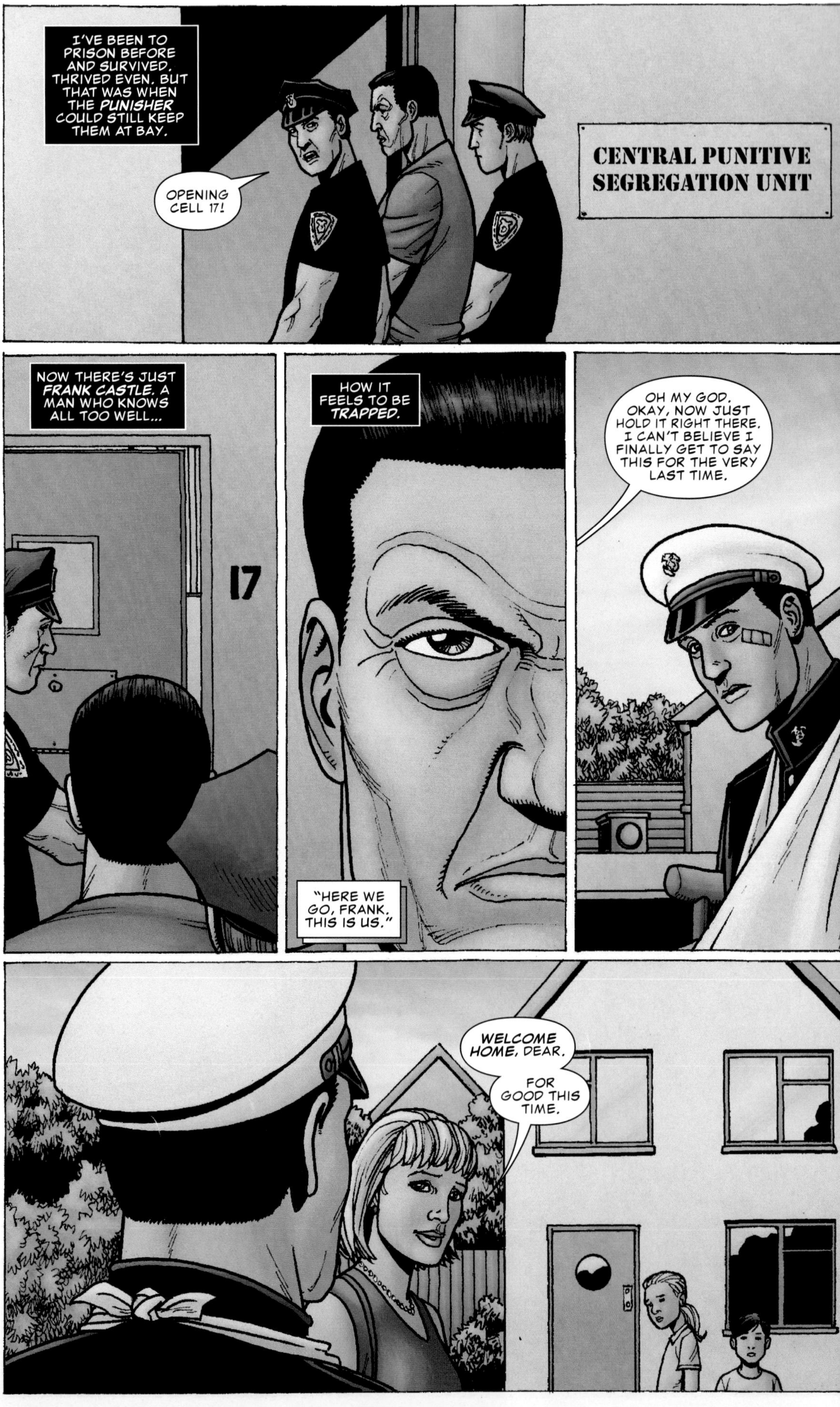
I'VE BEEN TO PRISON BEFORE AND SURVIVED. THRIVED EVEN. BUT THAT WAS WHEN THE *PUNISHER* COULD STILL KEEP THEM AT BAY.
OPENING CELL 17!
CENTRAL PUNITIVE SEGREGATION UNIT
NOW THERE'S JUST *FRANK CASTLE.* A MAN WHO KNOWS ALL TOO WELL...
17
HOW IT FEELS TO BE *TRAPPED.*
"HERE WE GO, FRANK. THIS IS US."
OH MY GOD. OKAY, NOW JUST HOLD IT RIGHT THERE. I CAN'T BELIEVE I FINALLY GET TO SAY THIS FOR THE VERY LAST TIME.
WELCOME HOME, DEAR.
FOR GOOD THIS TIME.

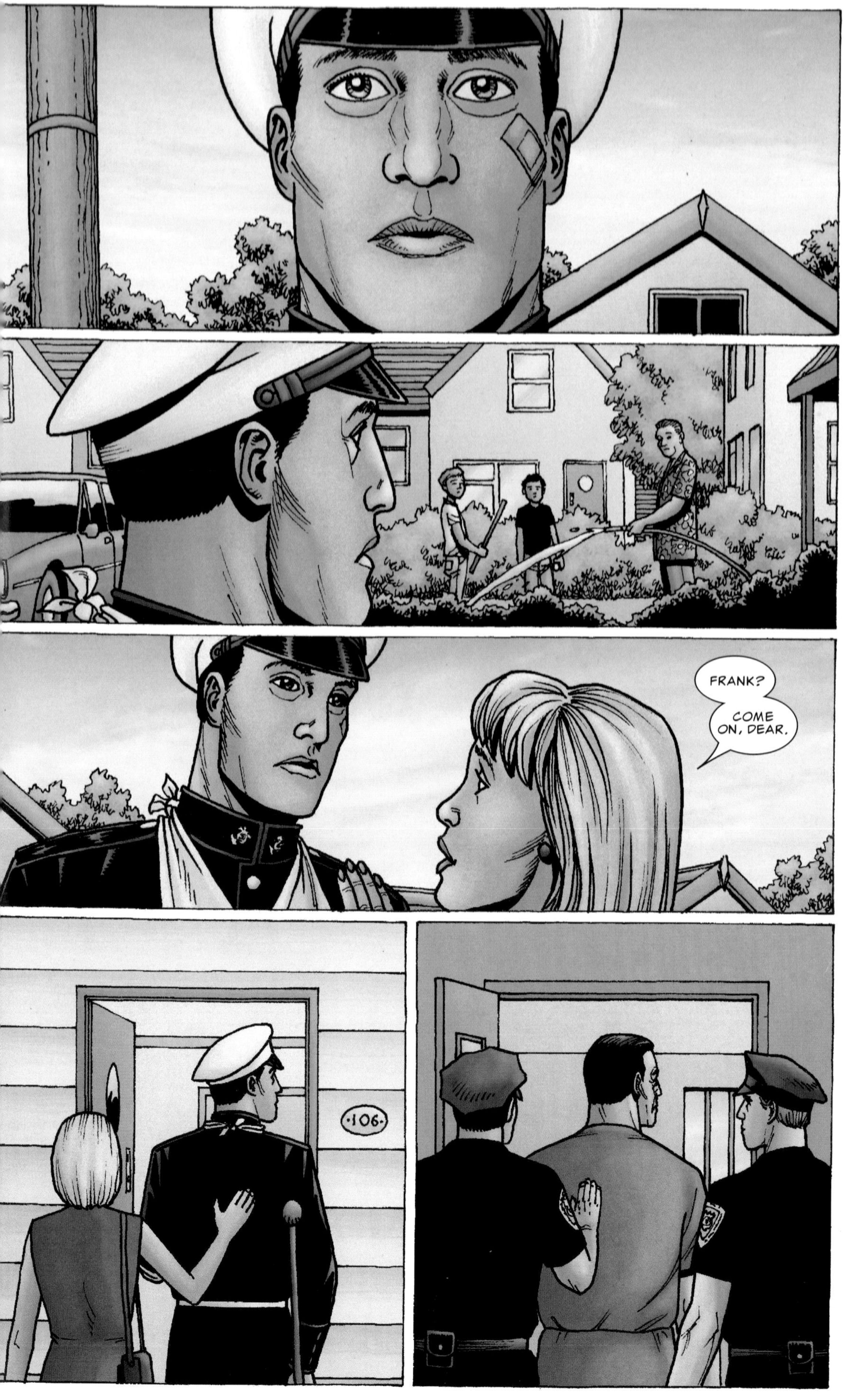
FRANK?
COME ON, DEAR.
·106·

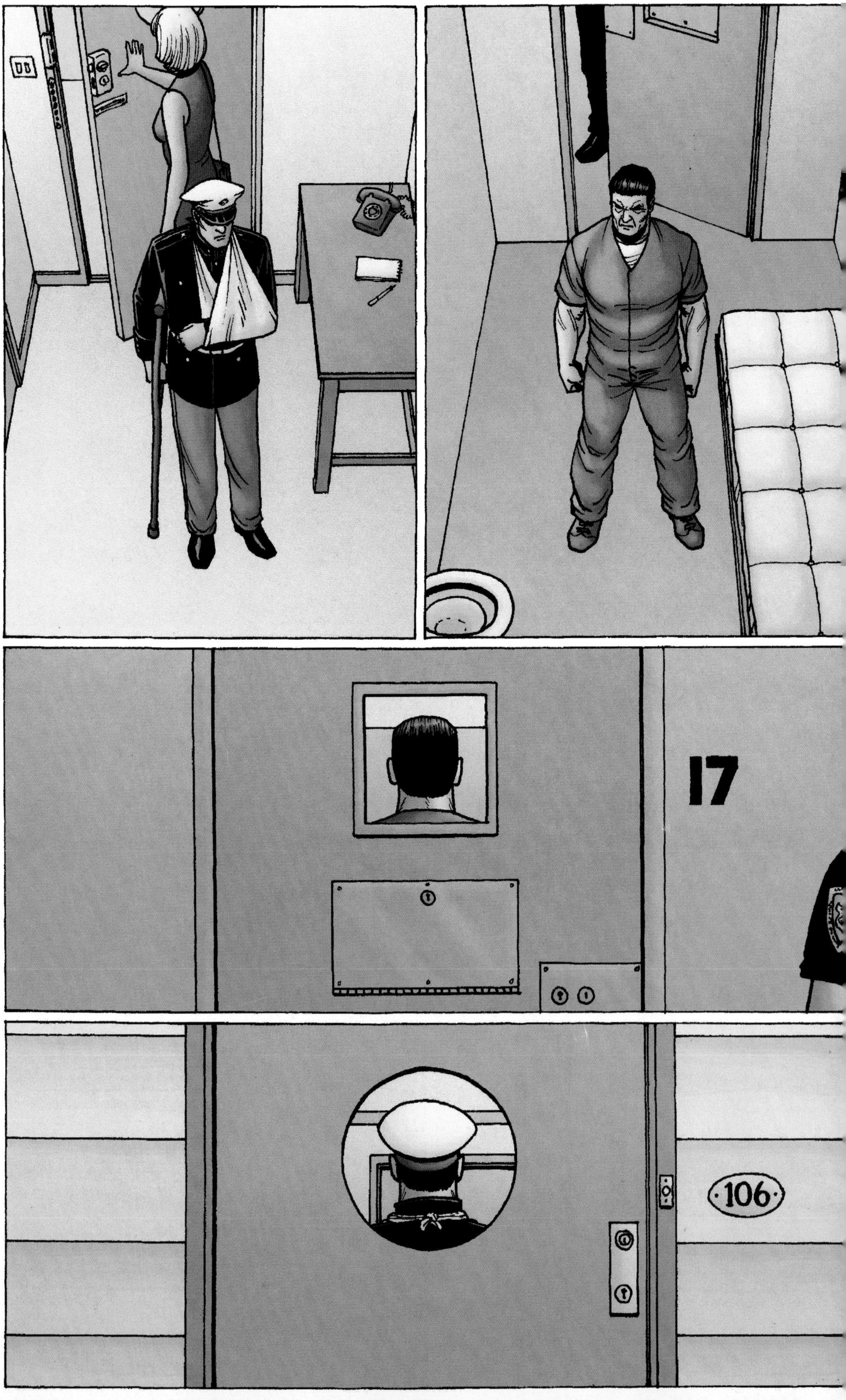
17
·106·

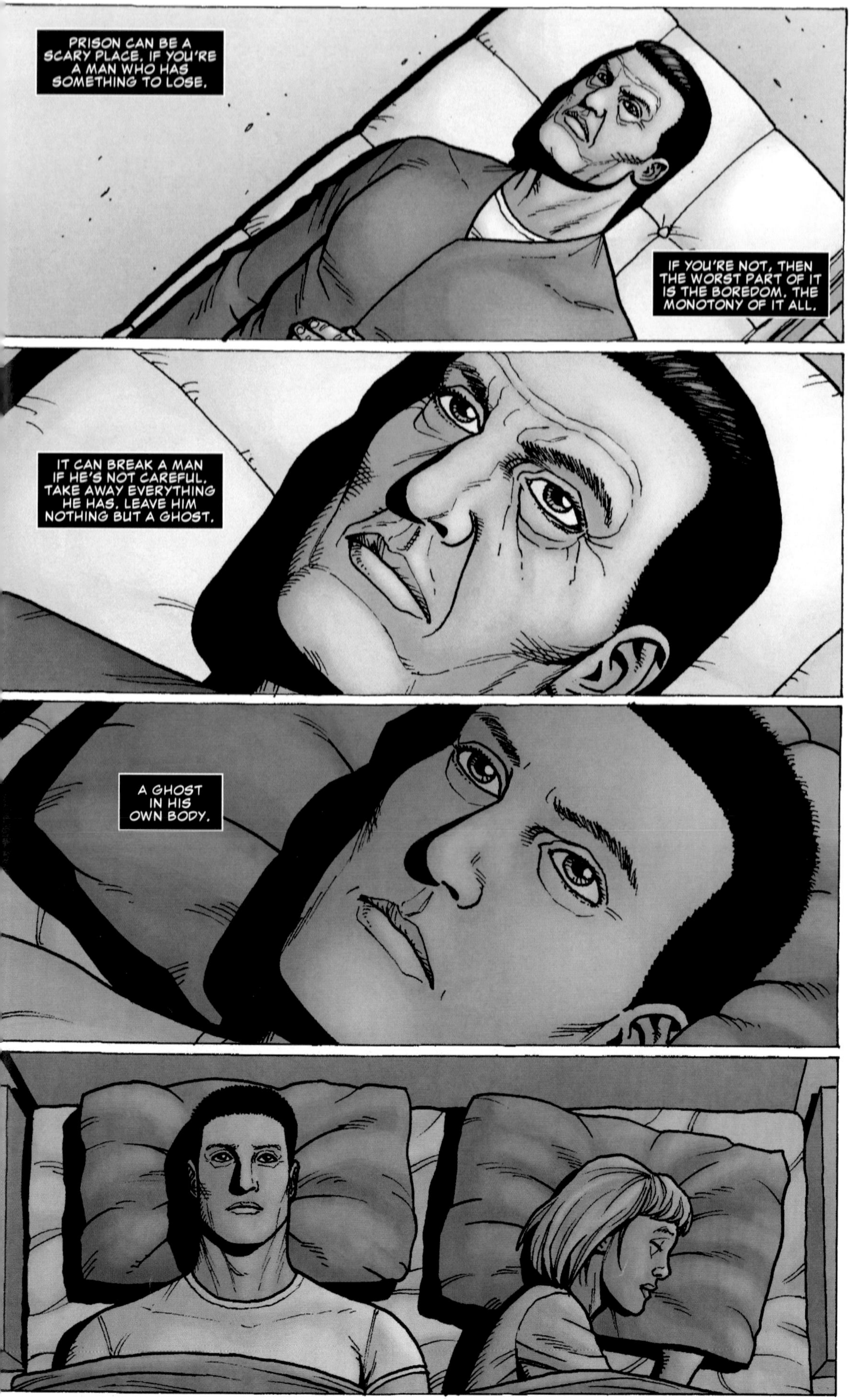
PRISON CAN BE A SCARY PLACE, IF YOU'RE A MAN WHO HAS SOMETHING TO LOSE.
IF YOU'RE NOT, THEN THE WORST PART OF IT IS THE BOREDOM. THE MONOTONY OF IT ALL.
IT CAN BREAK A MAN IF HE'S NOT CAREFUL. TAKE AWAY EVERYTHING HE HAS. LEAVE HIM NOTHING BUT A GHOST.
A GHOST IN HIS OWN BODY.

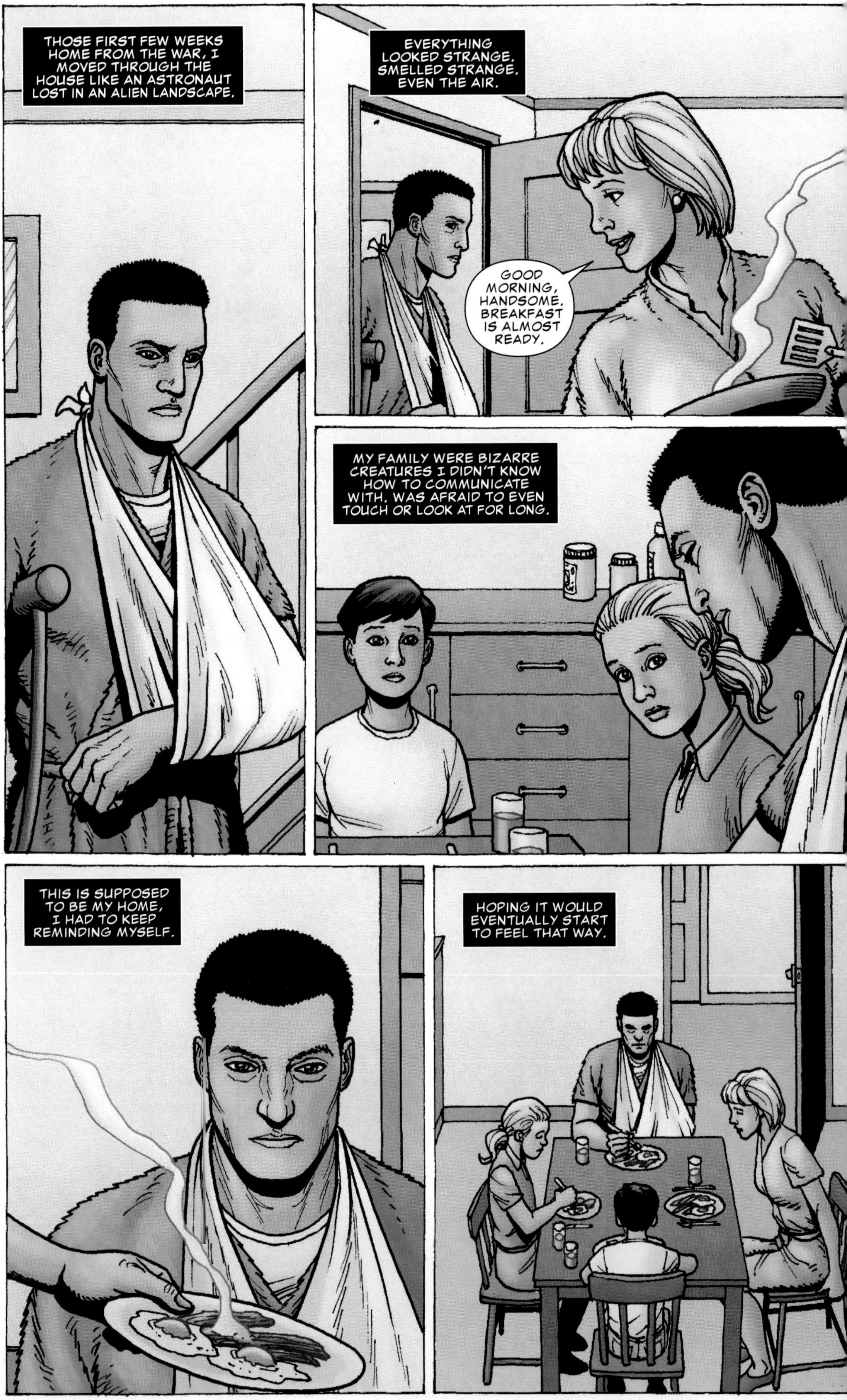
THOSE FIRST FEW WEEKS HOME FROM THE WAR, I MOVED THROUGH THE HOUSE LIKE AN ASTRONAUT LOST IN AN ALIEN LANDSCAPE.
EVERYTHING LOOKED STRANGE. SMELLED STRANGE. EVEN THE AIR.
GOOD MORNING, HANDSOME. BREAKFAST IS ALMOST READY.
MY FAMILY WERE BIZARRE CREATURES I DIDN'T KNOW HOW TO COMMUNICATE WITH. WAS AFRAID TO EVEN TOUCH OR LOOK AT FOR LONG.
THIS IS SUPPOSED TO BE MY HOME, I HAD TO KEEP REMINDING MYSELF.
HOPING IT WOULD EVENTUALLY START TO FEEL THAT WAY.

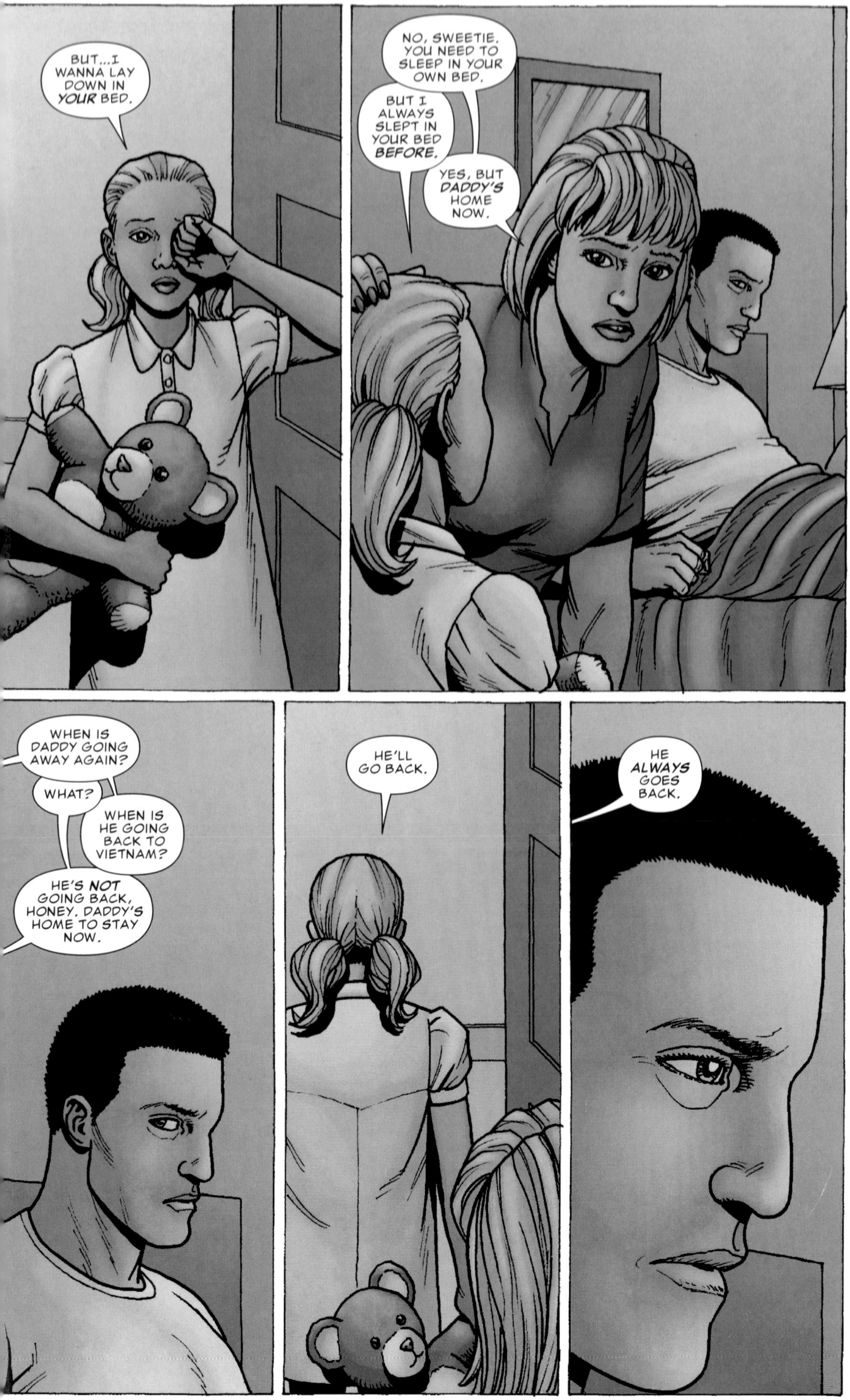
BUT...I WANNA LAY DOWN IN YOUR BED.
NO, SWEETIE, YOU NEED TO SLEEP IN YOUR OWN BED.
BUT I ALWAYS SLEPT IN YOUR BED BEFORE.
YES, BUT DADDY'S HOME NOW.
WHEN IS DADDY GOING AWAY AGAIN?
WHAT?
WHEN IS HE GOING BACK TO VIETNAM?
HE'S NOT GOING BACK, HONEY. DADDY'S HOME TO STAY NOW.
HE'LL GO BACK.
HE ALWAYS GOES BACK.

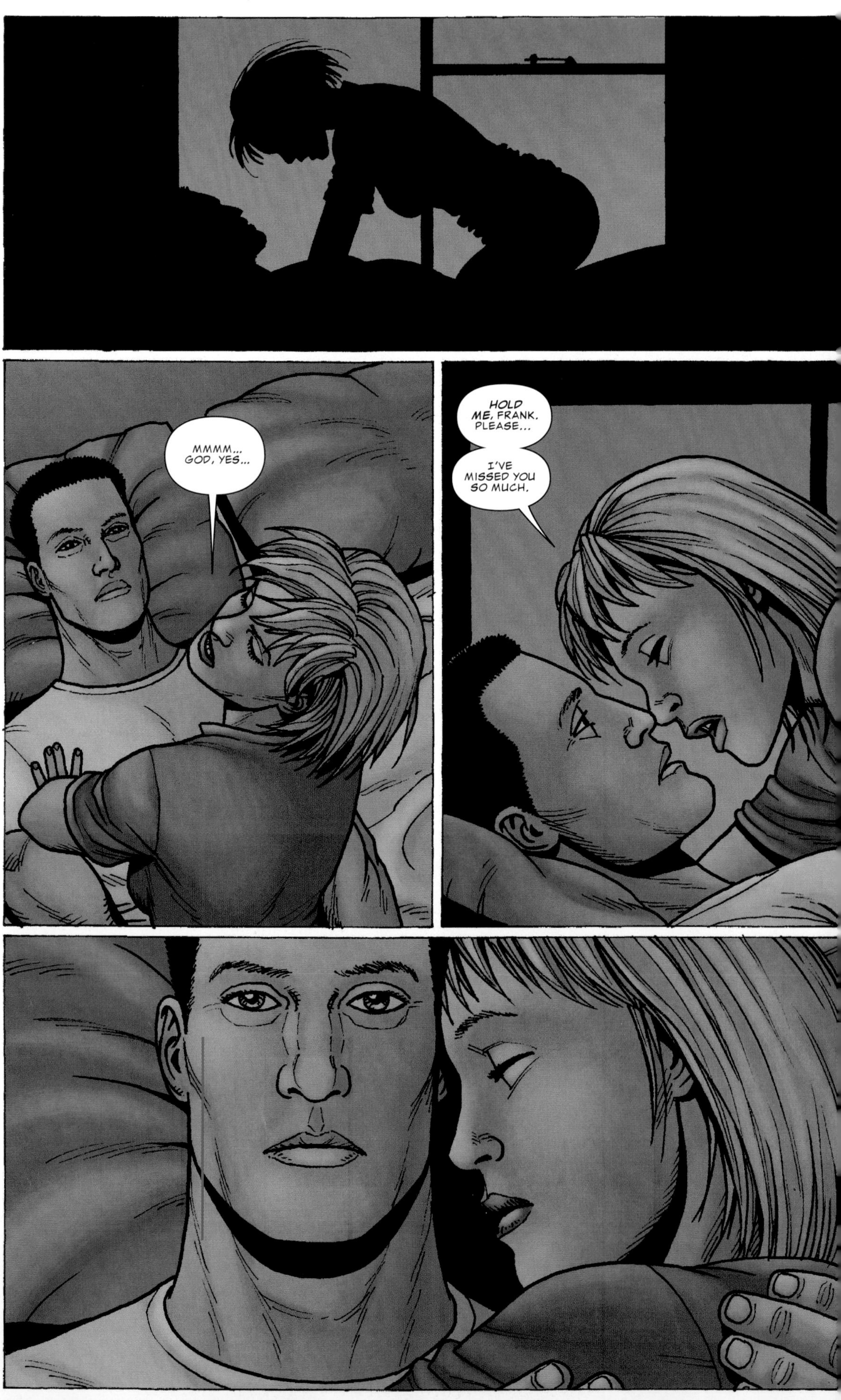

MMMM... GOD, YES...
HOLD ME, FRANK. PLEASE...
I'VE MISSED YOU SO MUCH.

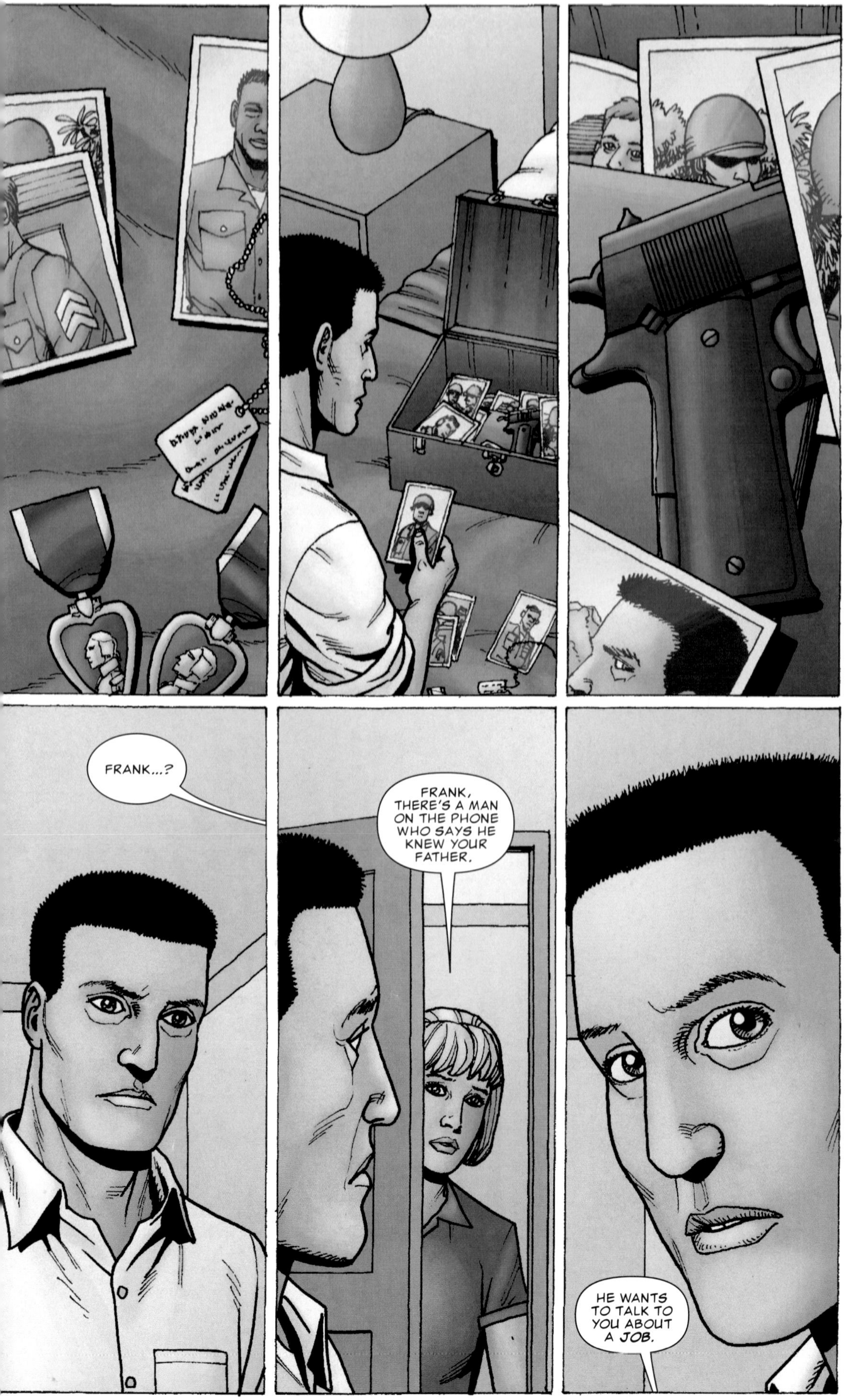
FRANK...?
FRANK, THERE'S A MAN ON THE PHONE WHO SAYS HE KNEW YOUR FATHER.
HE WANTS TO TALK TO YOU ABOUT A JOB.

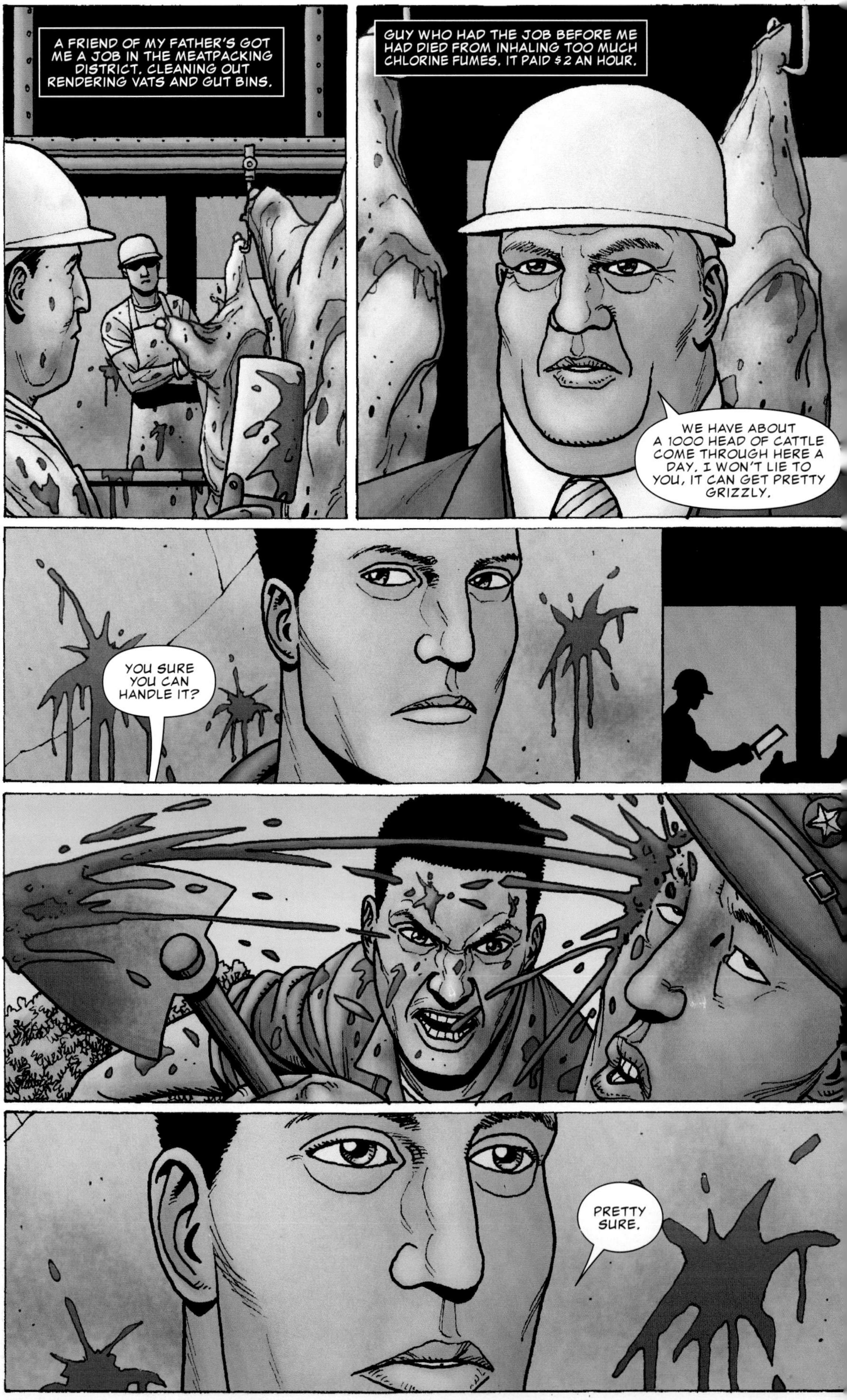
A FRIEND OF MY FATHER'S GOT ME A JOB IN THE MEATPACKING DISTRICT, CLEANING OUT RENDERING VATS AND GUT BINS.
GUY WHO HAD THE JOB BEFORE ME HAD DIED FROM INHALING TOO MUCH CHLORINE FUMES. IT PAID $2 AN HOUR.
WE HAVE ABOUT A 1000 HEAD OF CATTLE COME THROUGH HERE A DAY. I WON'T LIE TO YOU, IT CAN GET PRETTY GRIZZLY.
YOU SURE YOU CAN HANDLE IT?
PRETTY SURE.

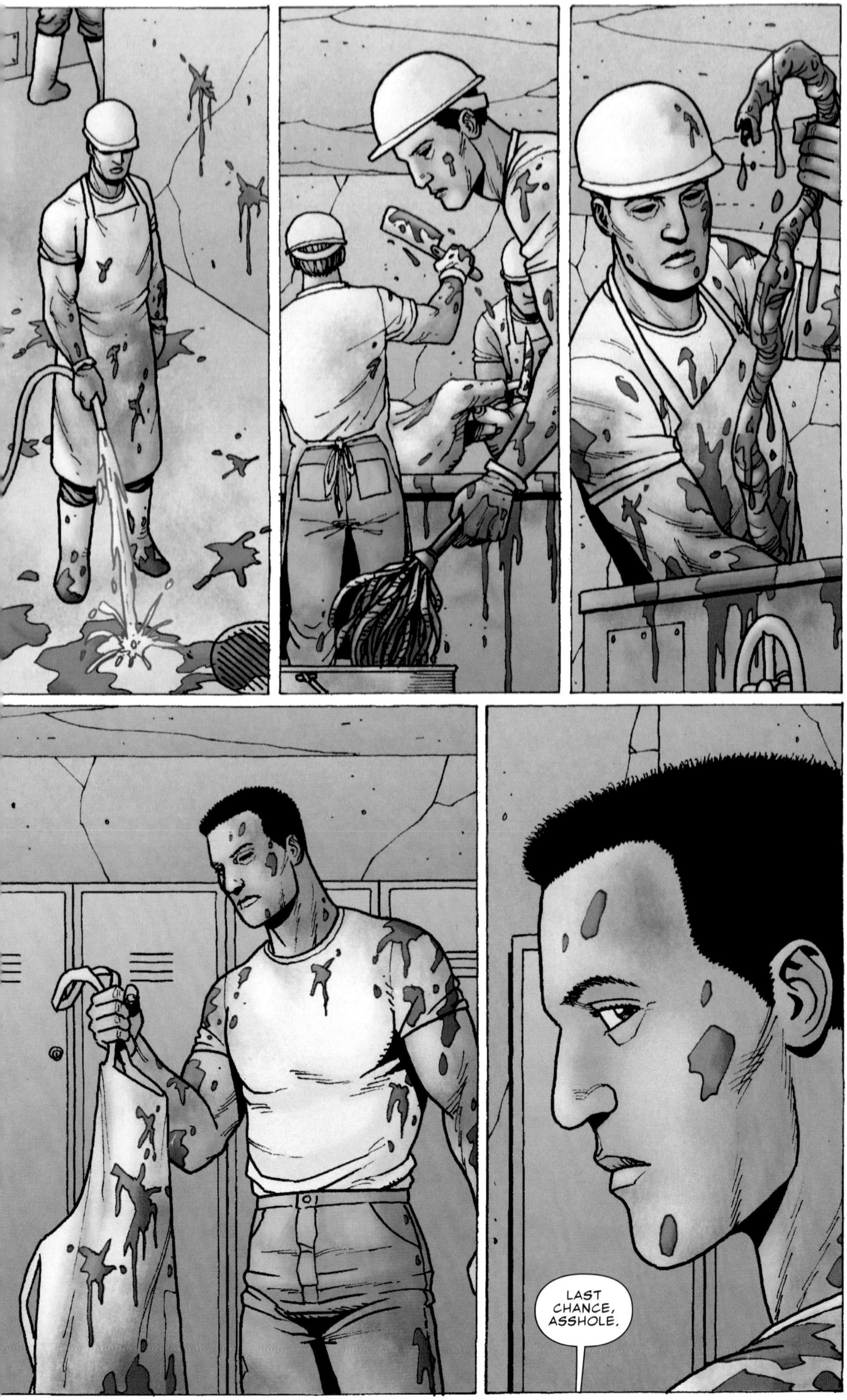
LAST CHANCE, ASSHOLE.

LICK 'EM CLEAN. DO IT OR YOU'RE *FUCKING* FIRED.

PLEASE, I NEED THIS JOB, YOU CAN'T--

I SEE YOUR MOUTH MOVING, BUT I DON'T FEEL NO *LICKIN'* GOING ON.

OH GOD...

THAT'S RIGHT. LICK IT UP *GOOD*.

THE OWNER'S SON, FUCKING ARROGANT LITTLE POGUE.

ONE OF THOSE GUYS WHO'S JUST BEGGING TO BE TAUGHT A FUCKING LESSON.

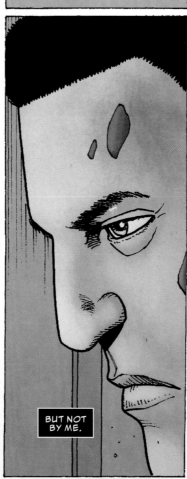

BUT NOT BY ME.

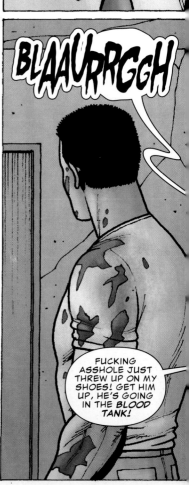

BLAAURRGGH

FUCKING ASSHOLE JUST THREW UP ON MY SHOES! GET HIM UP, HE'S GOING IN THE *BLOOD TANK!*

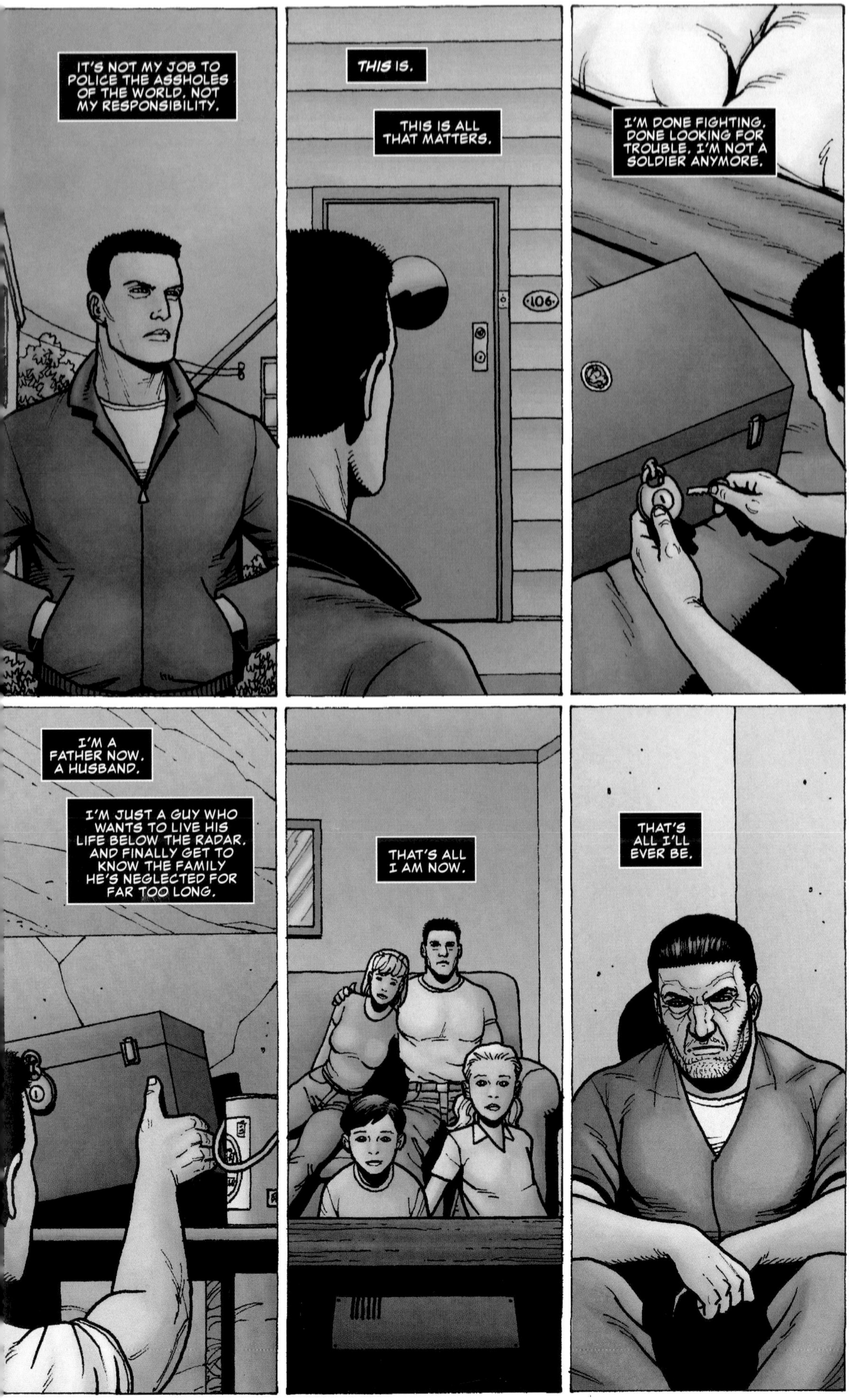
IT'S NOT MY JOB TO POLICE THE ASSHOLES OF THE WORLD. NOT MY RESPONSIBILITY.
THIS IS.
THIS IS ALL THAT MATTERS.
·106·
I'M DONE FIGHTING. DONE LOOKING FOR TROUBLE. I'M NOT A SOLDIER ANYMORE.
I'M A FATHER NOW. A HUSBAND.
I'M JUST A GUY WHO WANTS TO LIVE HIS LIFE BELOW THE RADAR, AND FINALLY GET TO KNOW THE FAMILY HE'S NEGLECTED FOR FAR TOO LONG.
THAT'S ALL I AM NOW.
THAT'S ALL I'LL EVER BE.

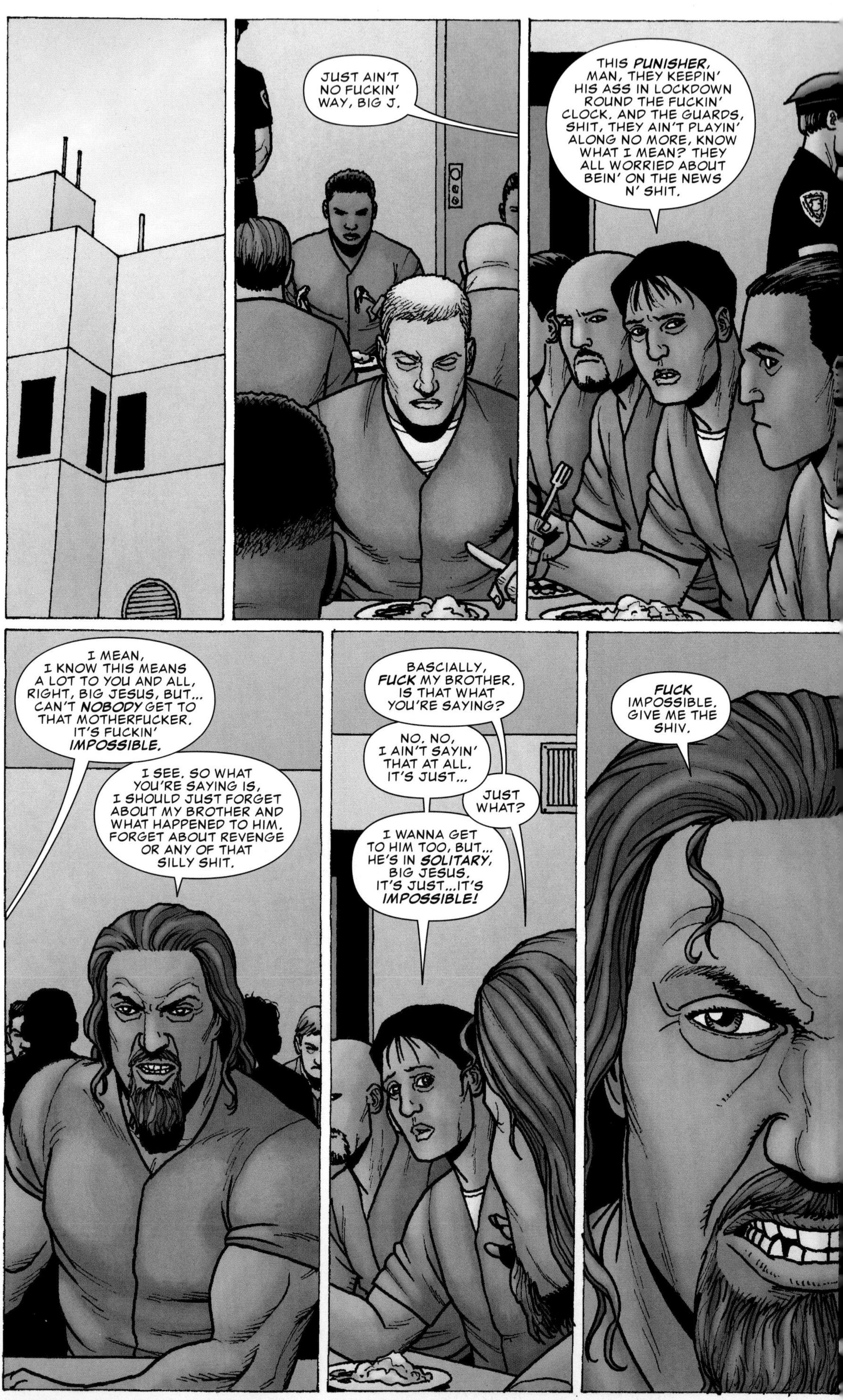

JUST AIN'T NO FUCKIN' WAY, BIG J.
THIS PUNISHER, MAN, THEY KEEPIN' HIS ASS IN LOCKDOWN ROUND THE FUCKIN' CLOCK. AND THE GUARDS, SHIT, THEY AIN'T PLAYIN' ALONG NO MORE, KNOW WHAT I MEAN? THEY ALL WORRIED ABOUT BEIN' ON THE NEWS N' SHIT.
I MEAN, I KNOW THIS MEANS A LOT TO YOU AND ALL, RIGHT, BIG JESUS, BUT... CAN'T NOBODY GET TO THAT MOTHERFUCKER. IT'S FUCKIN' IMPOSSIBLE.
I SEE. SO WHAT YOU'RE SAYING IS, I SHOULD JUST FORGET ABOUT MY BROTHER AND WHAT HAPPENED TO HIM. FORGET ABOUT REVENGE OR ANY OF THAT SILLY SHIT.
BASCIALLY, FUCK MY BROTHER. IS THAT WHAT YOU'RE SAYING?
NO, NO, I AIN'T SAYIN' THAT AT ALL. IT'S JUST...
JUST WHAT?
I WANNA GET TO HIM TOO, BUT... HE'S IN SOLITARY, BIG JESUS. IT'S JUST...IT'S IMPOSSIBLE!
FUCK IMPOSSIBLE. GIVE ME THE SHIV.

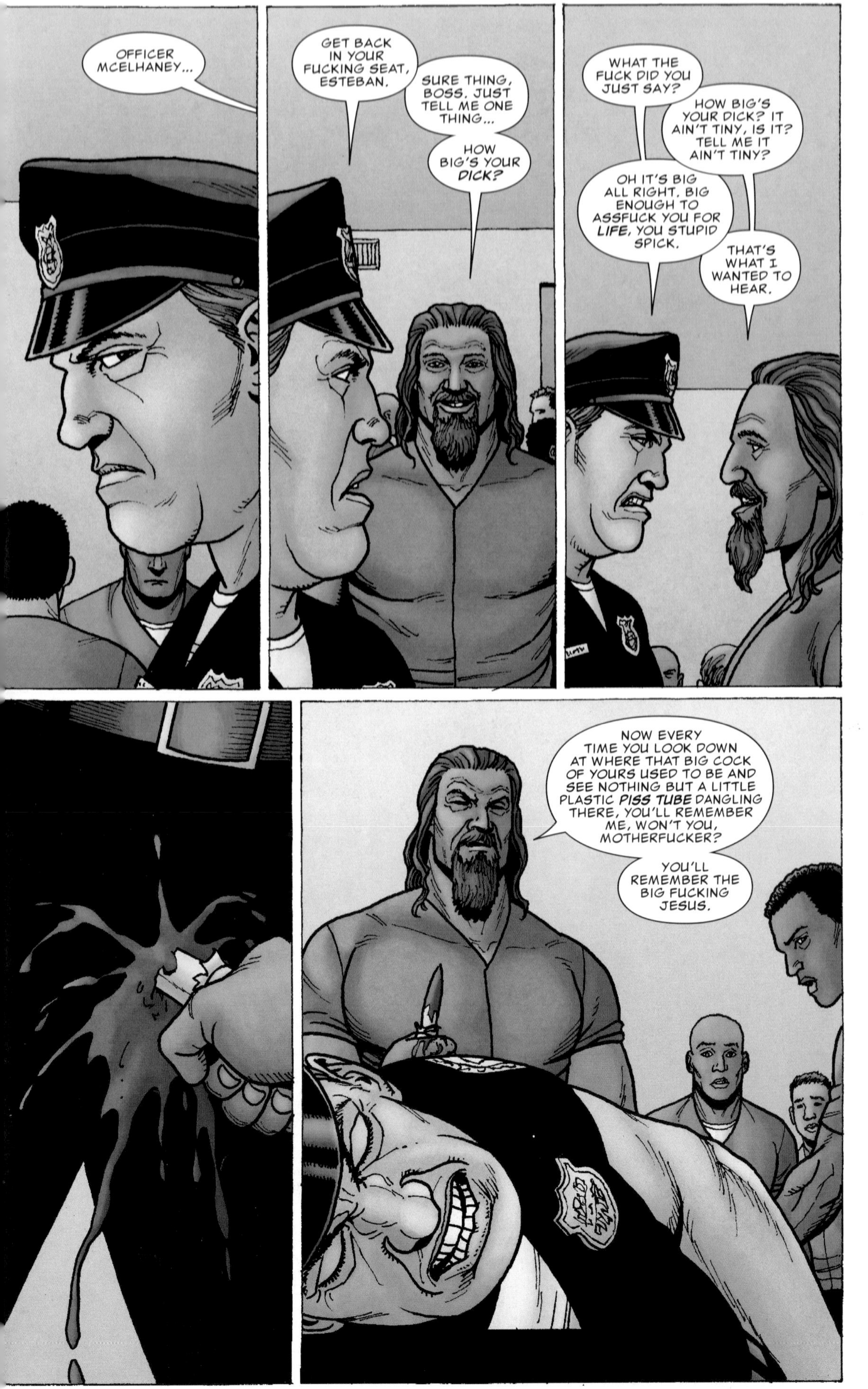

OFFICER MCELHANEY...
GET BACK IN YOUR FUCKING SEAT, ESTEBAN.
SURE THING, BOSS. JUST TELL ME ONE THING...
HOW BIG'S YOUR *DICK?*
WHAT THE FUCK DID YOU JUST SAY?
HOW BIG'S YOUR DICK? IT AIN'T TINY, IS IT? TELL ME IT AIN'T TINY?
OH IT'S BIG ALL RIGHT, BIG ENOUGH TO ASSFUCK YOU FOR *LIFE*, YOU STUPID SPICK.
THAT'S WHAT I WANTED TO HEAR.
NOW EVERY TIME YOU LOOK DOWN AT WHERE THAT BIG COCK OF YOURS USED TO BE AND SEE NOTHING BUT A LITTLE PLASTIC *PISS TUBE* DANGLING THERE, YOU'LL REMEMBER ME, WON'T YOU, MOTHERFUCKER?
YOU'LL REMEMBER THE BIG FUCKING JESUS.

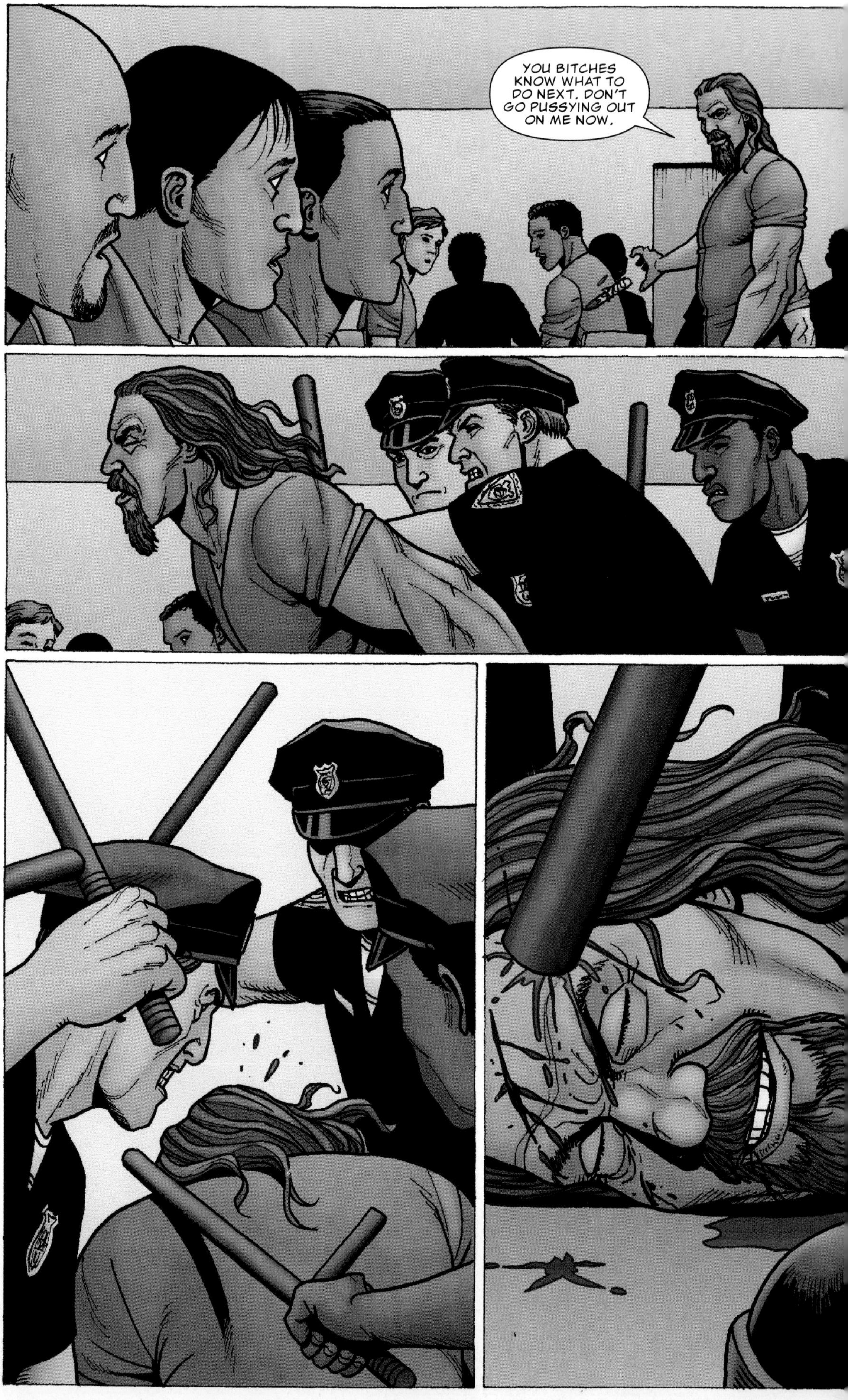
YOU BITCHES KNOW WHAT TO DO NEXT. DON'T GO PUSSYING OUT ON ME NOW.

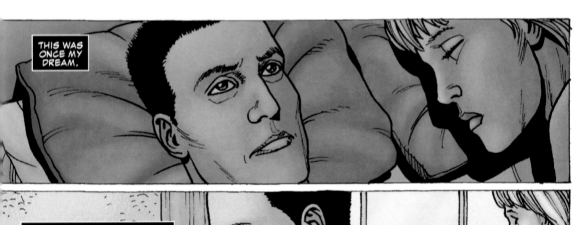

THIS WAS ONCE MY DREAM.

BACK IN VIETNAM, I WOULD DREAM OF THIS HOUSE. OF BEING HERE WITH MY FAMILY. OF BEING *HOME*.

BUT NOW THAT I'M HERE, EACH NIGHT I FIND MYSELF DREAMING THAT I WAS BACK OVER THERE.

DREAMING OF *WAR*. OF THE RUMBLE OF B-52s. THE SMELL OF WHITE PHOSPHORUS.

NEXT TIME I TELL YOU TO DO SOMETHING, YOU'RE GONNA FUCKING DO IT, *AREN'T* YOU, ASSHOLE?

THE BUCK OF AN M-60 AGAINST MY SIDE.

I DON'T UNDERSTAND WHAT'S WRONG WITH ME. WHY I STUMBLE THROUGH MY DAYS LIKE A ZOMBIE. UNABLE TO FEEL ANY OF THE THINGS I KNOW I'M SUPPOSED TO BE FEELING, UNABLE TO FEEL...ANYTHING.

FRANK, WHY DON'T WE ALL GET OUT THIS WEEKEND? MAYBE GO TO THE PARK OR... FRANK?

ANYTHING AT ALL.

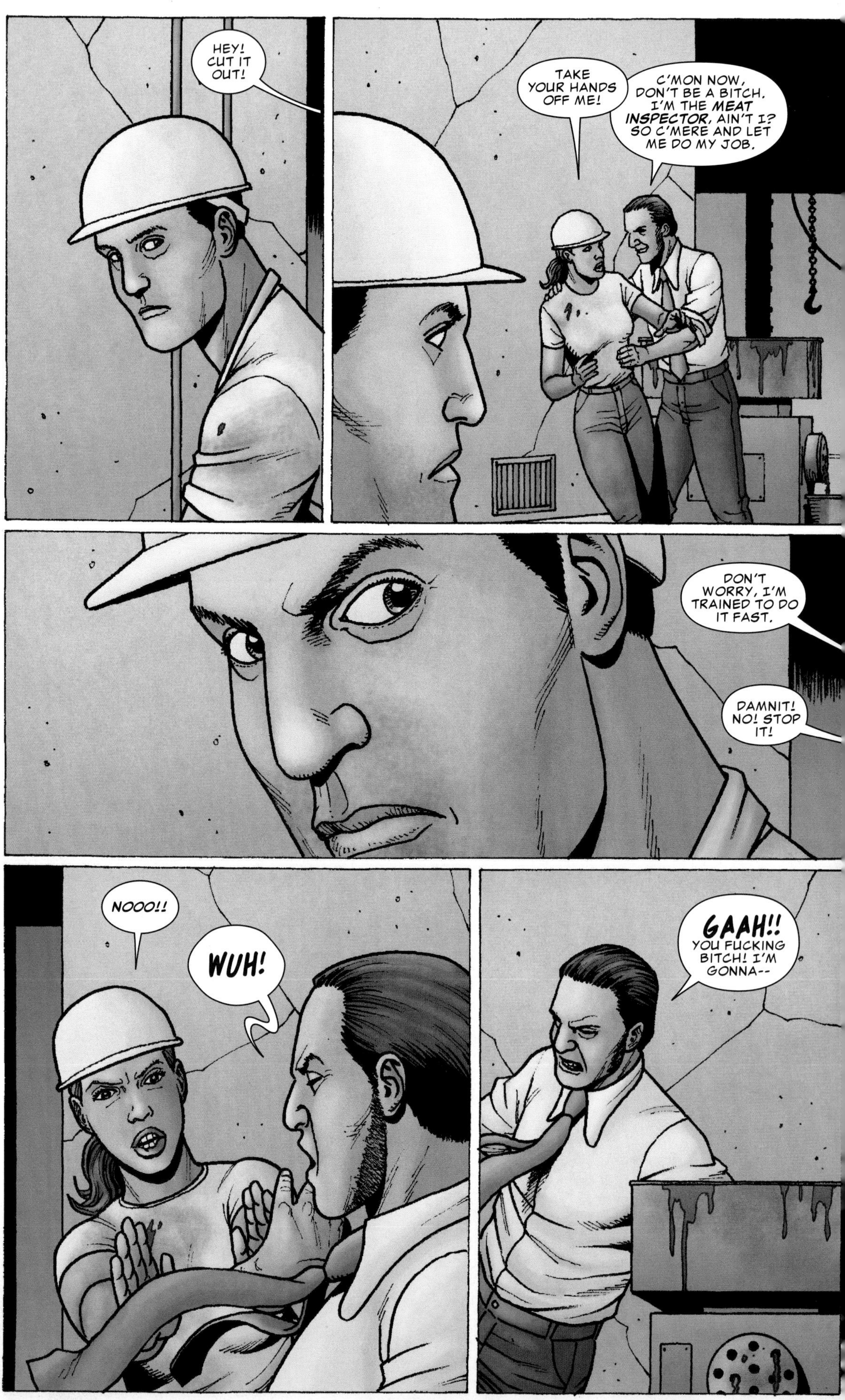

HEY! CUT IT OUT!
TAKE YOUR HANDS OFF ME!
C'MON NOW, DON'T BE A BITCH. I'M THE **MEAT INSPECTOR**, AIN'T I? SO C'MERE AND LET ME DO MY JOB.
DON'T WORRY, I'M TRAINED TO DO IT FAST.
DAMNIT! NO! STOP IT!
NOOO!!
WUH!
GAAH!! YOU FUCKING BITCH! I'M GONNA--

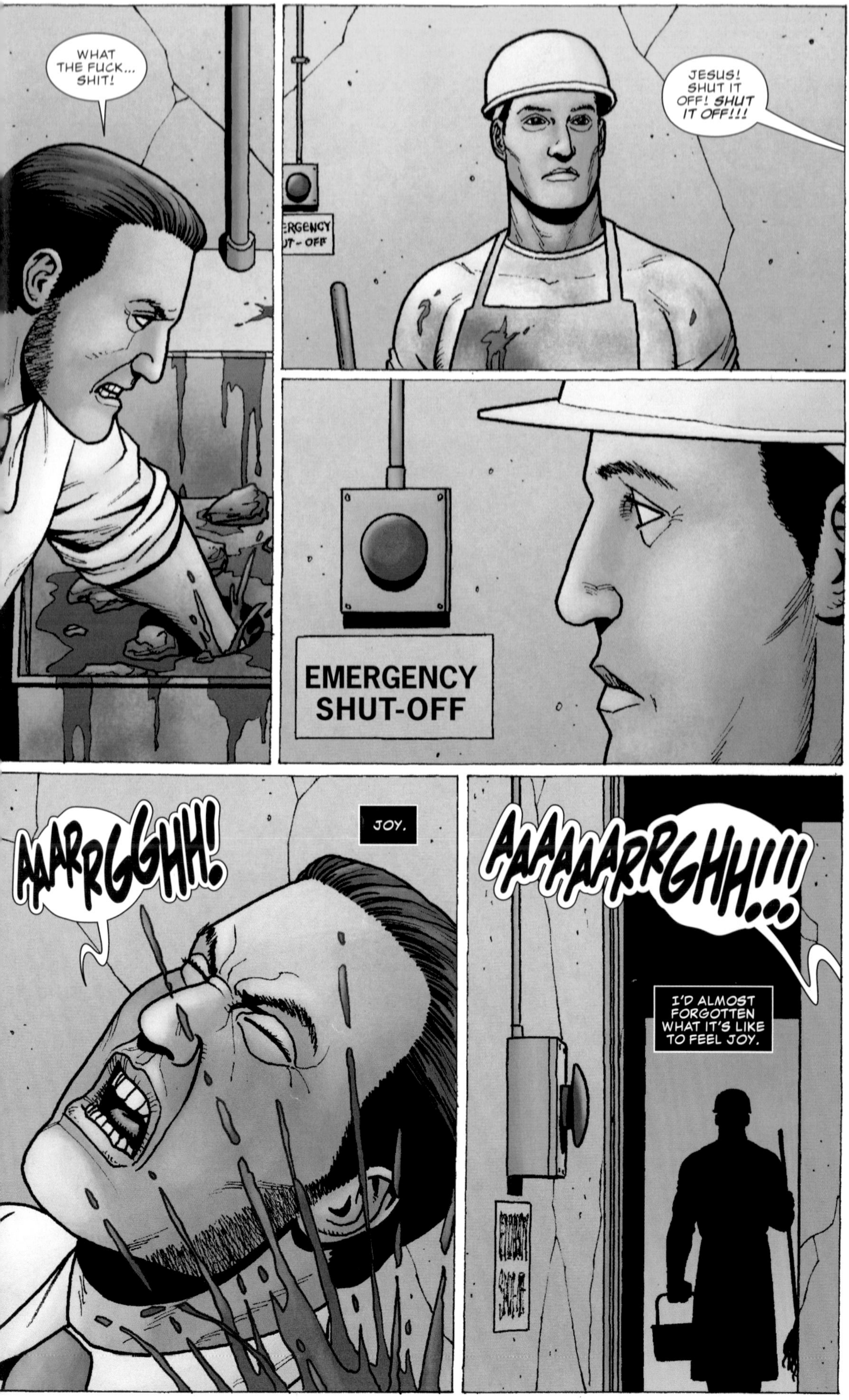
WHAT THE FUCK... SHIT!
JESUS! SHUT IT OFF! SHUT IT OFF!!!
ERGENCY UT-OFF
EMERGENCY SHUT-OFF
AAARRGGHH!
JOY.
AAAAAARRGHH!!!...
I'D ALMOST FORGOTTEN WHAT IT'S LIKE TO FEEL JOY.

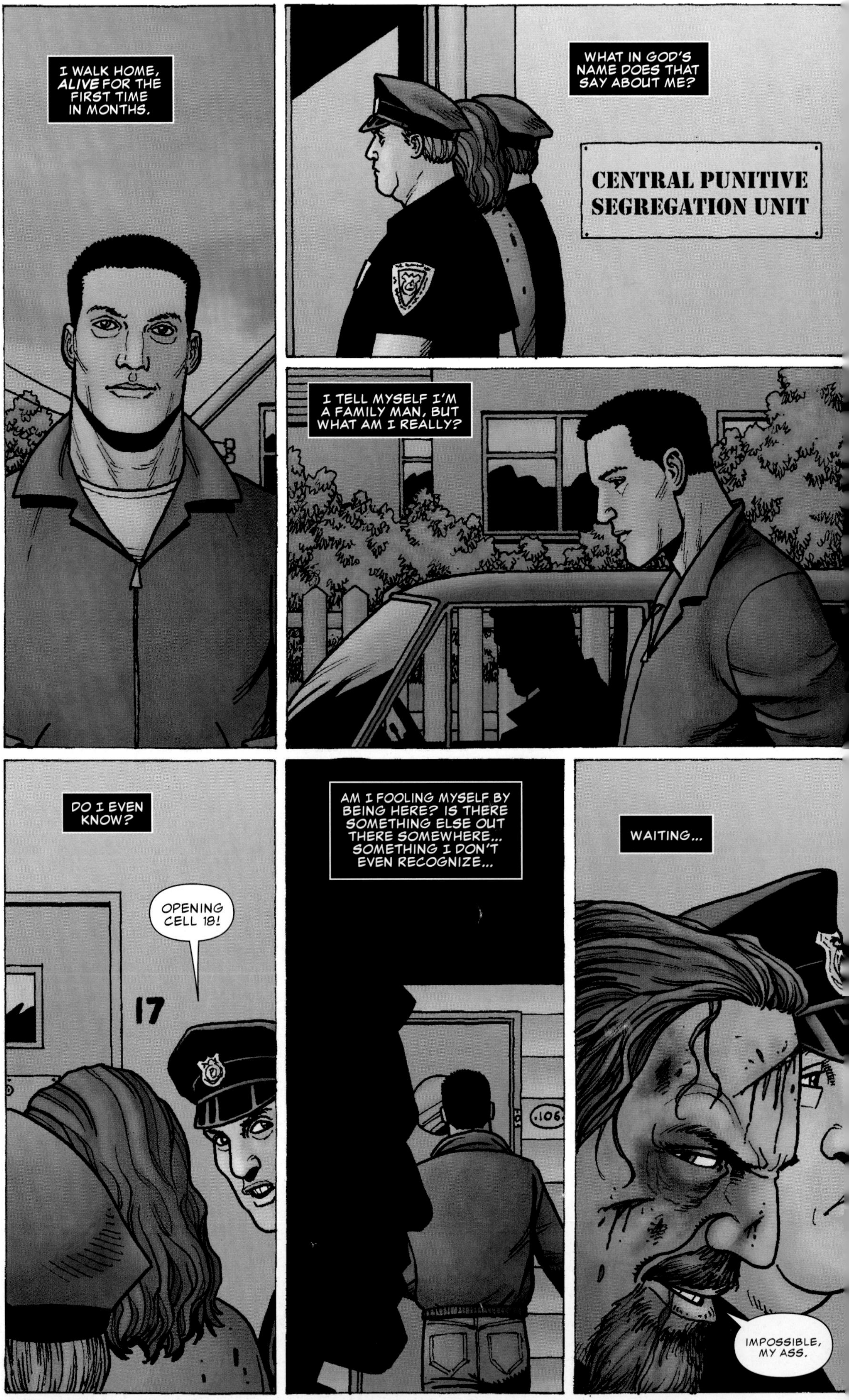
I WALK HOME, *ALIVE* FOR THE FIRST TIME IN MONTHS.
WHAT IN GOD'S NAME DOES THAT SAY ABOUT ME?
CENTRAL PUNITIVE SEGREGATION UNIT
I TELL MYSELF I'M A FAMILY MAN, BUT WHAT AM I REALLY?
DO I EVEN KNOW?
OPENING CELL 18!
17
AM I FOOLING MYSELF BY BEING HERE? IS THERE SOMETHING ELSE OUT THERE SOMEWHERE... SOMETHING I DON'T EVEN RECOGNIZE...
106
WAITING...
IMPOSSIBLE, MY ASS.

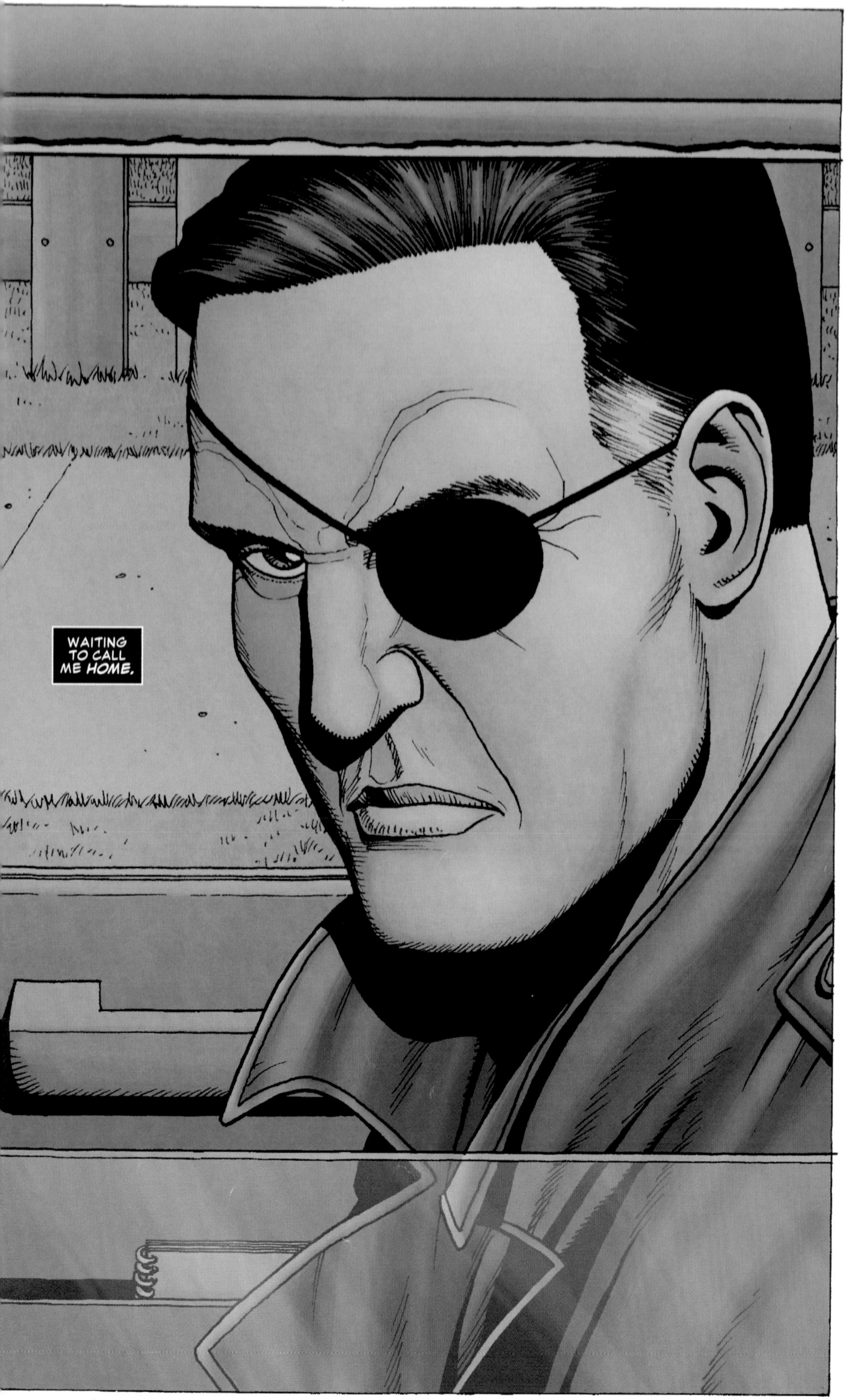
WAITING TO CALL ME HOME.

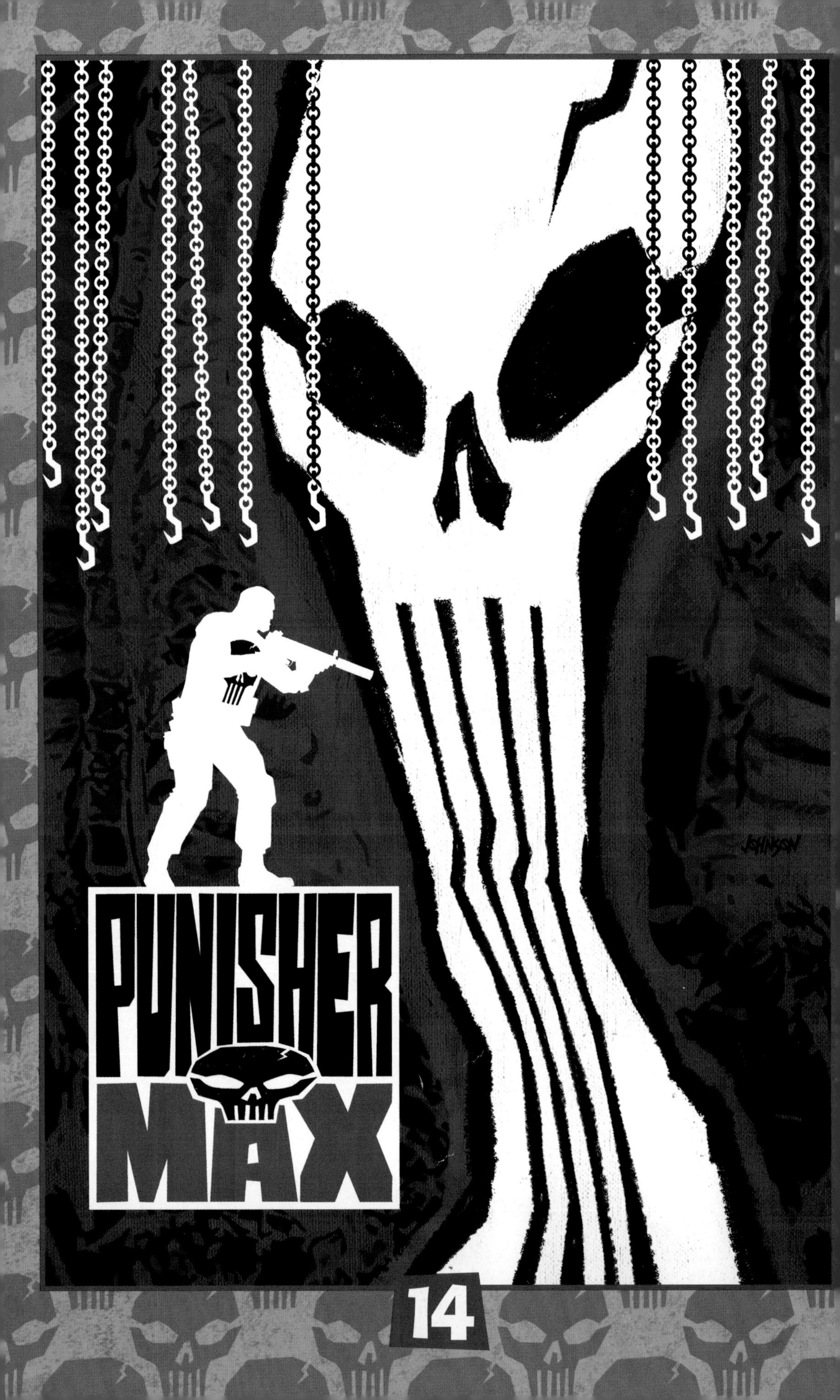
JOHNSON
PUNISHER
MAX
14

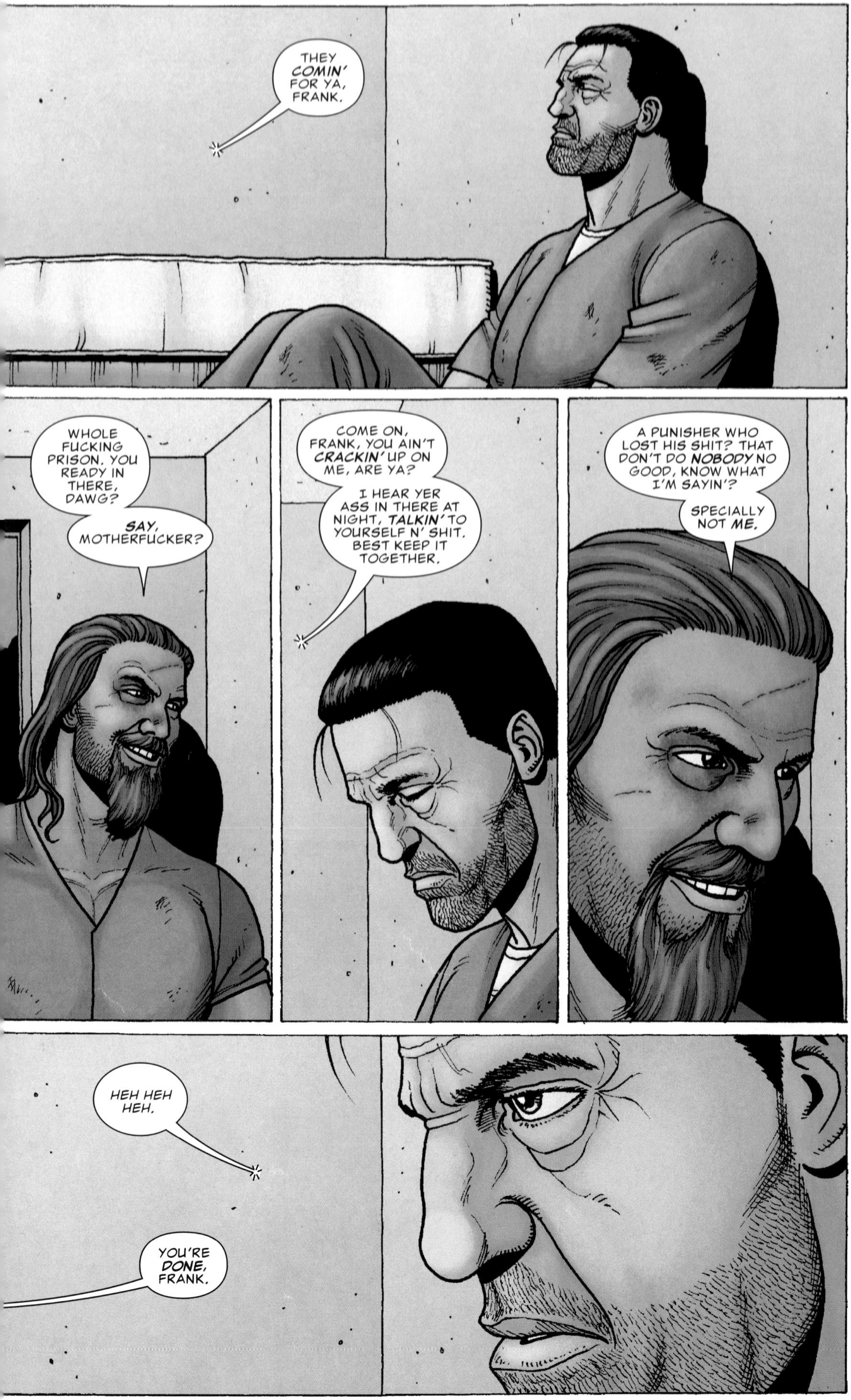

THEY COMIN' FOR YA, FRANK.
WHOLE FUCKING PRISON. YOU READY IN THERE, DAWG?
SAY, MOTHERFUCKER?
COME ON, FRANK, YOU AIN'T CRACKIN' UP ON ME, ARE YA?
I HEAR YER ASS IN THERE AT NIGHT, TALKIN' TO YOURSELF N' SHIT. BEST KEEP IT TOGETHER.
A PUNISHER WHO LOST HIS SHIT? THAT DON'T DO NOBODY NO GOOD, KNOW WHAT I'M SAYIN'?
SPECIALLY NOT ME.
HEH HEH HEH.
YOU'RE DONE, FRANK.

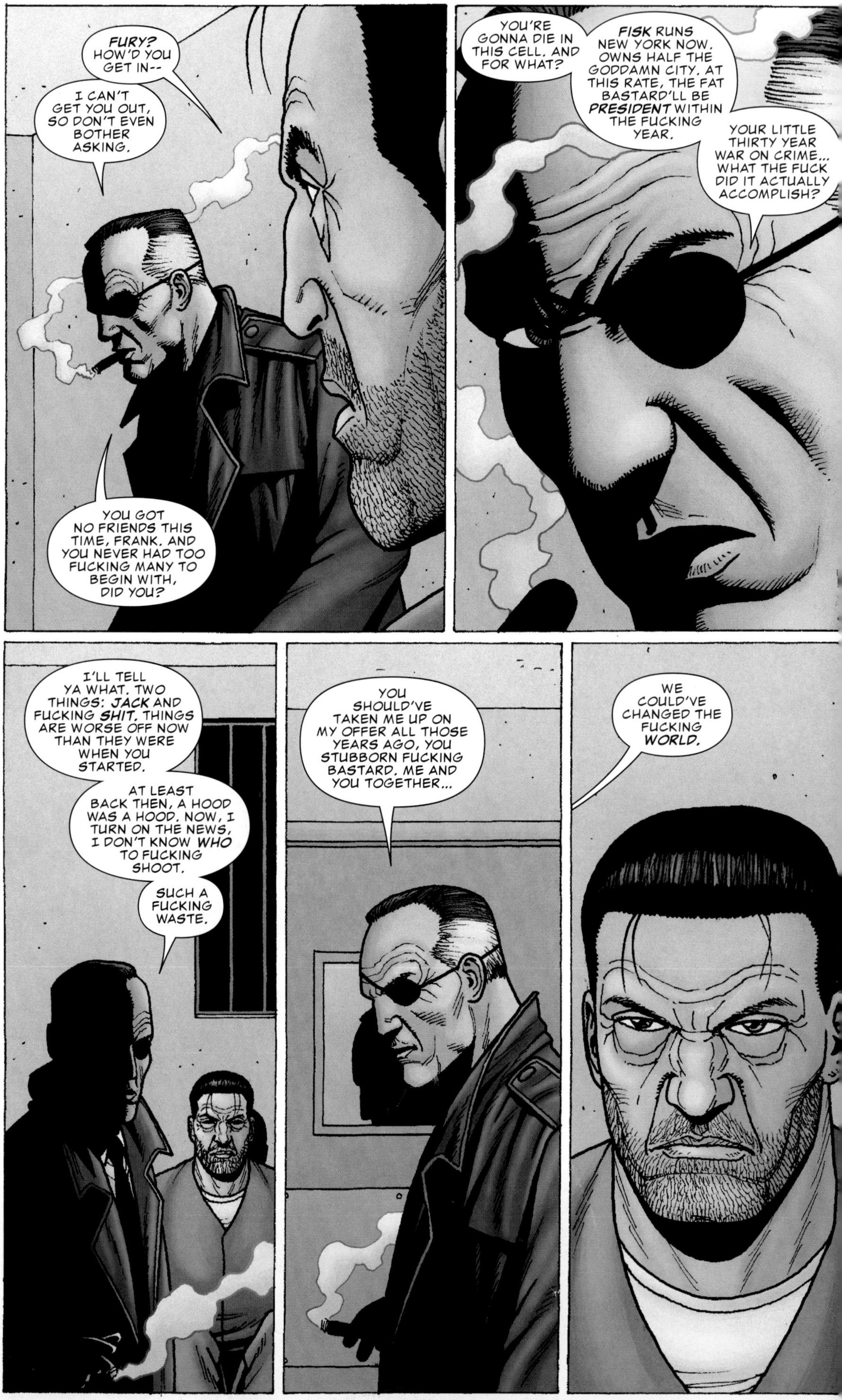
FURY? HOW'D YOU GET IN--
I CAN'T GET YOU OUT, SO DON'T EVEN BOTHER ASKING.
YOU GOT NO FRIENDS THIS TIME, FRANK. AND YOU NEVER HAD TOO FUCKING MANY TO BEGIN WITH, DID YOU?
YOU'RE GONNA DIE IN THIS CELL. AND FOR WHAT?
FISK RUNS NEW YORK NOW. OWNS HALF THE GODDAMN CITY. AT THIS RATE, THE FAT BASTARD'LL BE PRESIDENT WITHIN THE FUCKING YEAR.
YOUR LITTLE THIRTY YEAR WAR ON CRIME... WHAT THE FUCK DID IT ACTUALLY ACCOMPLISH?
I'LL TELL YA WHAT. TWO THINGS: JACK AND FUCKING SHIT. THINGS ARE WORSE OFF NOW THAN THEY WERE WHEN YOU STARTED.
AT LEAST BACK THEN, A HOOD WAS A HOOD. NOW, I TURN ON THE NEWS, I DON'T KNOW WHO TO FUCKING SHOOT.
SUCH A FUCKING WASTE.
YOU SHOULD'VE TAKEN ME UP ON MY OFFER ALL THOSE YEARS AGO, YOU STUBBORN FUCKING BASTARD. ME AND YOU TOGETHER...
WE COULD'VE CHANGED THE FUCKING WORLD.

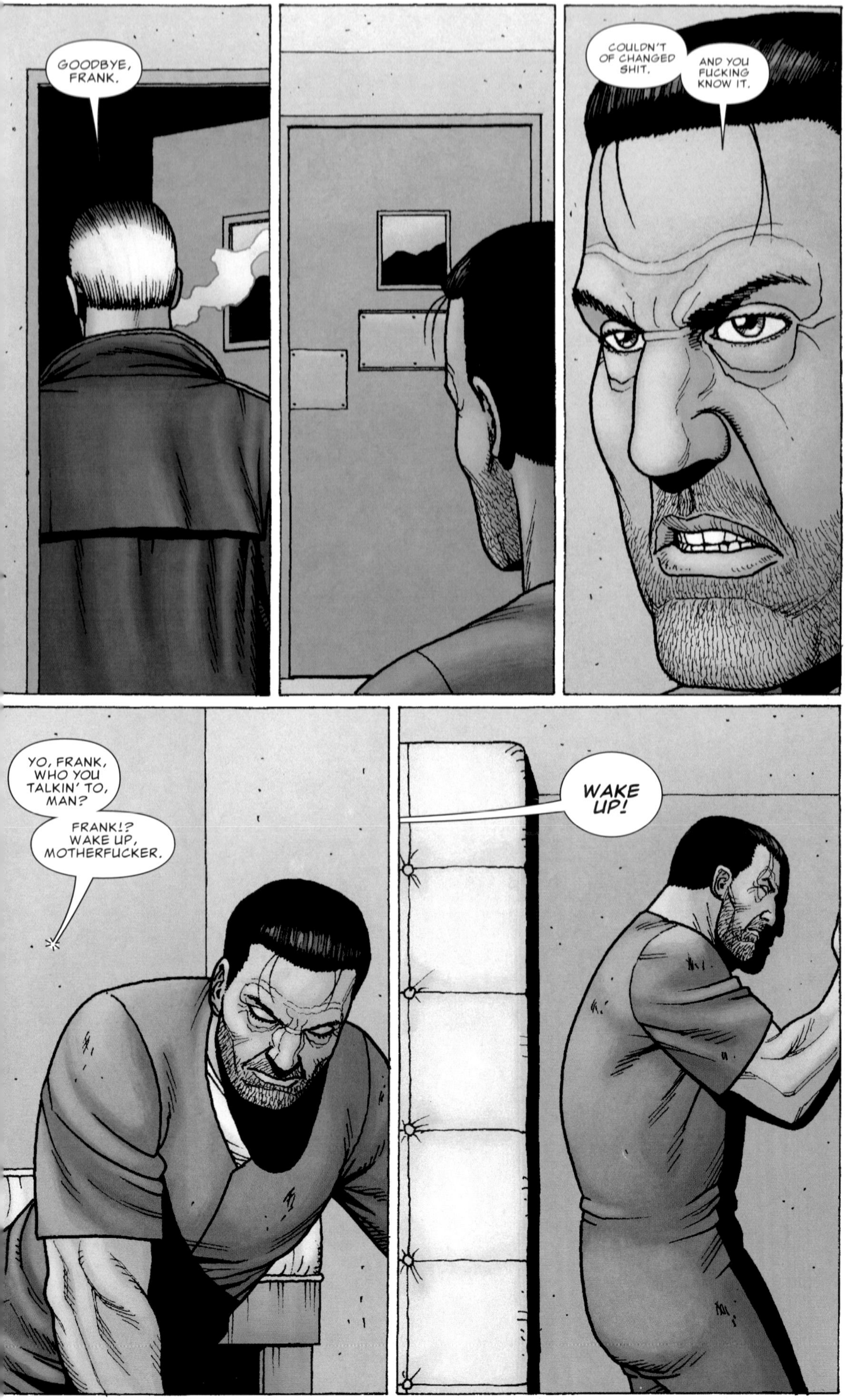
GOODBYE, FRANK.
COULDN'T OF CHANGED SHIT.
AND YOU FUCKING KNOW IT.
YO, FRANK, WHO YOU TALKIN' TO, MAN?
FRANK!? WAKE UP, MOTHERFUCKER.
WAKE UP!

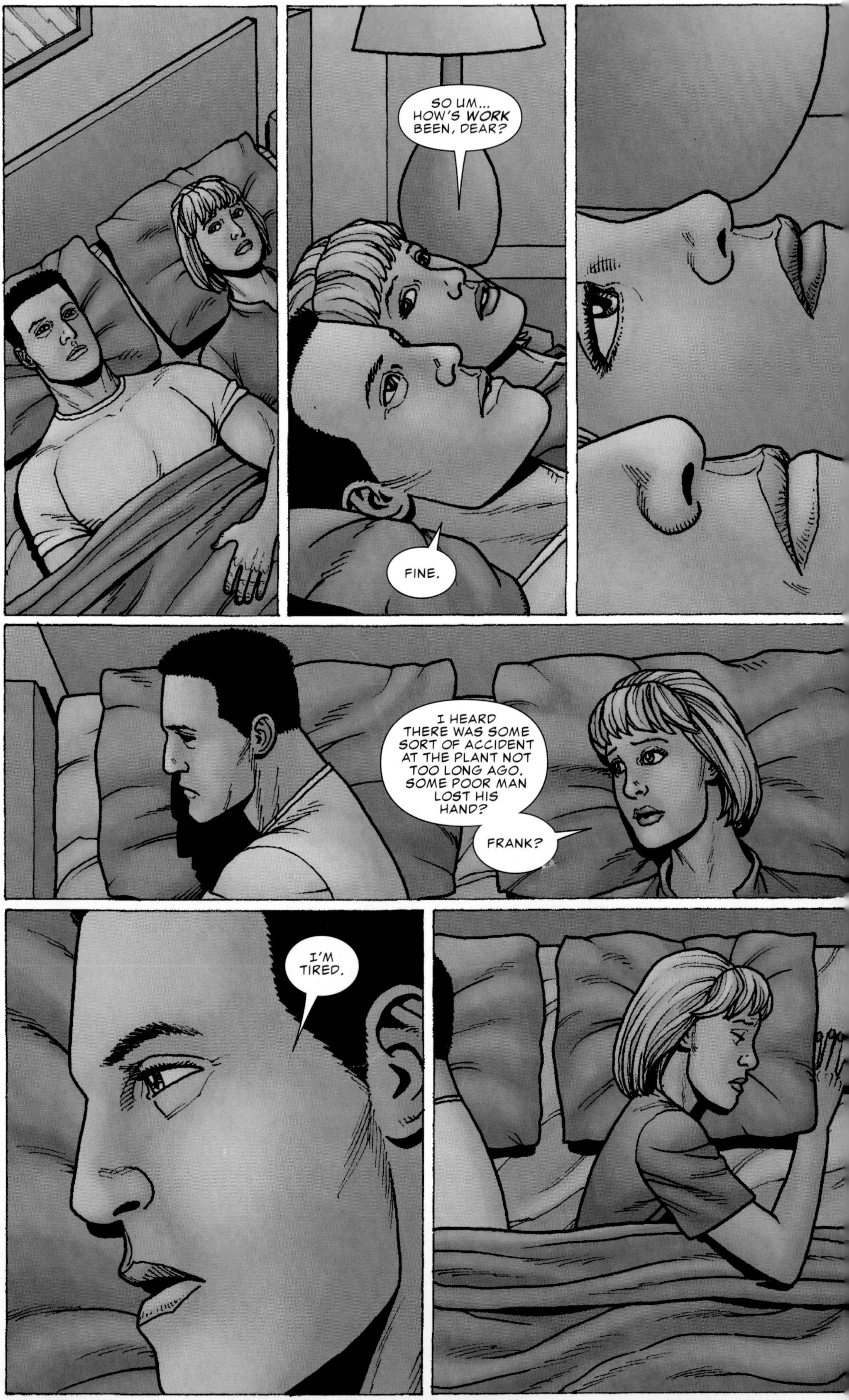
SO UM... HOW'S WORK BEEN, DEAR?
FINE.
I HEARD THERE WAS SOME SORT OF ACCIDENT AT THE PLANT NOT TOO LONG AGO. SOME POOR MAN LOST HIS HAND?
FRANK?
I'M TIRED.

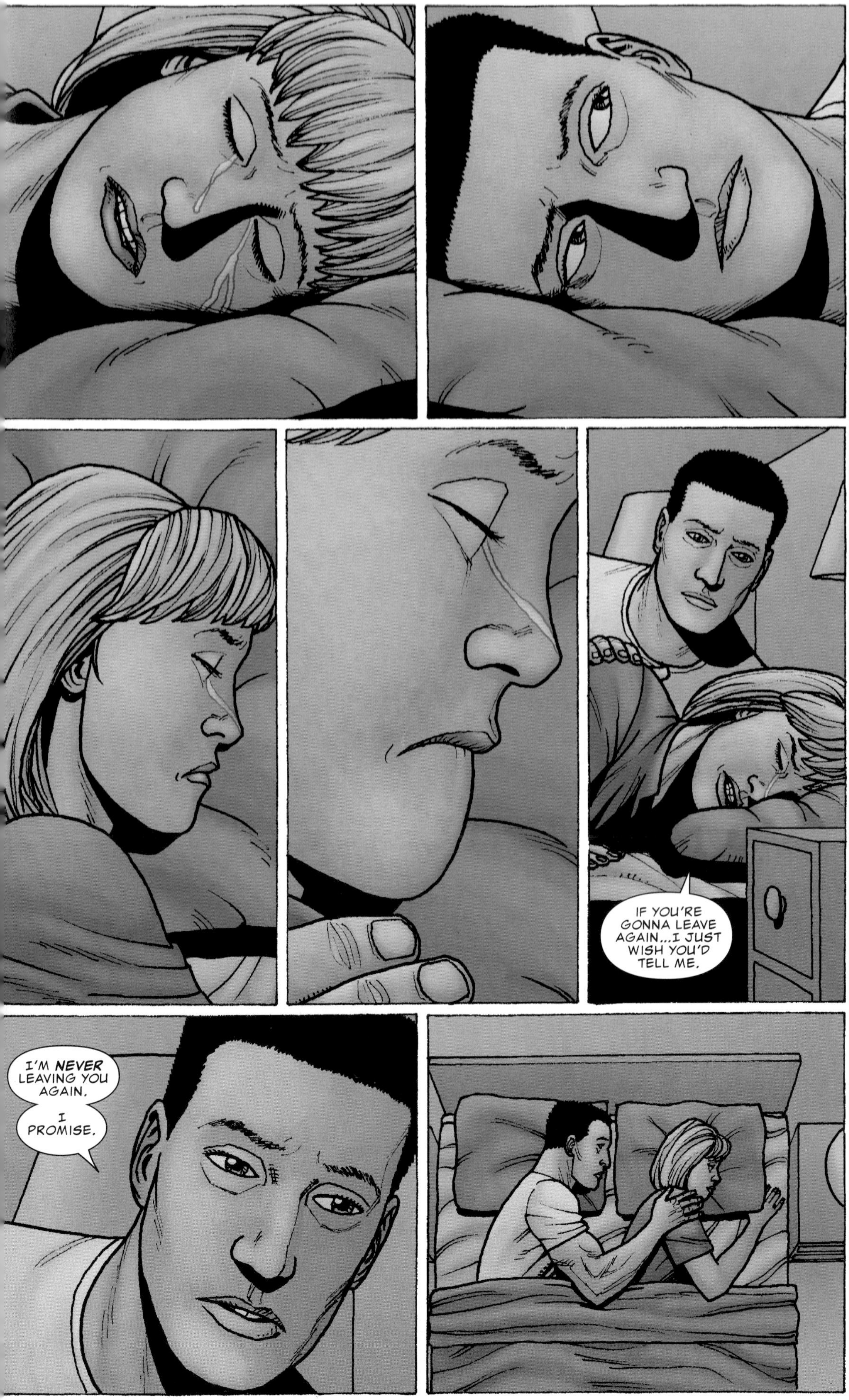
IF YOU'RE GONNA LEAVE AGAIN... I JUST WISH YOU'D TELL ME.
I'M NEVER LEAVING YOU AGAIN.
I PROMISE.

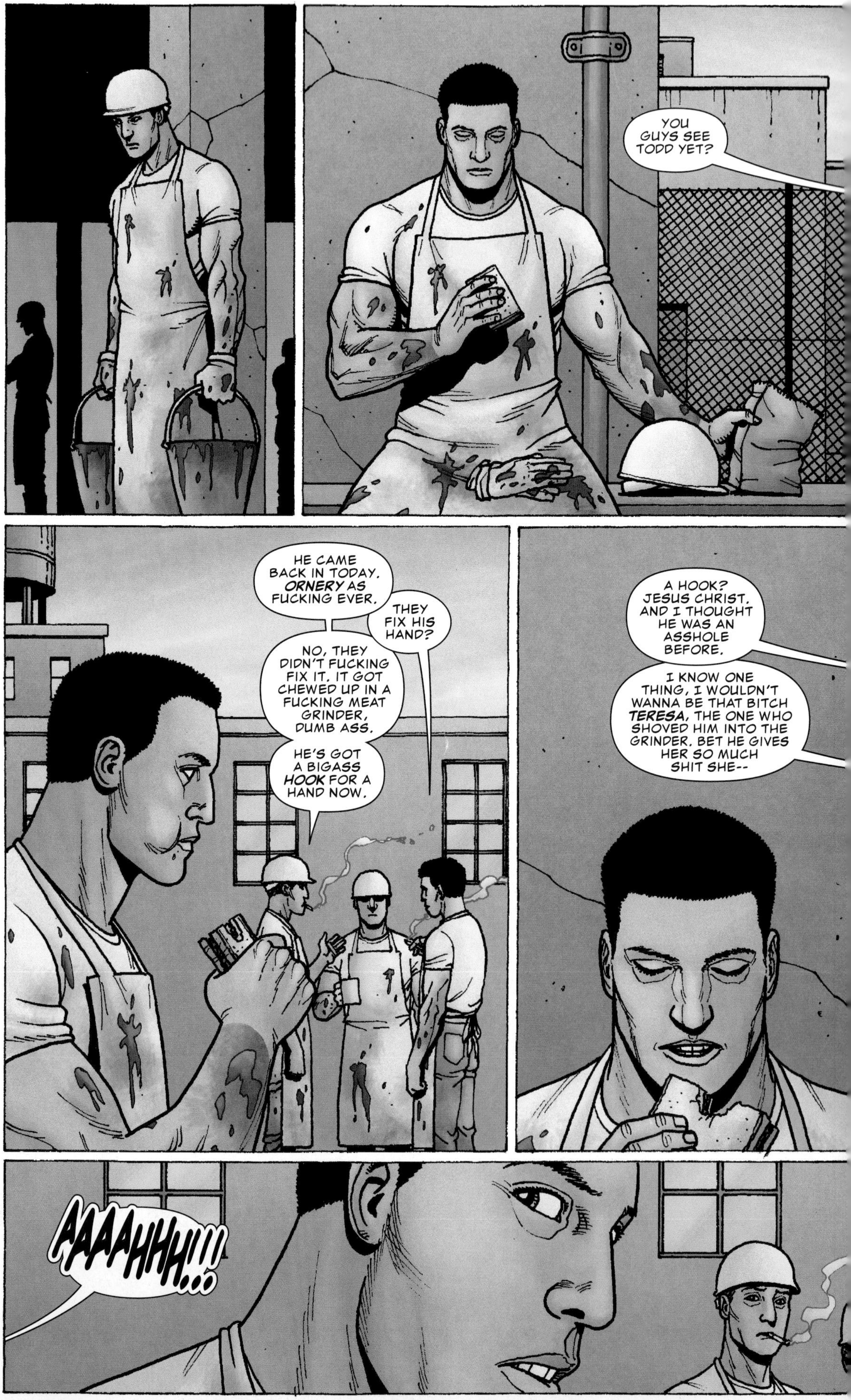

YOU GUYS SEE TODD YET?
HE CAME BACK IN TODAY. ORNERY AS FUCKING EVER.
THEY FIX HIS HAND?
NO, THEY DIDN'T FUCKING FIX IT. IT GOT CHEWED UP IN A FUCKING MEAT GRINDER, DUMB ASS.
HE'S GOT A BIGASS HOOK FOR A HAND NOW.
A HOOK? JESUS CHRIST. AND I THOUGHT HE WAS AN ASSHOLE BEFORE.
I KNOW ONE THING, I WOULDN'T WANNA BE THAT BITCH TERESA, THE ONE WHO SHOVED HIM INTO THE GRINDER. BET HE GIVES HER SO MUCH SHIT SHE--
AAAAHHH!!!..

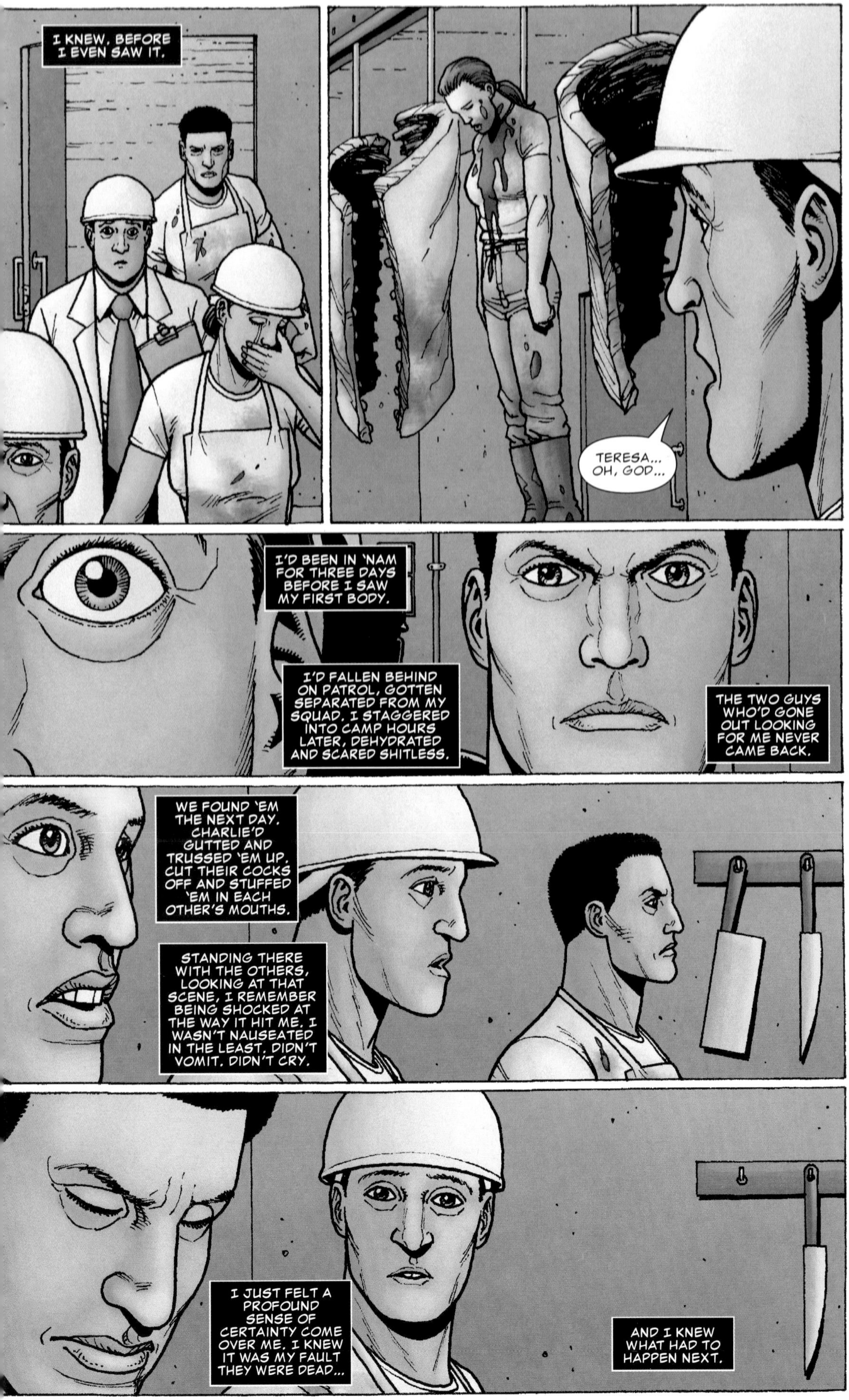
I KNEW, BEFORE I EVEN SAW IT.
TERESA... OH, GOD...
I'D BEEN IN 'NAM FOR THREE DAYS BEFORE I SAW MY FIRST BODY.
I'D FALLEN BEHIND ON PATROL, GOTTEN SEPARATED FROM MY SQUAD. I STAGGERED INTO CAMP HOURS LATER, DEHYDRATED AND SCARED SHITLESS.
THE TWO GUYS WHO'D GONE OUT LOOKING FOR ME NEVER CAME BACK.
WE FOUND 'EM THE NEXT DAY. CHARLIE'D GUTTED AND TRUSSED 'EM UP, CUT THEIR COCKS OFF AND STUFFED 'EM IN EACH OTHER'S MOUTHS.
STANDING THERE WITH THE OTHERS, LOOKING AT THAT SCENE, I REMEMBER BEING SHOCKED AT THE WAY IT HIT ME. I WASN'T NAUSEATED IN THE LEAST. DIDN'T VOMIT. DIDN'T CRY.
I JUST FELT A PROFOUND SENSE OF CERTAINTY COME OVER ME. I KNEW IT WAS MY FAULT THEY WERE DEAD...
AND I KNEW WHAT HAD TO HAPPEN NEXT.

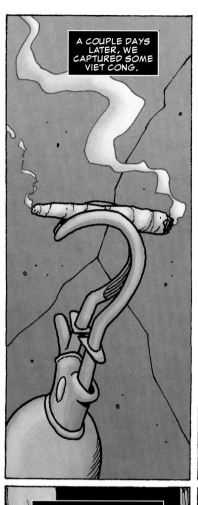

A COUPLE DAYS LATER, WE CAPTURED SOME VIET CONG.

THREE RAGGEDY, MALNOURISHED MEN WITH BARELY A DOZEN ROUNDS OF AMMO BETWEEN THEM.

GOT A FUCKING *ROACH CLIP* FOR A HAND NOW, JESUS.

SOME OF OUR GUYS SAID THEY HAD TO BE THE ONES, THE BASTARDS WHO'D BUTCHERED OUR FRIENDS. THERE WAS NO WAY OF KNOWING FOR SURE.

THE WHOLE SQUAD WAS SHOVING THEM AROUND, TALKING LOUDLY, MAKING THREATS.

WHEN I STEPPED TO THE FRONT OF THE CROWD, EVERYTHING WENT QUIET.

WHILE EVERYONE ELSE STOOD AROUND AND WATCHED, I TOOK MY K-BAR TO THOSE THREE MEN...

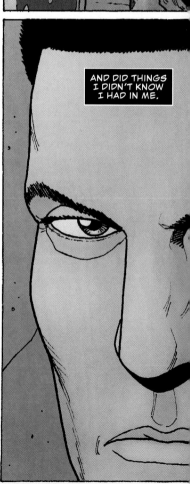

AND DID THINGS I DIDN'T KNOW I HAD IN ME.

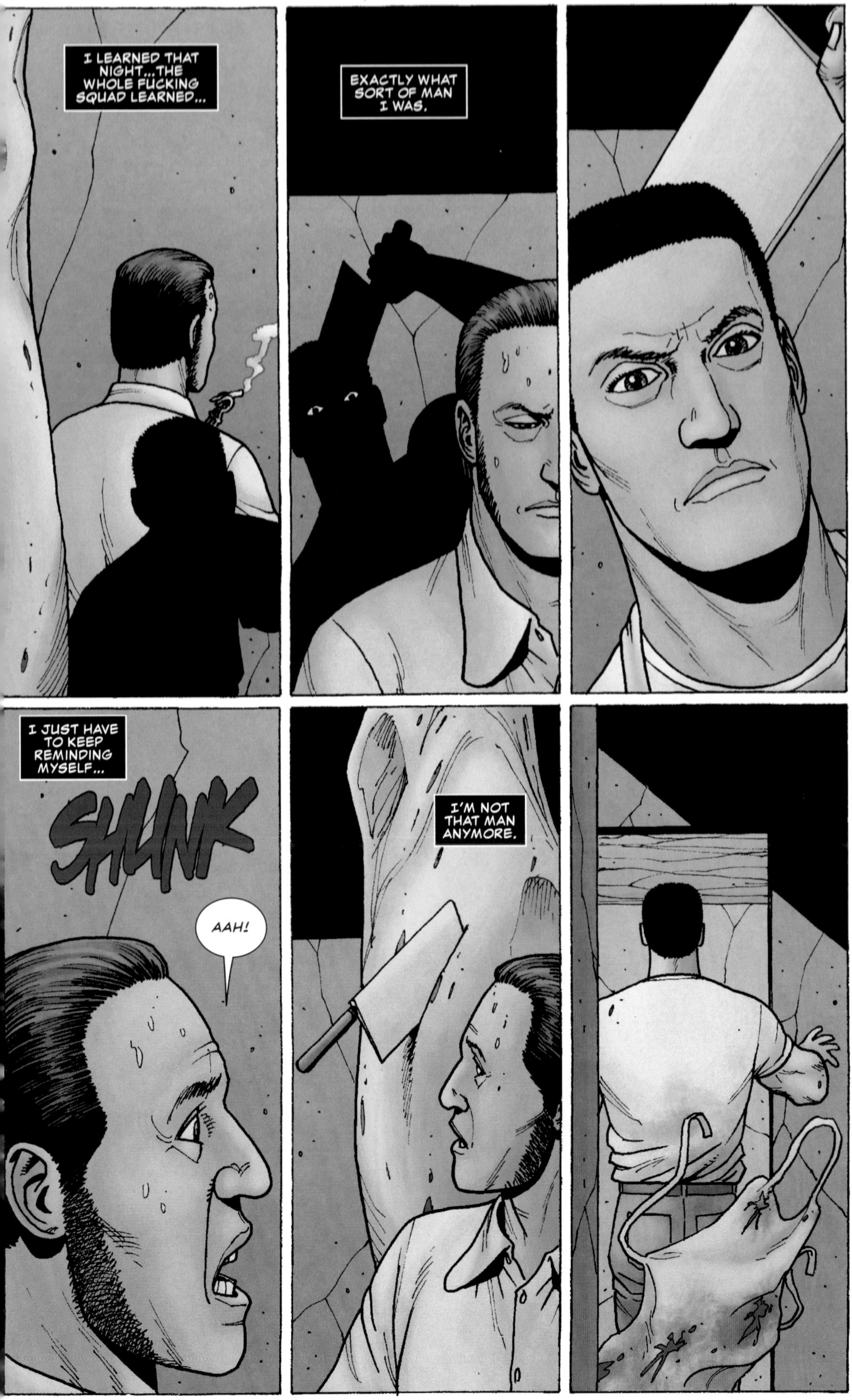
I LEARNED THAT NIGHT...THE WHOLE FUCKING SQUAD LEARNED...
EXACTLY WHAT SORT OF MAN I WAS.
I JUST HAVE TO KEEP REMINDING MYSELF...
SHUNK
AAH!
I'M NOT THAT MAN ANYMORE.

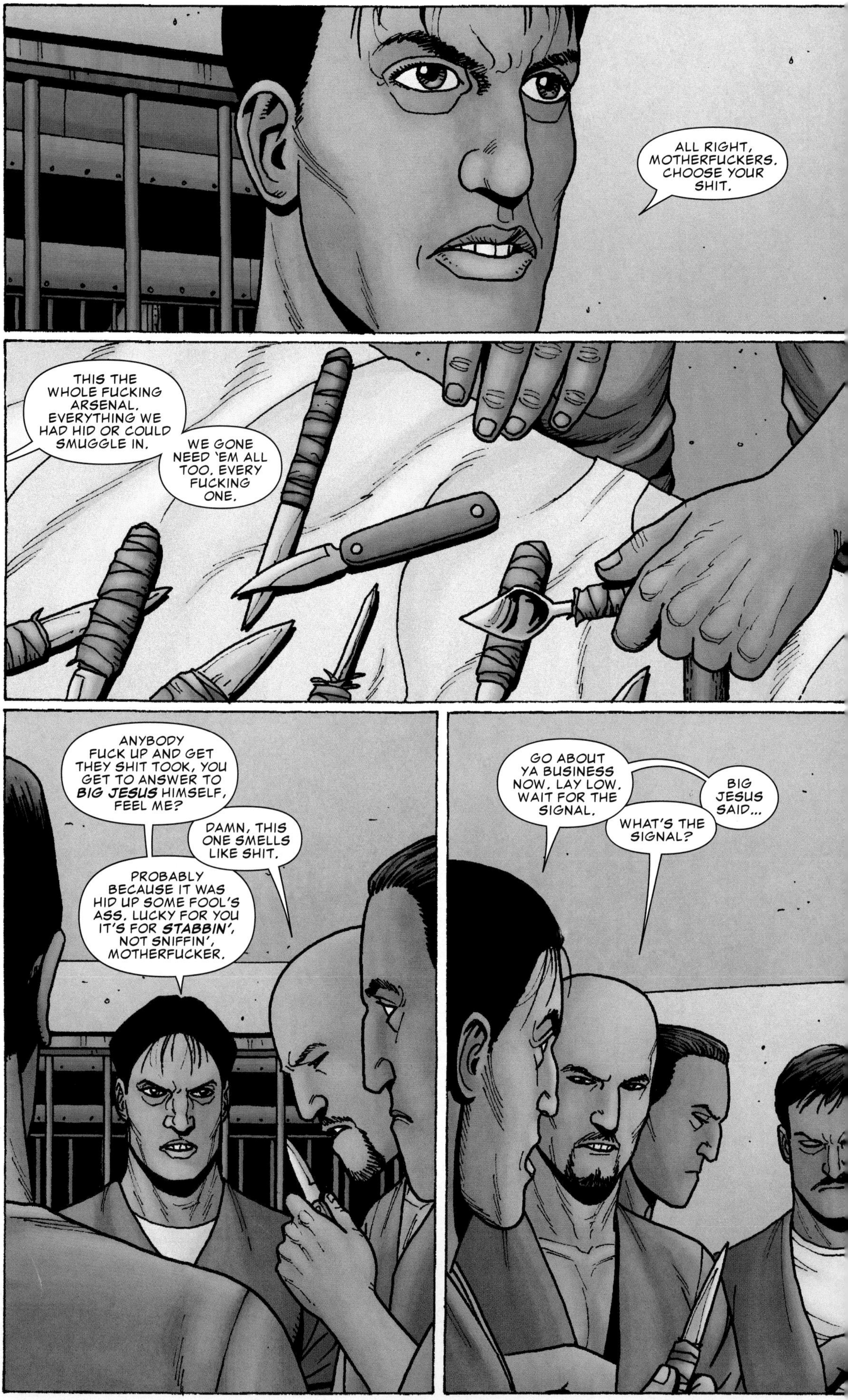
ALL RIGHT, MOTHERFUCKERS. CHOOSE YOUR SHIT.
THIS THE WHOLE FUCKING ARSENAL, EVERYTHING WE HAD HID OR COULD SMUGGLE IN.
WE GONE NEED 'EM ALL TOO. EVERY FUCKING ONE.
ANYBODY FUCK UP AND GET THEY SHIT TOOK, YOU GET TO ANSWER TO BIG JESUS HIMSELF, FEEL ME?
DAMN, THIS ONE SMELLS LIKE SHIT.
PROBABLY BECAUSE IT WAS HID UP SOME FOOL'S ASS. LUCKY FOR YOU IT'S FOR STABBIN', NOT SNIFFIN', MOTHERFUCKER.
GO ABOUT YA BUSINESS NOW. LAY LOW. WAIT FOR THE SIGNAL.
WHAT'S THE SIGNAL?
BIG JESUS SAID...

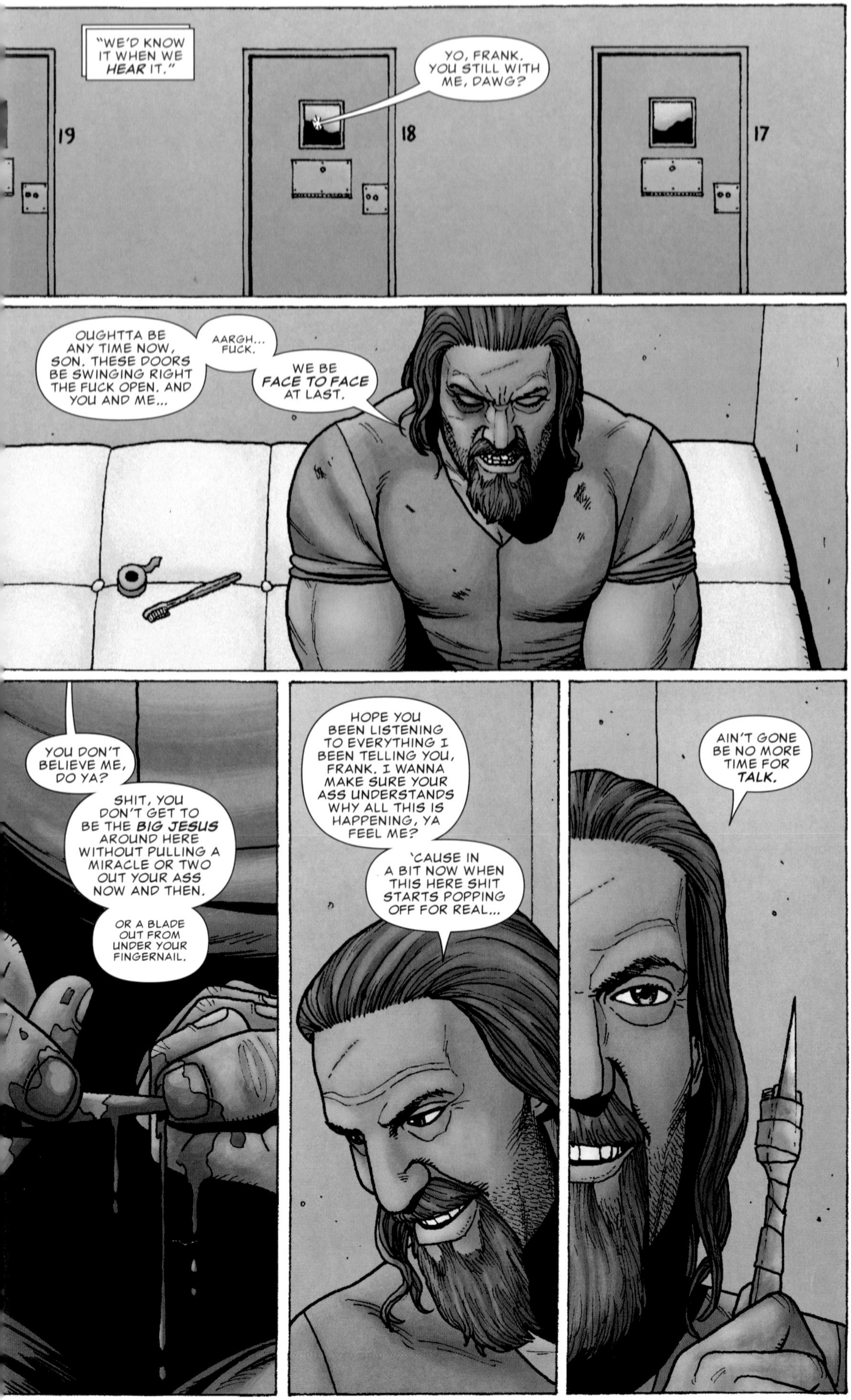
"WE'D KNOW IT WHEN WE HEAR IT."
YO, FRANK. YOU STILL WITH ME, DAWG?
19
18
17
OUGHTTA BE ANY TIME NOW, SON. THESE DOORS BE SWINGING RIGHT THE FUCK OPEN. AND YOU AND ME...
AARGH... FUCK.
WE BE FACE TO FACE AT LAST.
YOU DON'T BELIEVE ME, DO YA?
SHIT, YOU DON'T GET TO BE THE BIG JESUS AROUND HERE WITHOUT PULLING A MIRACLE OR TWO OUT YOUR ASS NOW AND THEN.
OR A BLADE OUT FROM UNDER YOUR FINGERNAIL.
HOPE YOU BEEN LISTENING TO EVERYTHING I BEEN TELLING YOU, FRANK. I WANNA MAKE SURE YOUR ASS UNDERSTANDS WHY ALL THIS IS HAPPENING, YA FEEL ME?
'CAUSE IN A BIT NOW WHEN THIS HERE SHIT STARTS POPPING OFF FOR REAL...
AIN'T GONE BE NO MORE TIME FOR TALK.

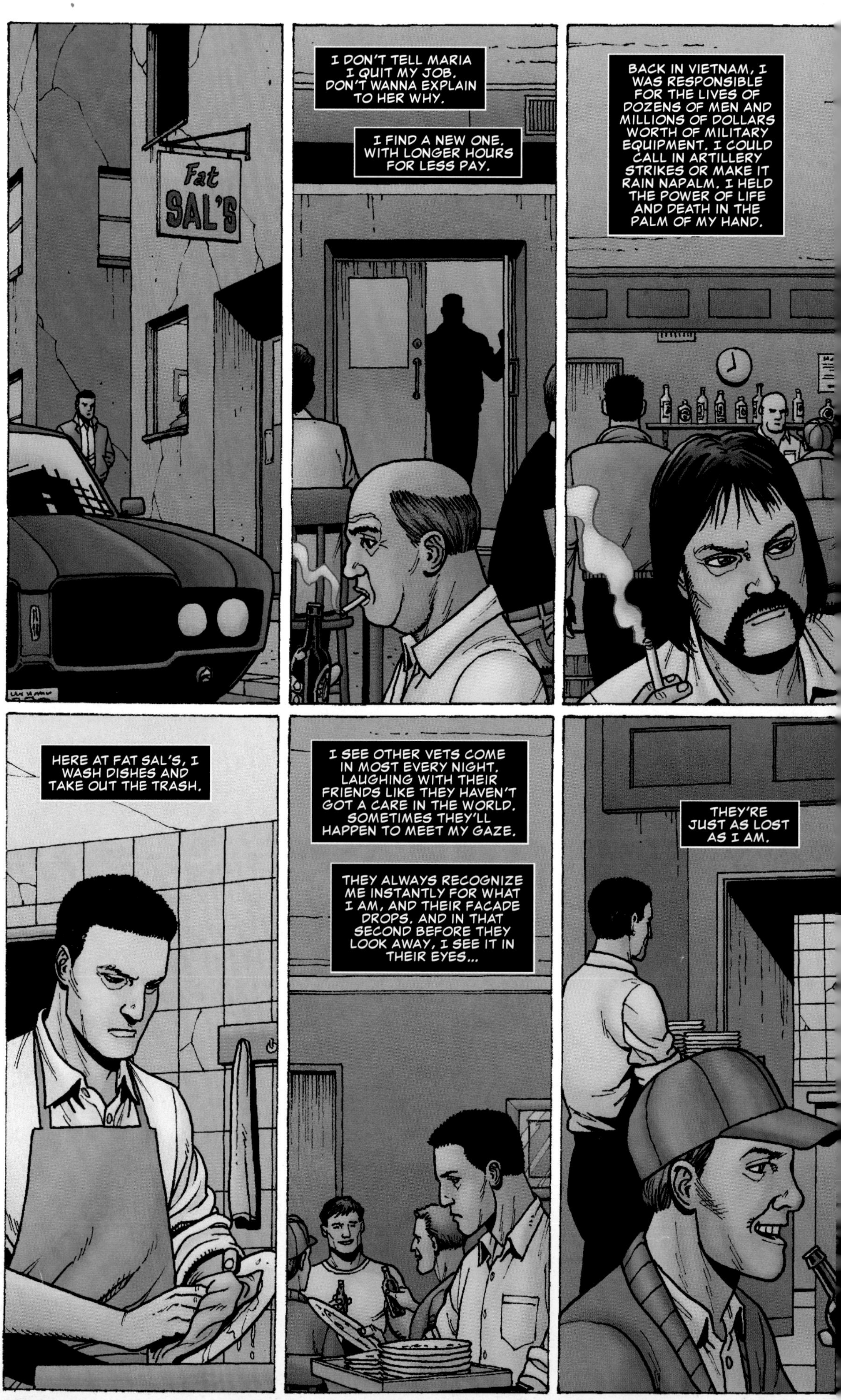
Fat SAL'S
I DON'T TELL MARIA I QUIT MY JOB. DON'T WANNA EXPLAIN TO HER WHY.
I FIND A NEW ONE. WITH LONGER HOURS FOR LESS PAY.
BACK IN VIETNAM, I WAS RESPONSIBLE FOR THE LIVES OF DOZENS OF MEN AND MILLIONS OF DOLLARS WORTH OF MILITARY EQUIPMENT. I COULD CALL IN ARTILLERY STRIKES OR MAKE IT RAIN NAPALM. I HELD THE POWER OF LIFE AND DEATH IN THE PALM OF MY HAND.
HERE AT FAT SAL'S, I WASH DISHES AND TAKE OUT THE TRASH.
I SEE OTHER VETS COME IN MOST EVERY NIGHT, LAUGHING WITH THEIR FRIENDS LIKE THEY HAVEN'T GOT A CARE IN THE WORLD. SOMETIMES THEY'LL HAPPEN TO MEET MY GAZE.
THEY ALWAYS RECOGNIZE ME INSTANTLY FOR WHAT I AM, AND THEIR FACADE DROPS. AND IN THAT SECOND BEFORE THEY LOOK AWAY, I SEE IT IN THEIR EYES...
THEY'RE JUST AS LOST AS I AM.

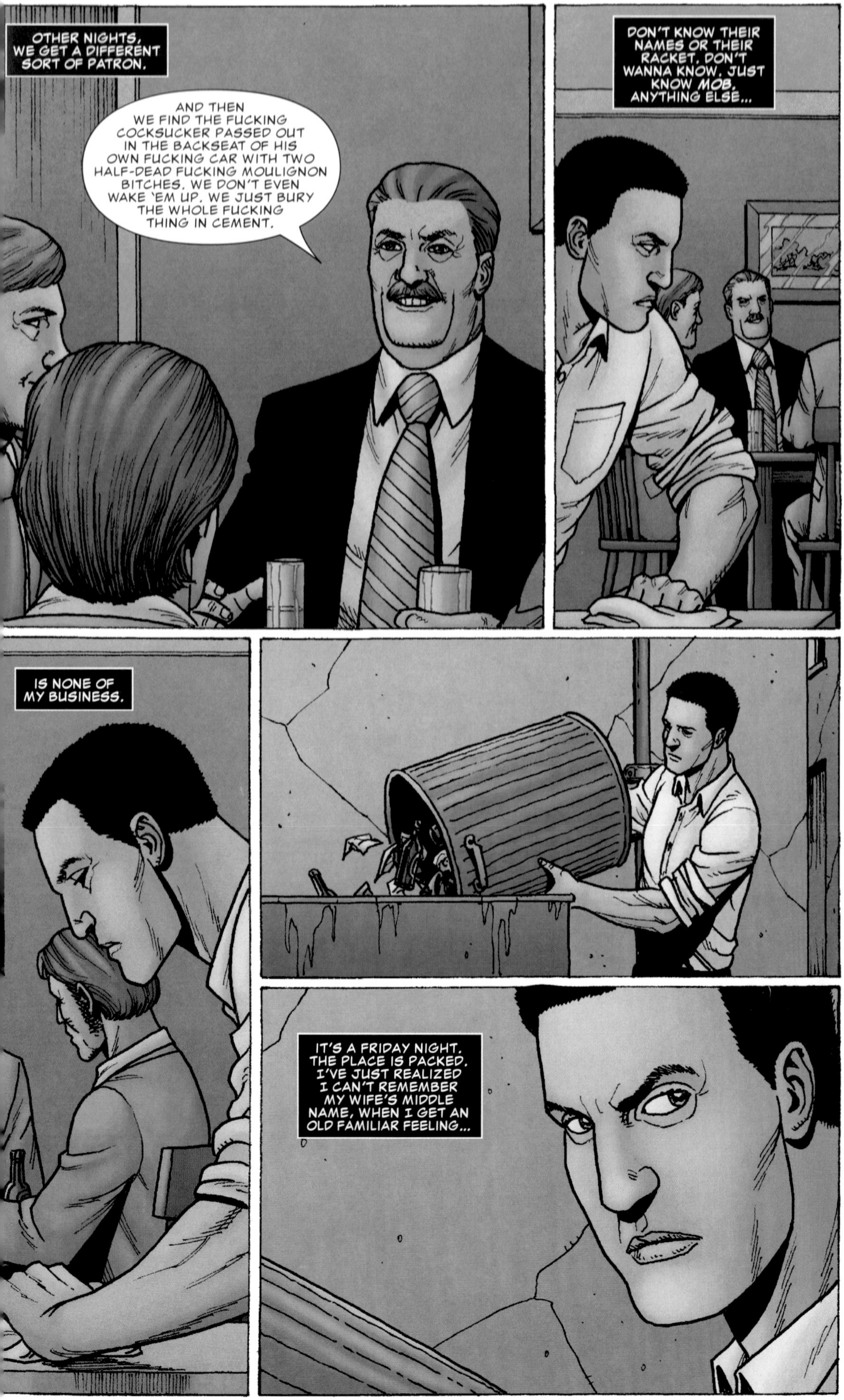
OTHER NIGHTS, WE GET A DIFFERENT SORT OF PATRON.
AND THEN WE FIND THE FUCKING COCKSUCKER PASSED OUT IN THE BACKSEAT OF HIS OWN FUCKING CAR WITH TWO HALF-DEAD FUCKING MOULIGNON BITCHES. WE DON'T EVEN WAKE 'EM UP. WE JUST BURY THE WHOLE FUCKING THING IN CEMENT.
DON'T KNOW THEIR NAMES OR THEIR RACKET. DON'T WANNA KNOW. JUST KNOW *MOB*. ANYTHING ELSE...
IS NONE OF MY BUSINESS.
IT'S A FRIDAY NIGHT. THE PLACE IS PACKED. I'VE JUST REALIZED I CAN'T REMEMBER MY WIFE'S MIDDLE NAME, WHEN I GET AN OLD FAMILIAR FEELING...

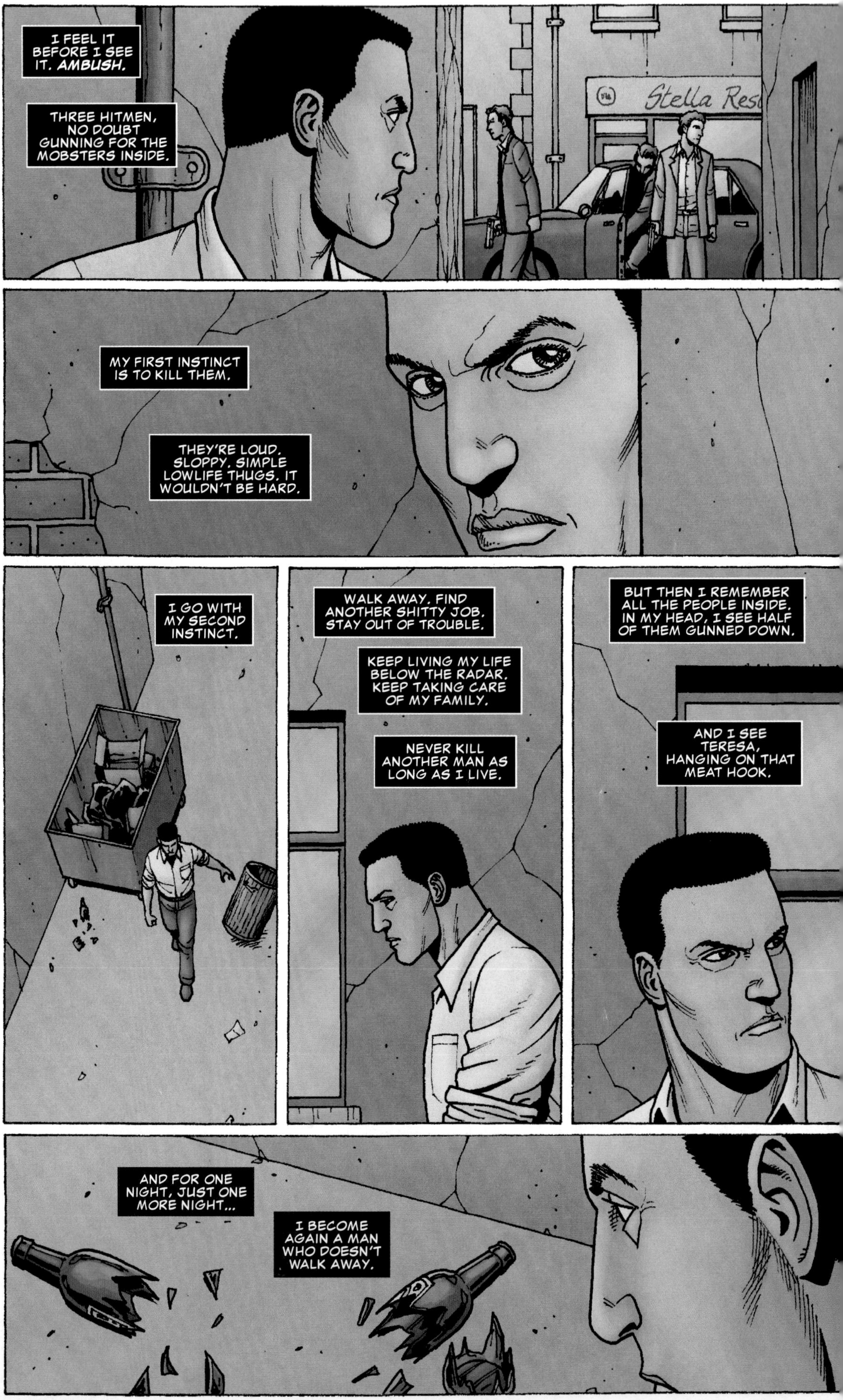
I FEEL IT BEFORE I SEE IT. AMBUSH.
THREE HITMEN, NO DOUBT GUNNING FOR THE MOBSTERS INSIDE.
Stella Res
MY FIRST INSTINCT IS TO KILL THEM.
THEY'RE LOUD. SLOPPY. SIMPLE LOWLIFE THUGS. IT WOULDN'T BE HARD.
I GO WITH MY SECOND INSTINCT.
WALK AWAY. FIND ANOTHER SHITTY JOB. STAY OUT OF TROUBLE.
KEEP LIVING MY LIFE BELOW THE RADAR. KEEP TAKING CARE OF MY FAMILY.
NEVER KILL ANOTHER MAN AS LONG AS I LIVE.
BUT THEN I REMEMBER ALL THE PEOPLE INSIDE. IN MY HEAD, I SEE HALF OF THEM GUNNED DOWN.
AND I SEE TERESA, HANGING ON THAT MEAT HOOK.
AND FOR ONE NIGHT, JUST ONE MORE NIGHT...
I BECOME AGAIN A MAN WHO DOESN'T WALK AWAY.

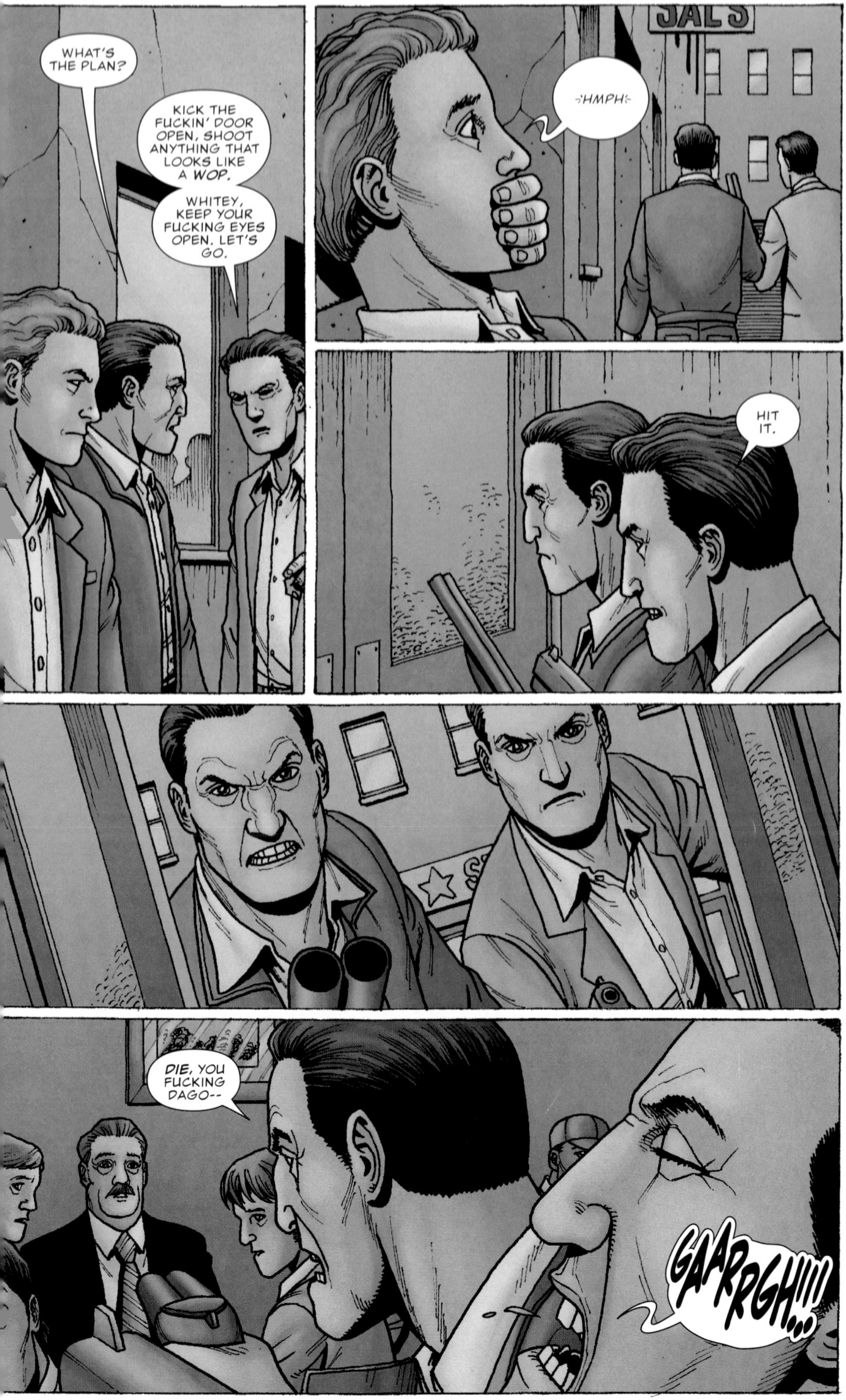
WHAT'S THE PLAN?
KICK THE FUCKIN' DOOR OPEN, SHOOT ANYTHING THAT LOOKS LIKE A WOP.
WHITEY, KEEP YOUR FUCKING EYES OPEN. LET'S GO.
HMPH
SAL'S
HIT IT.
DIE, YOU FUCKING DAGO--
GAARRGH!!!!

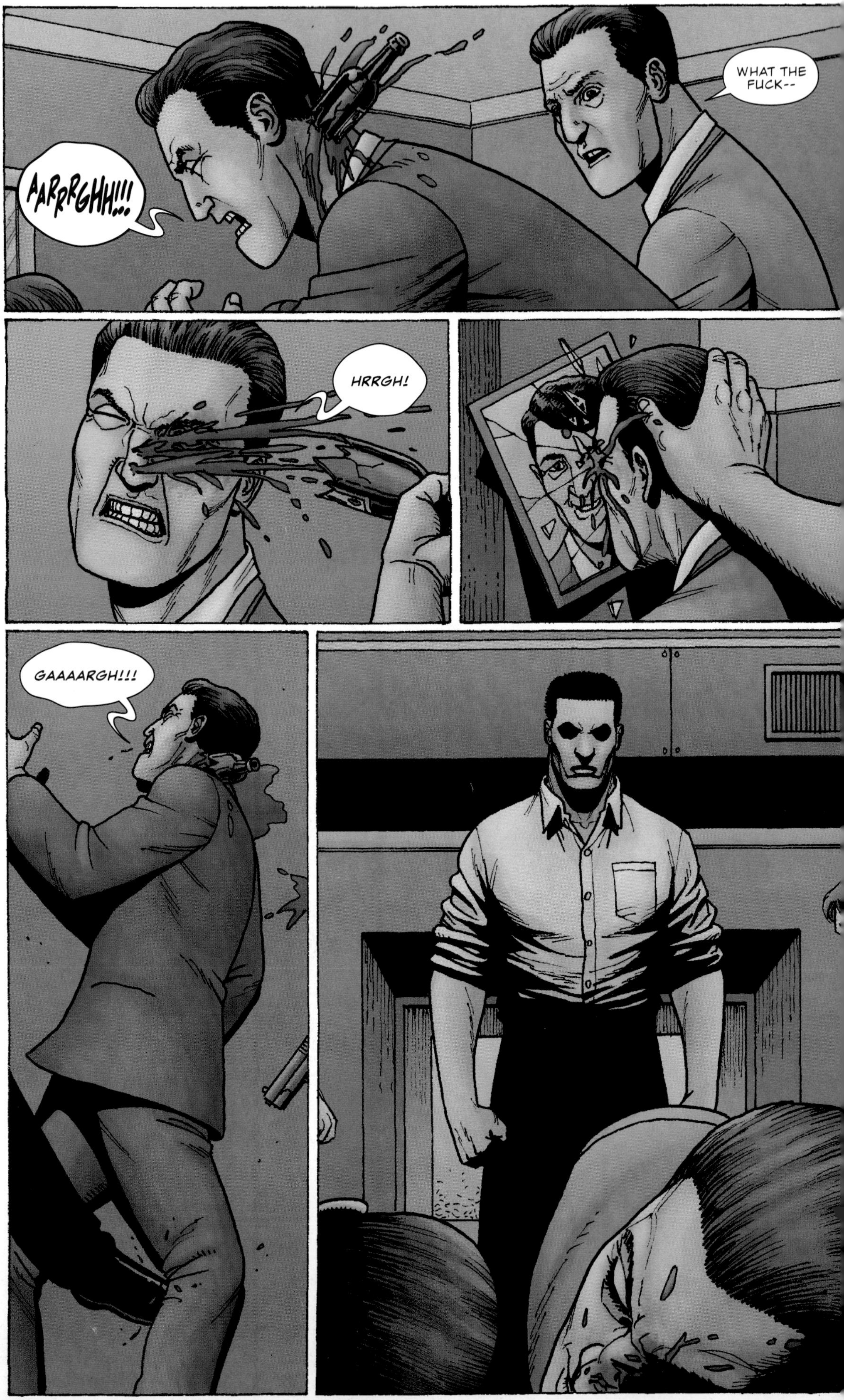
AARRRGHH!!!
WHAT THE FUCK--
HRRGH!
GAAAARGH!!!

WHAT THE FUCK?!

FUCKIN' *WESTIES*! GODDAMN IRISH COCKSUCKERS!

AND WHO THE FUCK IS *THIS*?!

WAIT, STOP! HE WORKS HERE! HE'S THE *DISHWASHER*!

PICK 'EM UP. GET 'EM THE FUCK OUTTA HERE.

THERE'S ANOTHER ONE IN THE ALLEY WITH HIS LEGS BROKEN.

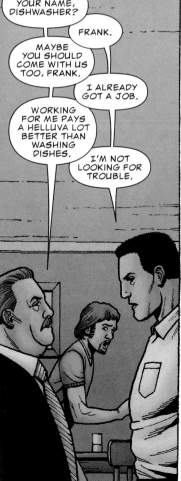

WHAT'S YOUR NAME, DISHWASHER?

FRANK.

MAYBE YOU SHOULD COME WITH US TOO, FRANK.

I ALREADY GOT A JOB.

WORKING FOR ME PAYS A HELLUVA LOT BETTER THAN WASHING DISHES.

I'M NOT LOOKING FOR TROUBLE.

WHO IS?

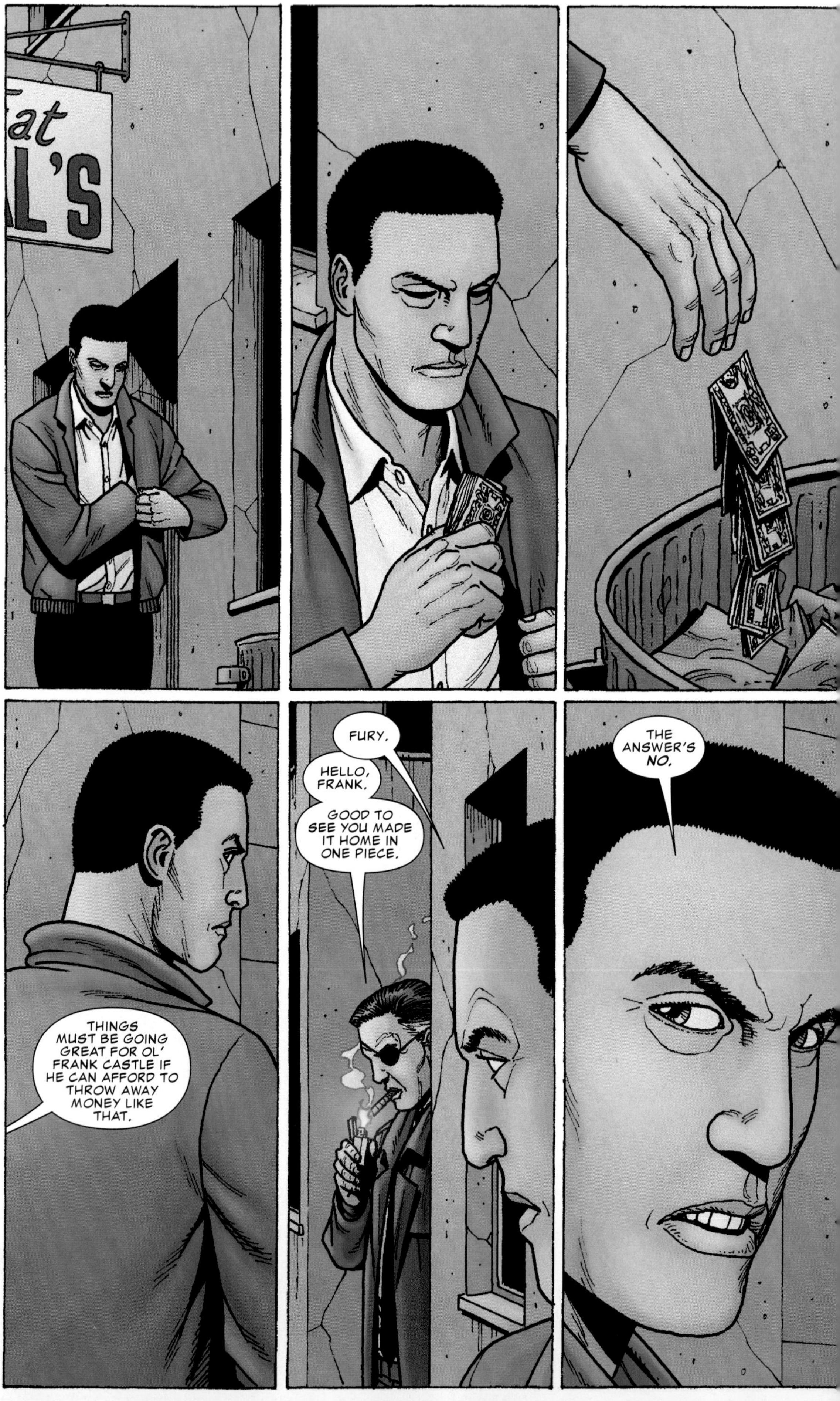

at
L'S
THINGS MUST BE GOING GREAT FOR OL' FRANK CASTLE IF HE CAN AFFORD TO THROW AWAY MONEY LIKE THAT.
FURY.
HELLO, FRANK.
GOOD TO SEE YOU MADE IT HOME IN ONE PIECE.
THE ANSWER'S *NO.*

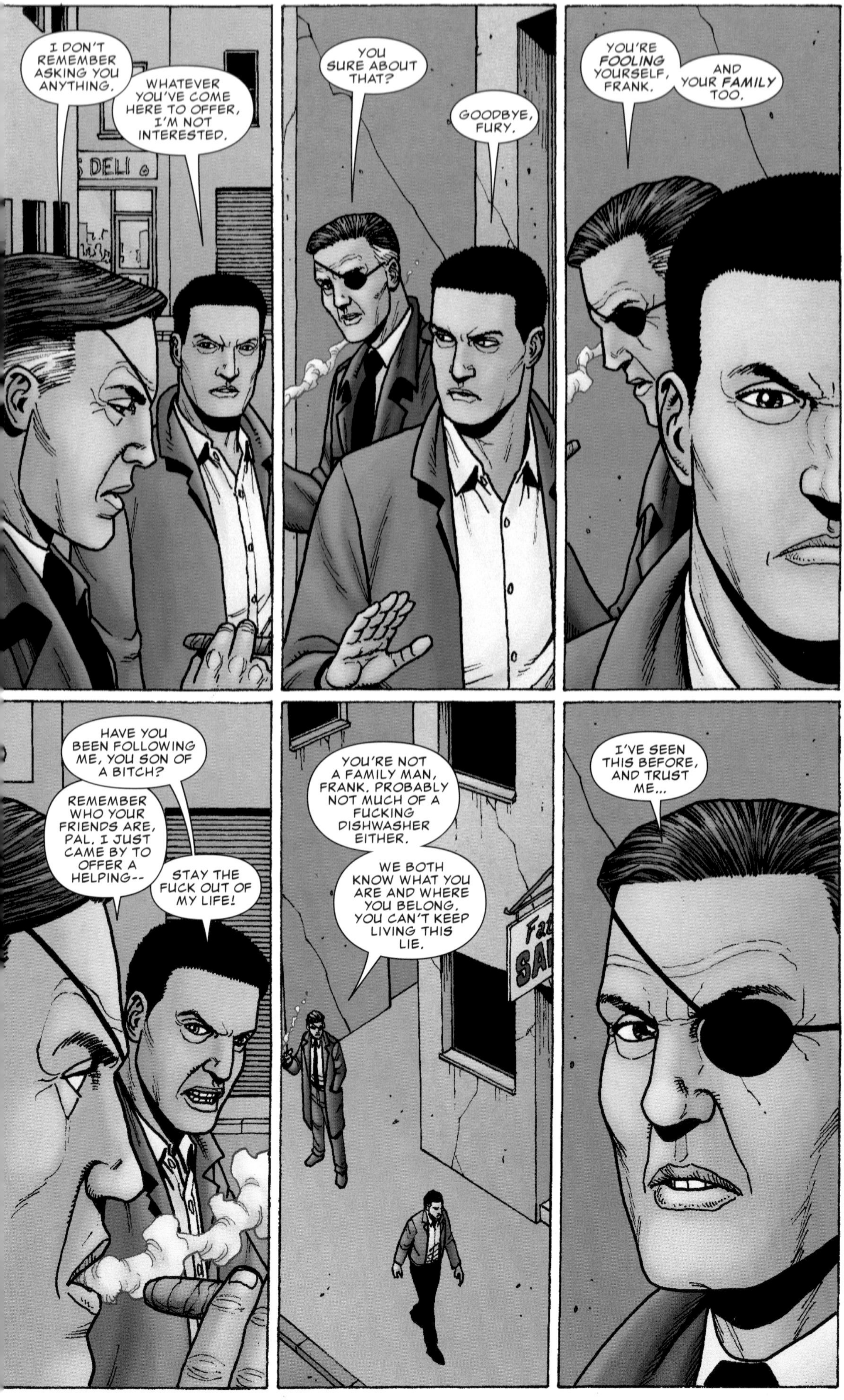

I DON'T REMEMBER ASKING YOU ANYTHING.
WHATEVER YOU'VE COME HERE TO OFFER, I'M NOT INTERESTED.
S DELI
YOU SURE ABOUT THAT?
GOODBYE, FURY.
YOU'RE *FOOLING* YOURSELF, FRANK.
AND YOUR **FAMILY** TOO.
HAVE YOU BEEN FOLLOWING ME, YOU SON OF A BITCH?
REMEMBER WHO YOUR FRIENDS ARE, PAL. I JUST CAME BY TO OFFER A HELPING--
STAY THE FUCK OUT OF MY LIFE!
YOU'RE NOT A FAMILY MAN, FRANK. PROBABLY NOT MUCH OF A FUCKING DISHWASHER EITHER.
WE BOTH KNOW WHAT YOU ARE AND WHERE YOU BELONG. YOU CAN'T KEEP LIVING THIS LIE.
I'VE SEEN THIS BEFORE, AND TRUST ME...

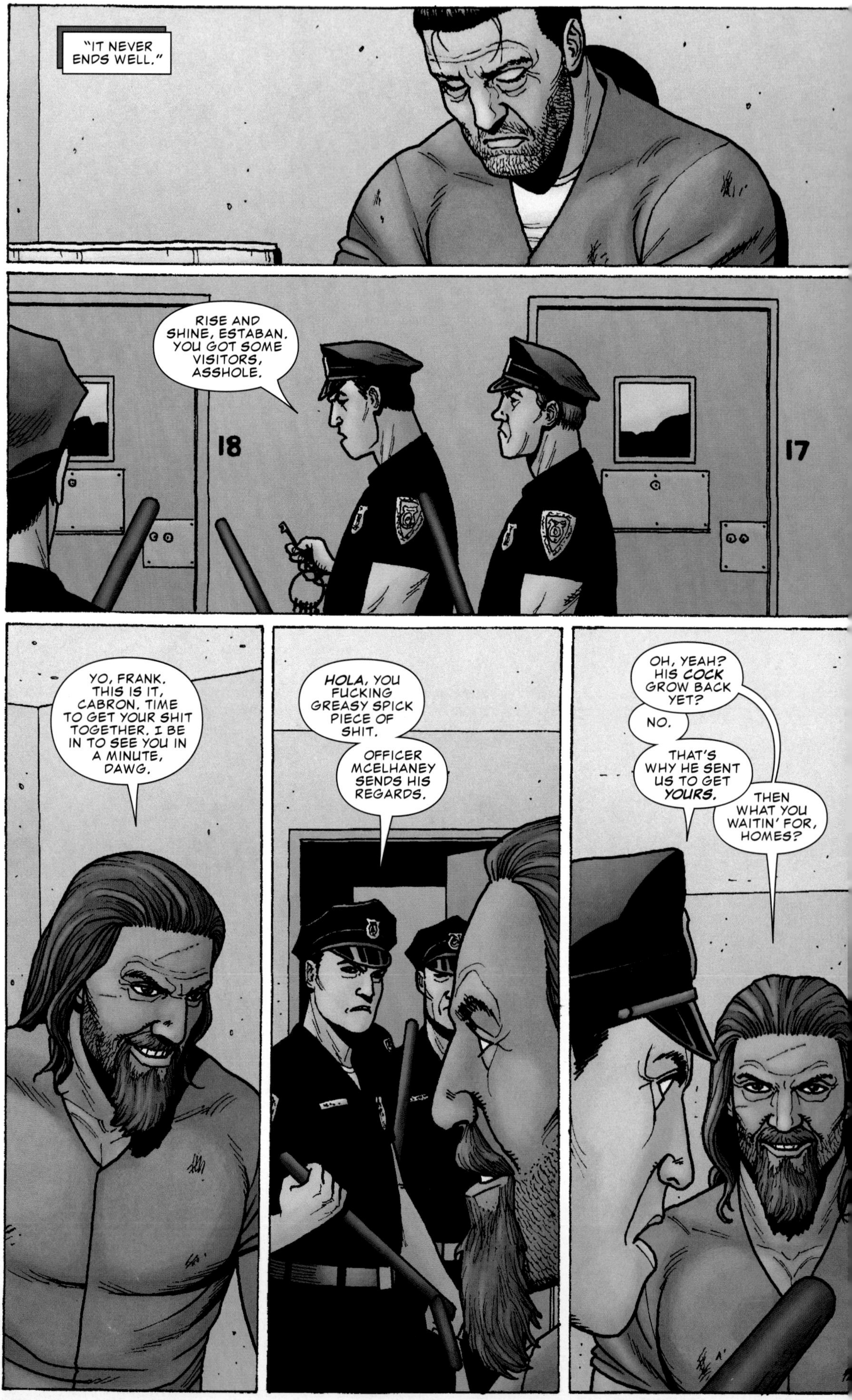
"IT NEVER ENDS WELL."
RISE AND SHINE, ESTABAN. YOU GOT SOME VISITORS, ASSHOLE.
18
17
YO, FRANK. THIS IS IT, CABRON. TIME TO GET YOUR SHIT TOGETHER. I BE IN TO SEE YOU IN A MINUTE, DAWG.
HOLA, YOU FUCKING GREASY SPICK PIECE OF SHIT.
OFFICER MCELHANEY SENDS HIS REGARDS.
OH, YEAH? HIS COCK GROW BACK YET?
NO.
THAT'S WHY HE SENT US TO GET YOURS.
THEN WHAT YOU WAITIN' FOR, HOMES?

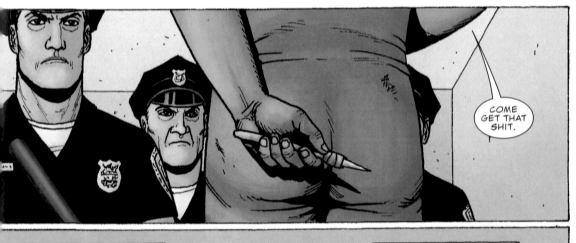

COME GET THAT SHIT.

AAAAHHH!!!

18

17

OH, SHIT, THAT'S GOTTA BE--

THIS IS IT. TAKE THE FUCKING TIER!

AARRGH!!!

FRANK! IT'S ALL FOR YOU, MOTHERFUCKER!

YOU GOTTA REMEMBER WHO YOU ARE!

FRANK!

FRANK...

JUST THE MAN WE BEEN LOOKING FOR. GET IN, PAL.

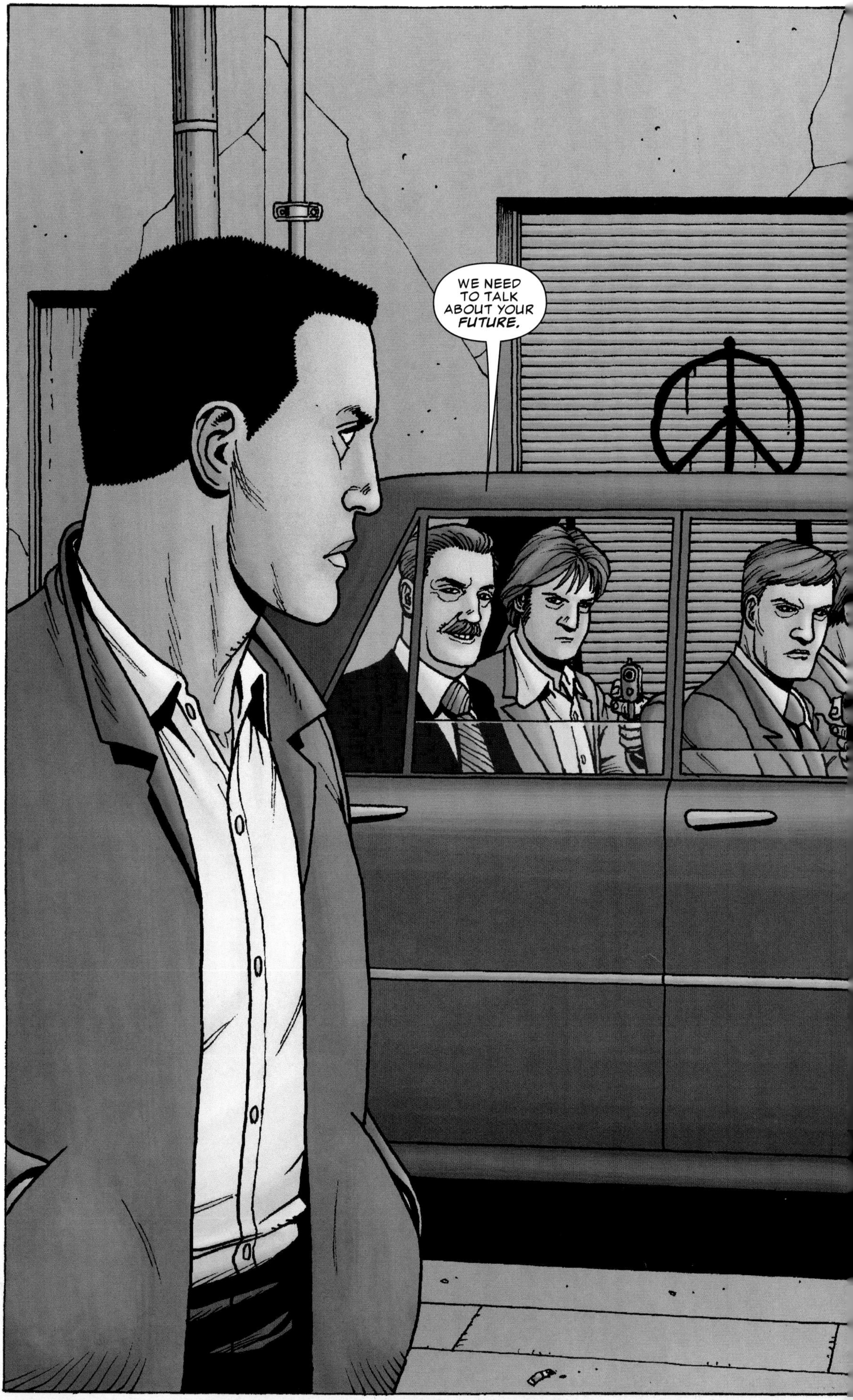
WE NEED TO TALK ABOUT YOUR *FUTURE.*

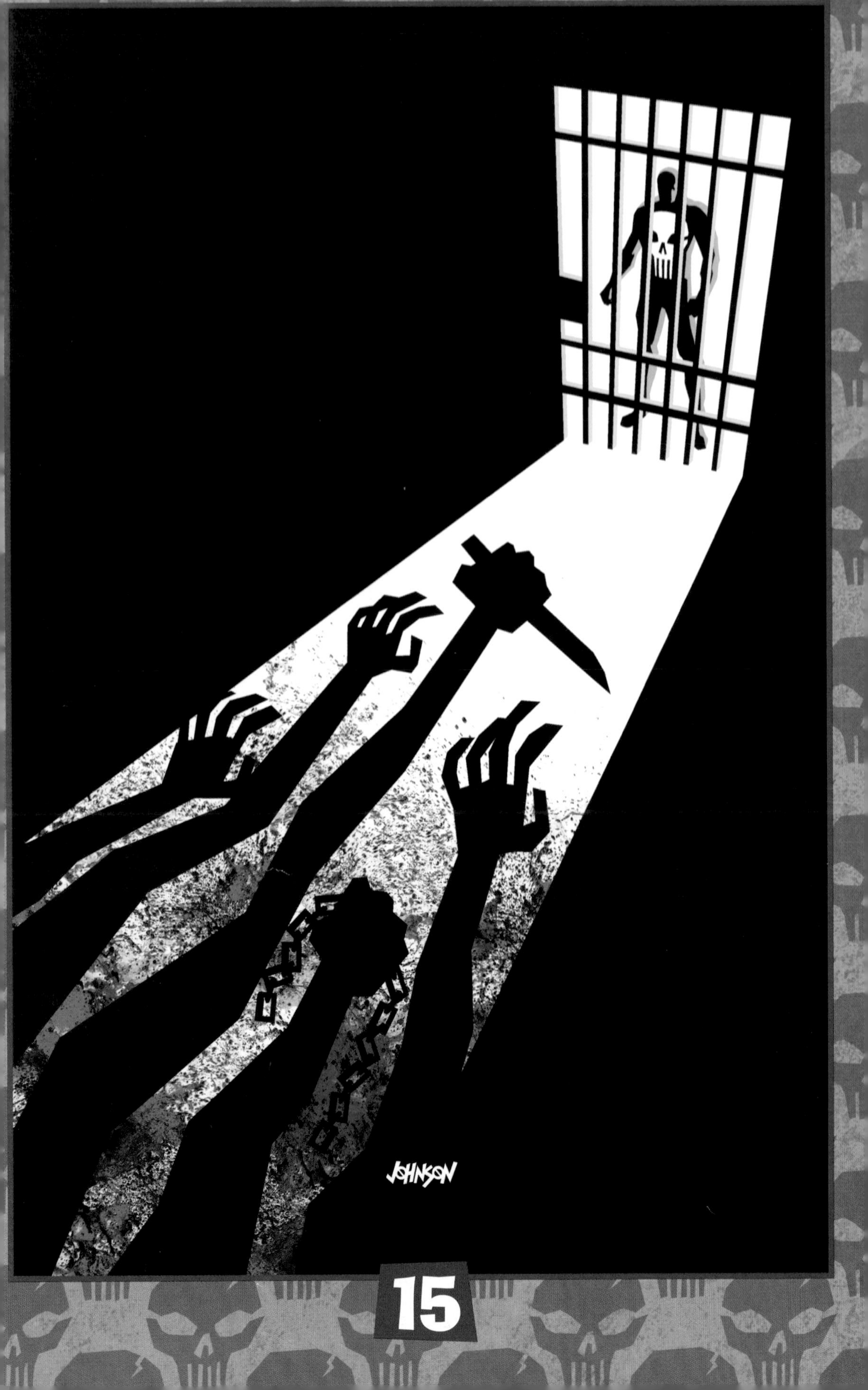
JOHNSON

15

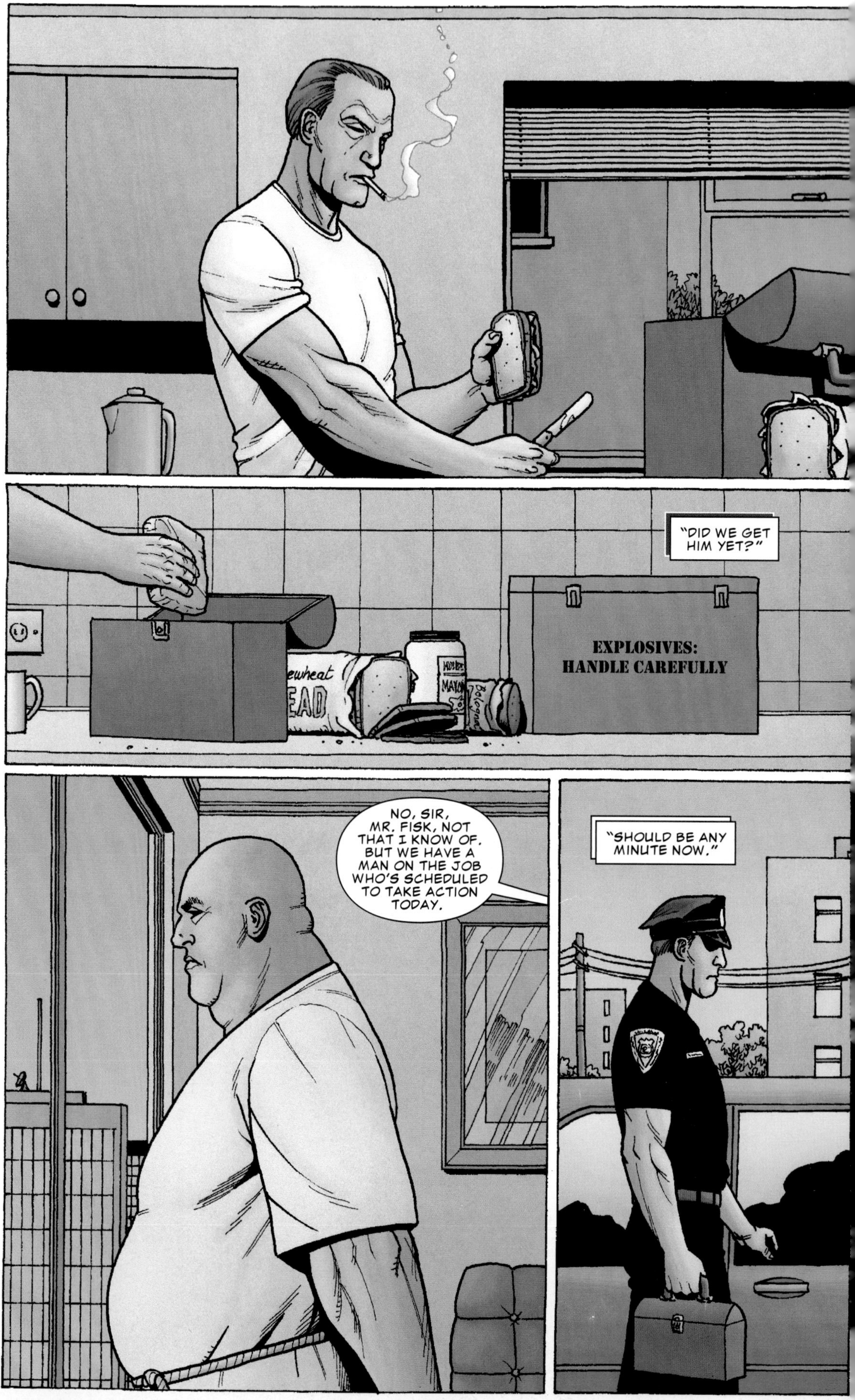
"DID WE GET HIM YET?"
EXPLOSIVES: HANDLE CAREFULLY
NO, SIR, MR. FISK, NOT THAT I KNOW OF. BUT WE HAVE A MAN ON THE JOB WHO'S SCHEDULED TO TAKE ACTION TODAY.
"SHOULD BE ANY MINUTE NOW."

I'LL LET YOU KNOW AS SOON AS I HEAR SOMETHING, SIR, IN THE MEANTIME... PERHAPS YOU SHOULD TRY GETTING SOME REST.

I'LL REST...

ONCE I KNOW HE'S DEAD.

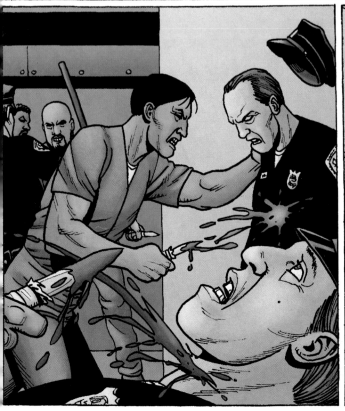

I REPEAT, WE HAVE A FULL-SCALE *RIOT* IN BUILDING 3! GUARDS DOWN, IN NEED OF ASSISTANCE!

OH SHIT...

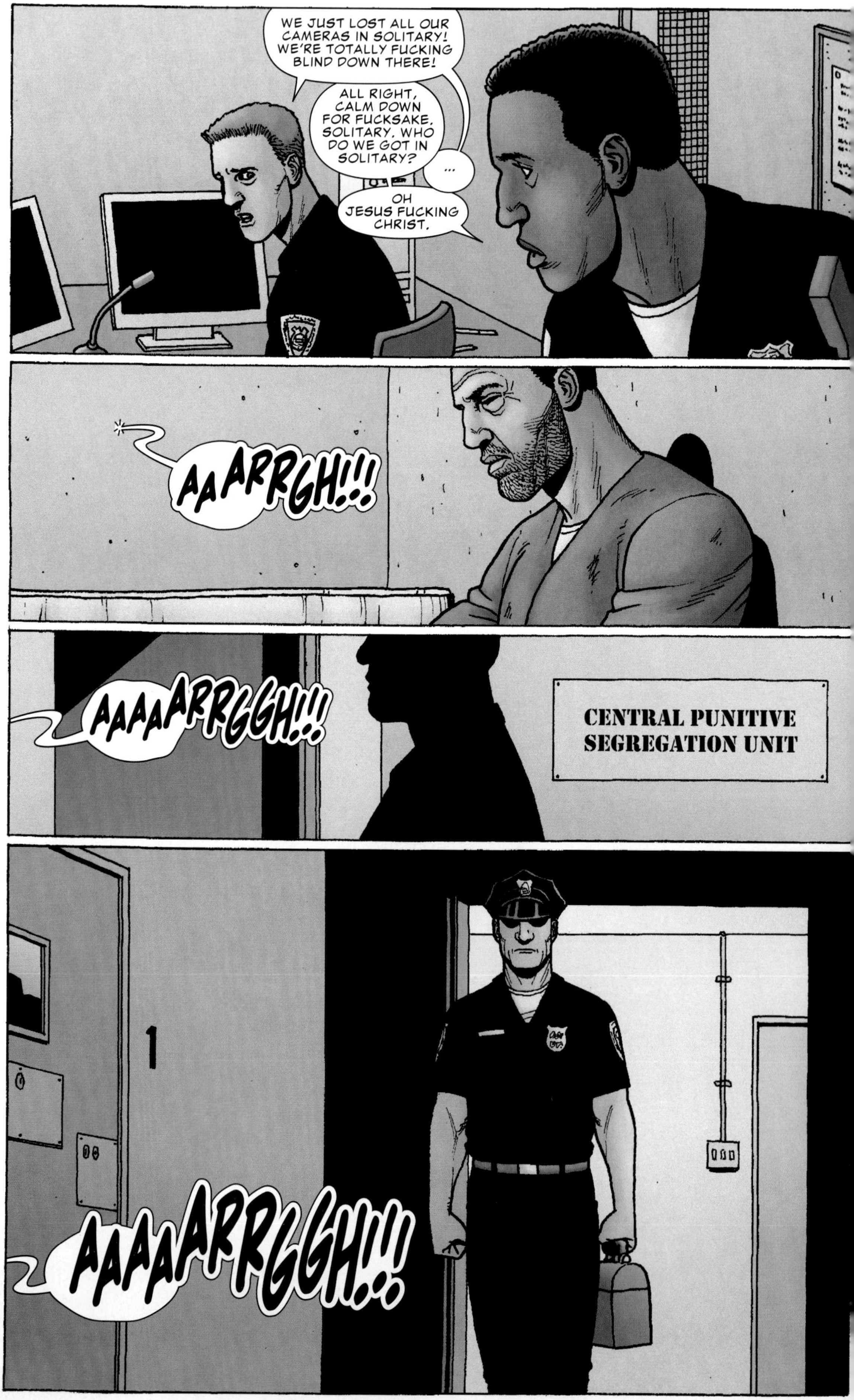
WE JUST LOST ALL OUR CAMERAS IN SOLITARY! WE'RE TOTALLY FUCKING BLIND DOWN THERE!
ALL RIGHT, CALM DOWN FOR FUCKSAKE. SOLITARY. WHO DO WE GOT IN SOLITARY?
...
OH JESUS FUCKING CHRIST.
AAARRRGH!!!
AAAAARRRGGH!!!
CENTRAL PUNITIVE SEGREGATION UNIT
1
AAAAARRRGGH!!!

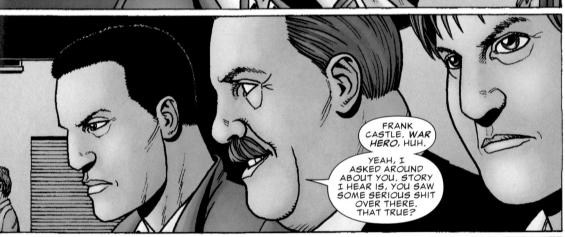

FRANK CASTLE. *WAR HERO*, HUH.

YEAH, I ASKED AROUND ABOUT YOU. STORY I HEAR IS, YOU SAW SOME SERIOUS SHIT OVER THERE. THAT TRUE?

DON MARGELLO ASKED YOU A FUCKING QUESTION, ASSHOLE.

TAKE IT EASY, JIMMY.

YOU'RE A SERIOUS MAN, FRANK, I RESPECT THAT. I'M NOT HERE TO BULLSHIT YOU OR PLAY GAMES. I'M JUST GONNA TELL YOU HOW IT IS.

YOU'RE GONNA DO A *JOB* FOR ME.

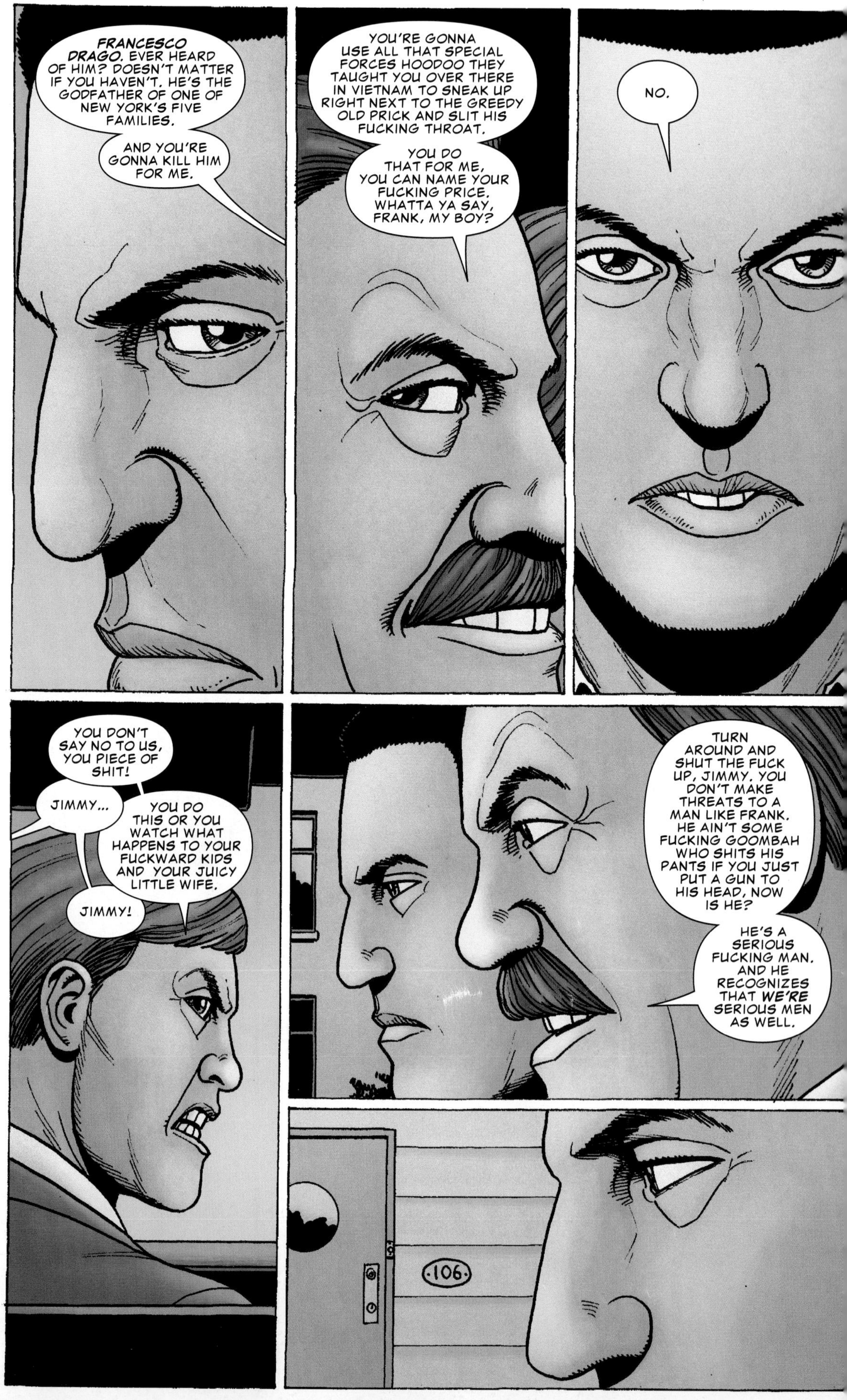
FRANCESCO DRAGO. EVER HEARD OF HIM? DOESN'T MATTER IF YOU HAVEN'T. HE'S THE GODFATHER OF ONE OF NEW YORK'S FIVE FAMILIES.
AND YOU'RE GONNA KILL HIM FOR ME.
YOU'RE GONNA USE ALL THAT SPECIAL FORCES HOODOO THEY TAUGHT YOU OVER THERE IN VIETNAM TO SNEAK UP RIGHT NEXT TO THE GREEDY OLD PRICK AND SLIT HIS FUCKING THROAT.
YOU DO THAT FOR ME, YOU CAN NAME YOUR FUCKING PRICE. WHATTA YA SAY, FRANK, MY BOY?
NO.
YOU DON'T SAY NO TO US, YOU PIECE OF SHIT!
JIMMY...
YOU DO THIS OR YOU WATCH WHAT HAPPENS TO YOUR FUCKWARD KIDS AND YOUR JUICY LITTLE WIFE.
JIMMY!
TURN AROUND AND SHUT THE FUCK UP, JIMMY. YOU DON'T MAKE THREATS TO A MAN LIKE FRANK. HE AIN'T SOME FUCKING GOOMBAH WHO SHITS HIS PANTS IF YOU JUST PUT A GUN TO HIS HEAD, NOW IS HE?
HE'S A SERIOUS FUCKING MAN. AND HE RECOGNIZES THAT WE'RE SERIOUS MEN AS WELL.
106

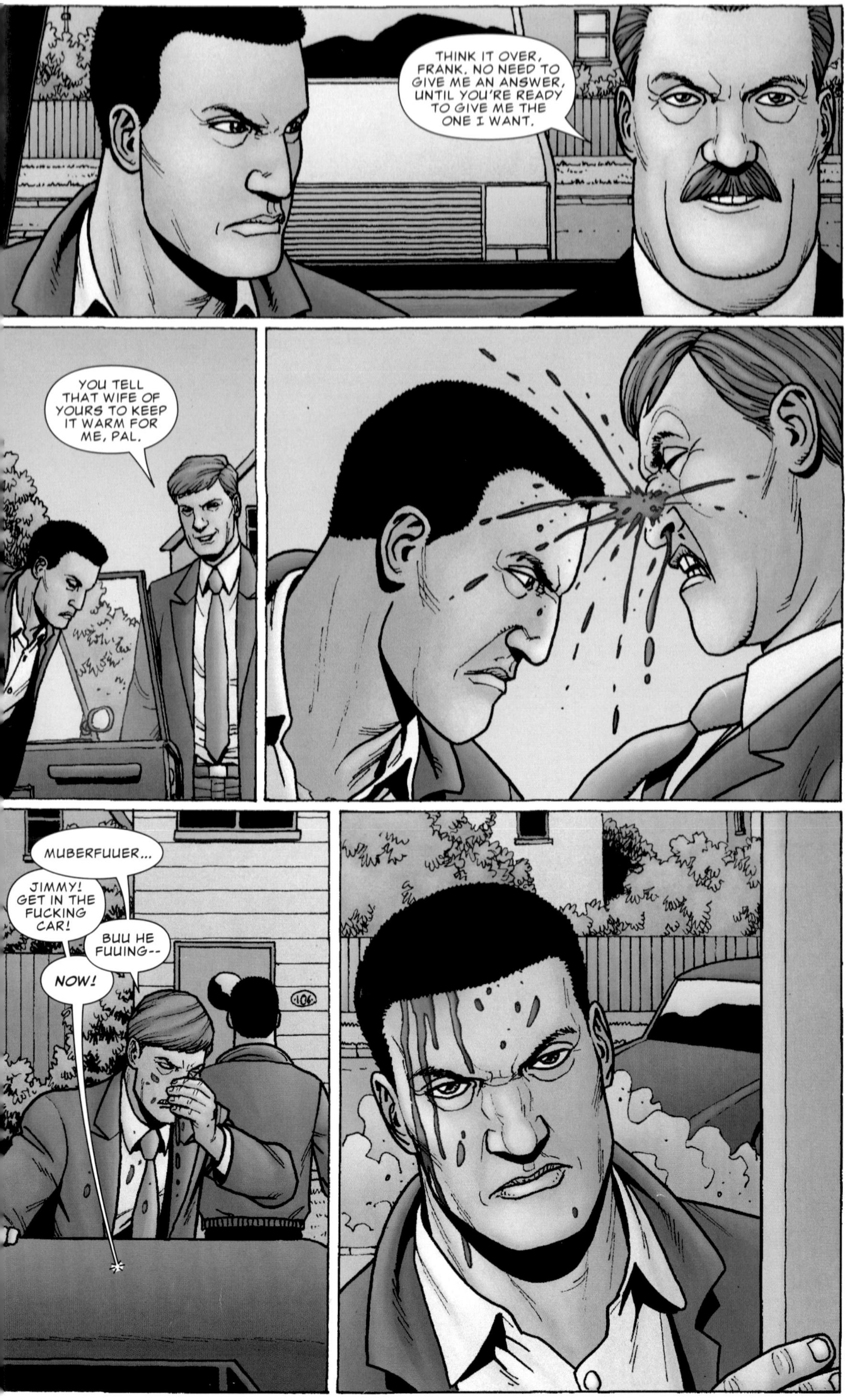
THINK IT OVER, FRANK. NO NEED TO GIVE ME AN ANSWER, UNTIL YOU'RE READY TO GIVE ME THE ONE I WANT.
YOU TELL THAT WIFE OF YOURS TO KEEP IT WARM FOR ME, PAL.
MUBERFUUER...
JIMMY! GET IN THE FUCKING CAR!
BUU HE FUUING--
NOW!
106

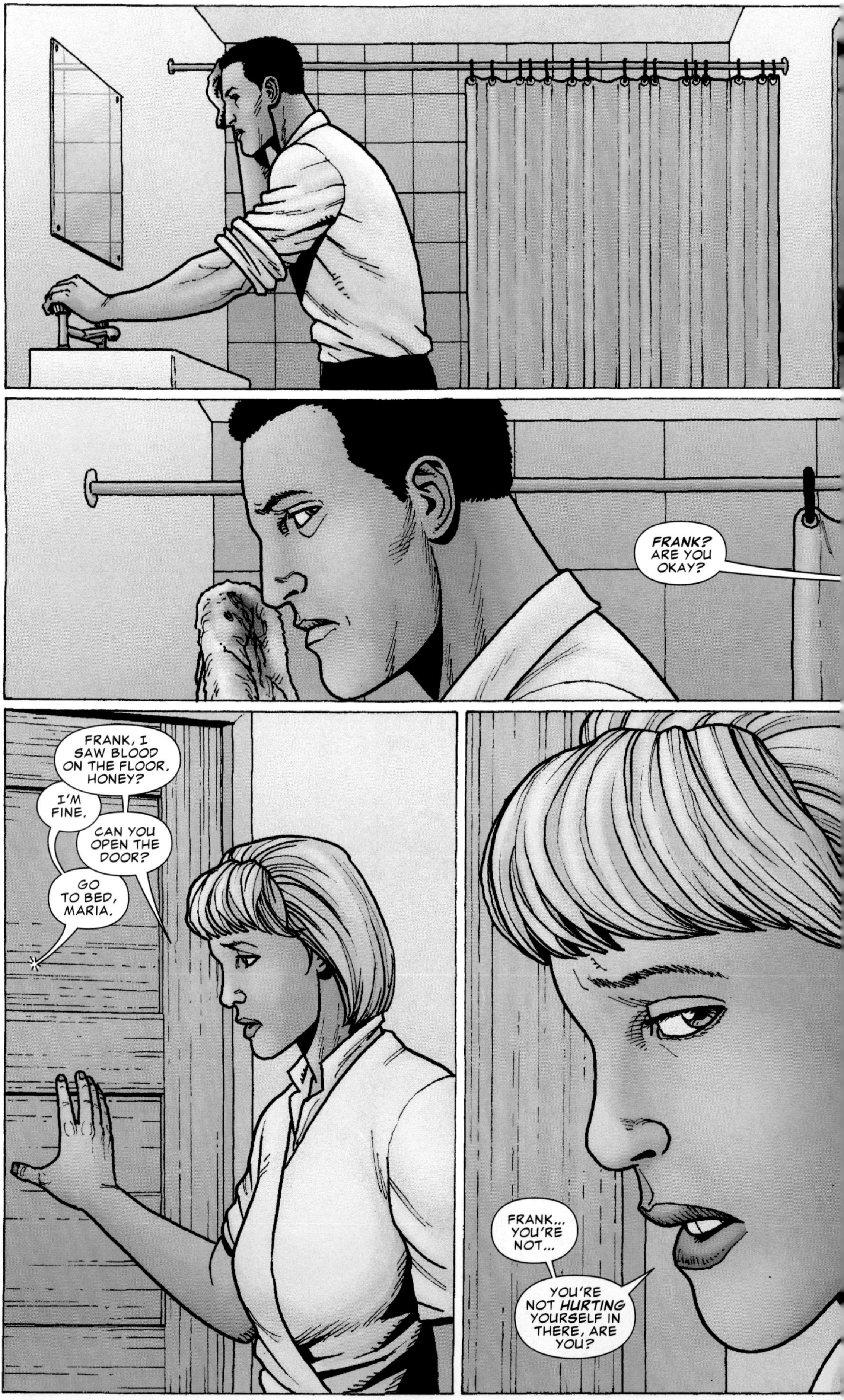

FRANK? ARE YOU OKAY?
FRANK, I SAW BLOOD ON THE FLOOR. HONEY?
I'M FINE.
CAN YOU OPEN THE DOOR?
GO TO BED, MARIA.
FRANK... YOU'RE NOT...
YOU'RE NOT *HURTING* YOURSELF IN THERE, ARE YOU?

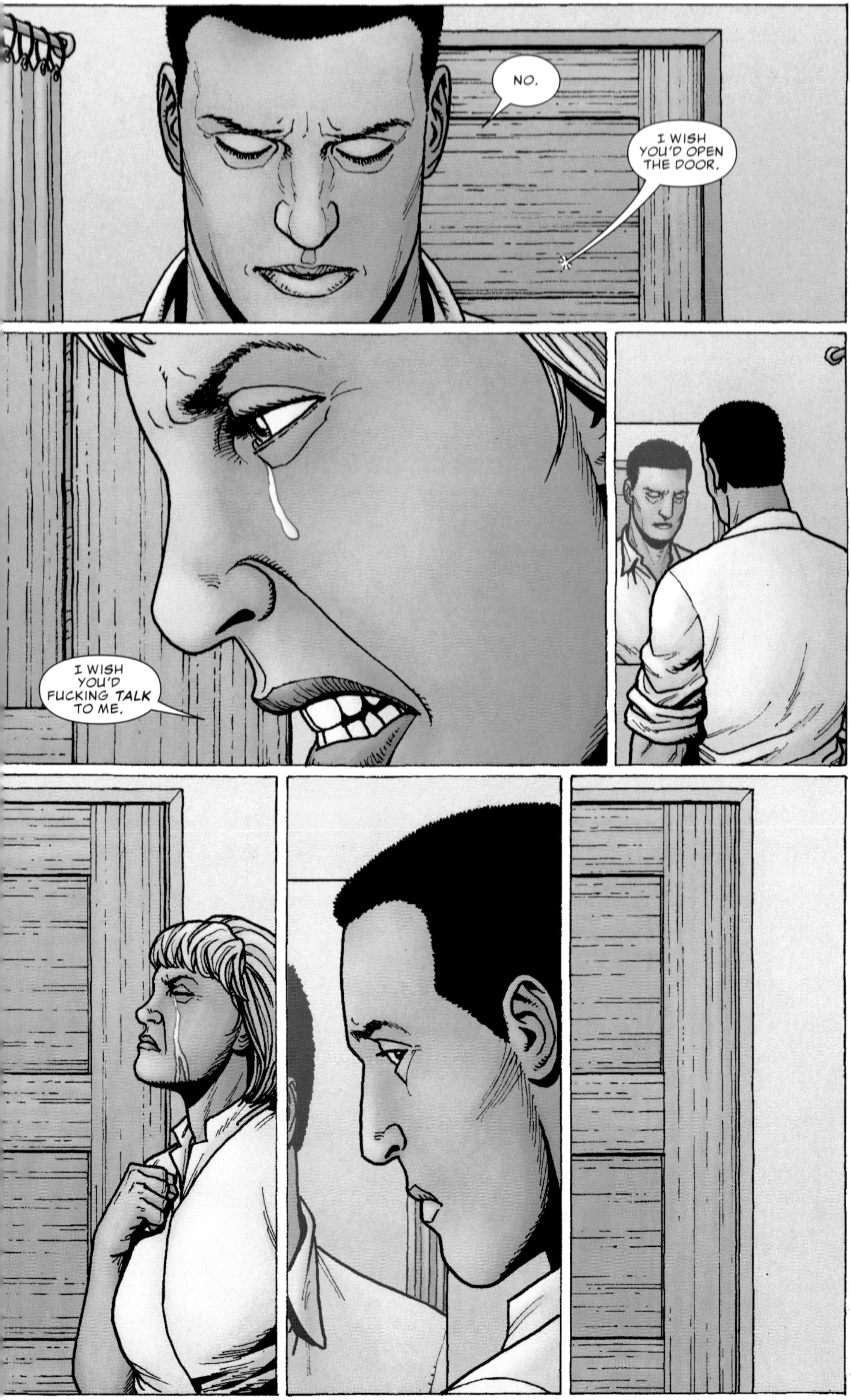
NO.
I WISH YOU'D OPEN THE DOOR.
I WISH YOU'D FUCKING TALK TO ME.

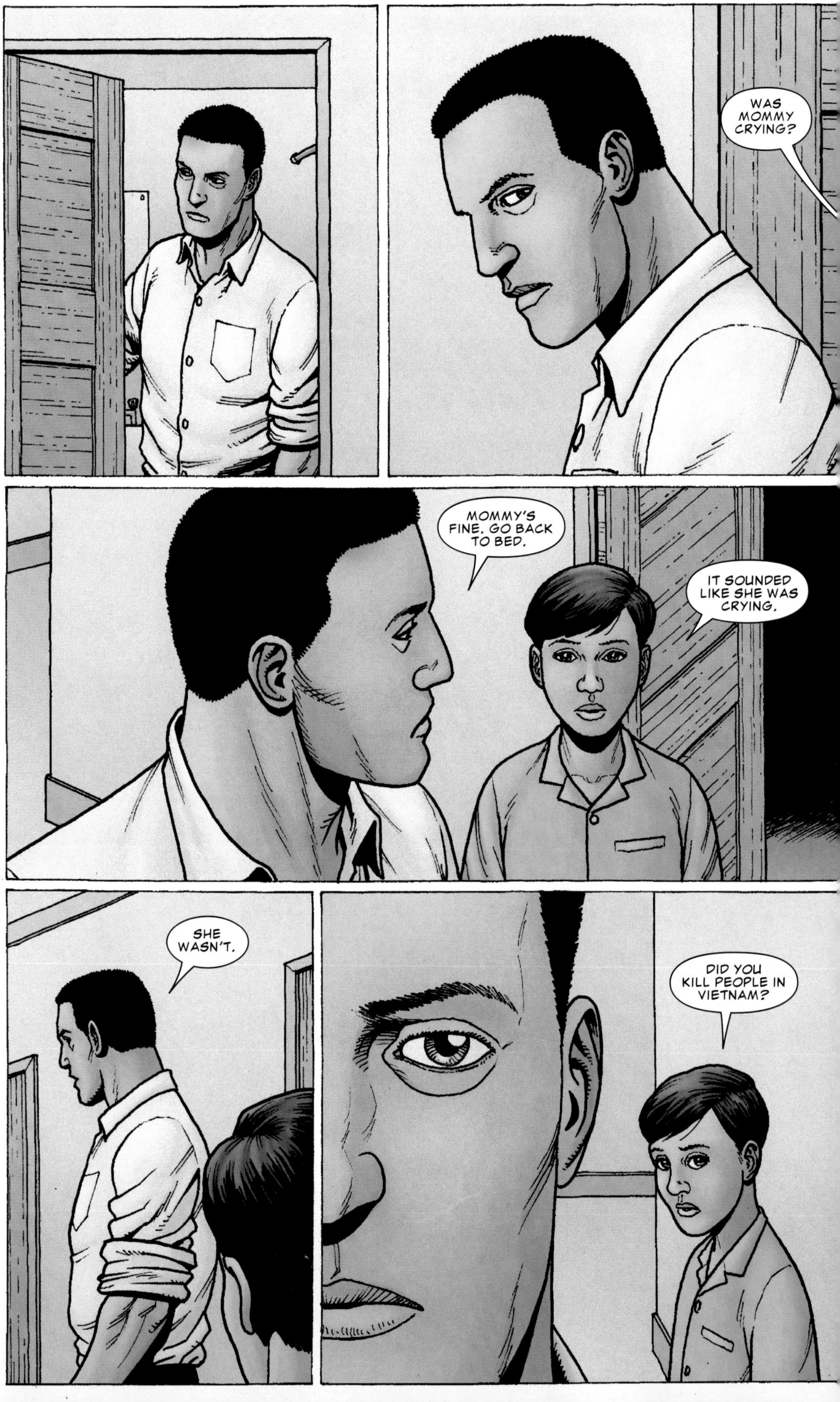
WAS MOMMY CRYING?
MOMMY'S FINE. GO BACK TO BED.
IT SOUNDED LIKE SHE WAS CRYING.
SHE WASN'T.
DID YOU KILL PEOPLE IN VIETNAM?

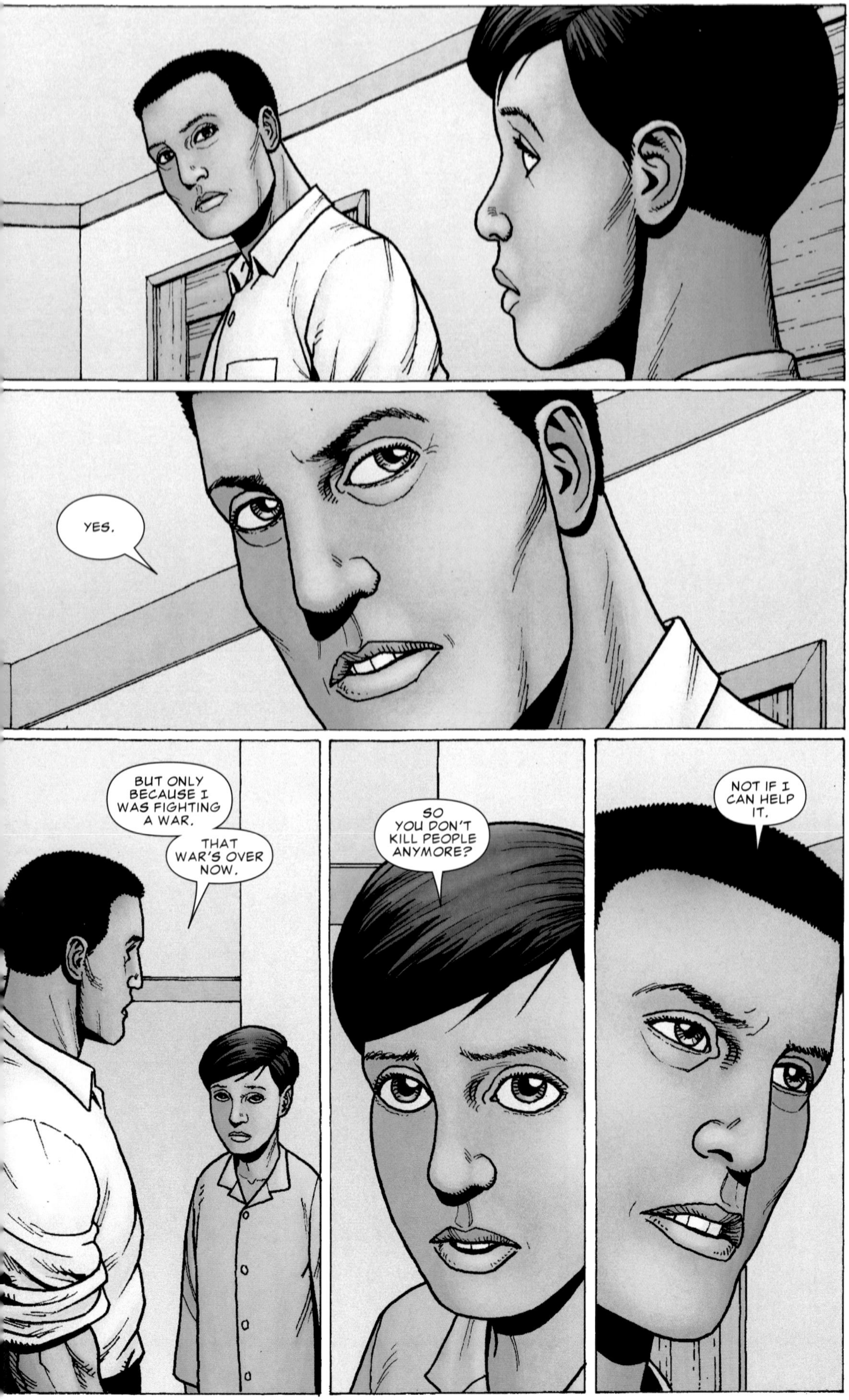
YES.
BUT ONLY BECAUSE I WAS FIGHTING A WAR.
THAT WAR'S OVER NOW.
SO YOU DON'T KILL PEOPLE ANYMORE?
NOT IF I CAN HELP IT.

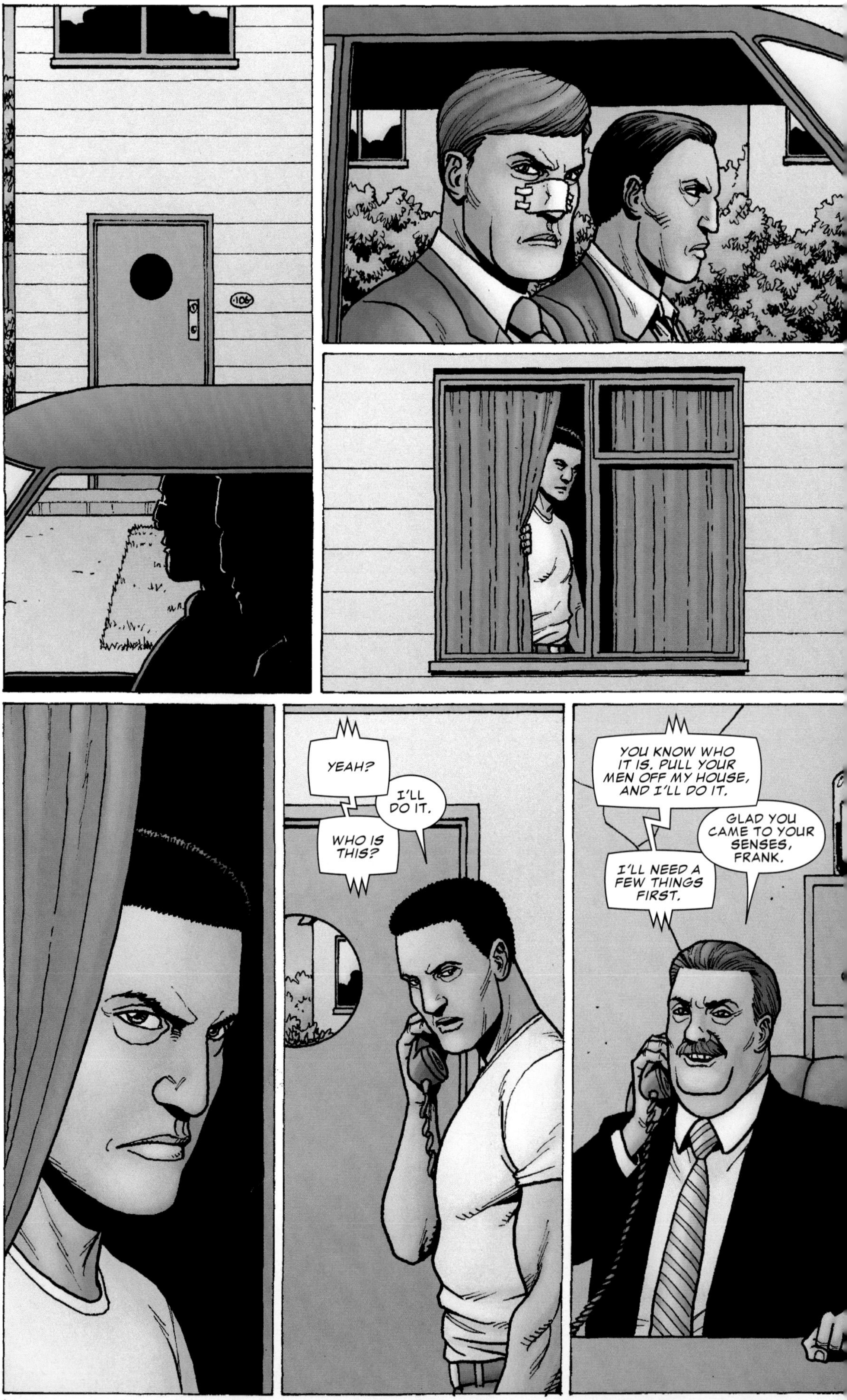

·106·
YEAH?
WHO IS THIS?
I'LL DO IT.
YOU KNOW WHO IT IS. PULL YOUR MEN OFF MY HOUSE, AND I'LL DO IT.
I'LL NEED A FEW THINGS FIRST.
GLAD YOU CAME TO YOUR SENSES, FRANK.

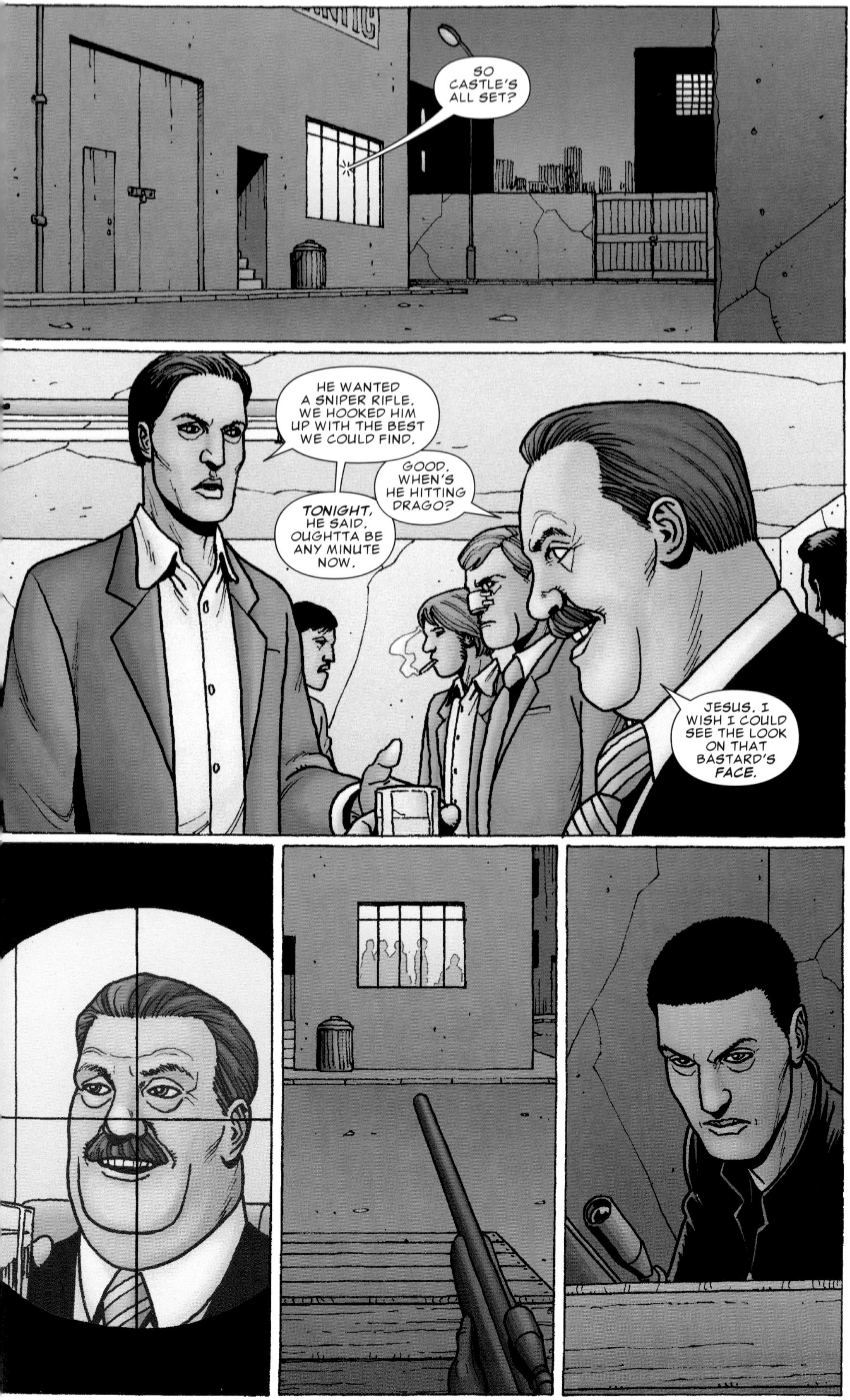
SO CASTLE'S ALL SET?
HE WANTED A SNIPER RIFLE. WE HOOKED HIM UP WITH THE BEST WE COULD FIND.
GOOD. WHEN'S HE HITTING DRAGO?
TONIGHT, HE SAID. OUGHTTA BE ANY MINUTE NOW.
JESUS. I WISH I COULD SEE THE LOOK ON THAT BASTARD'S FACE.

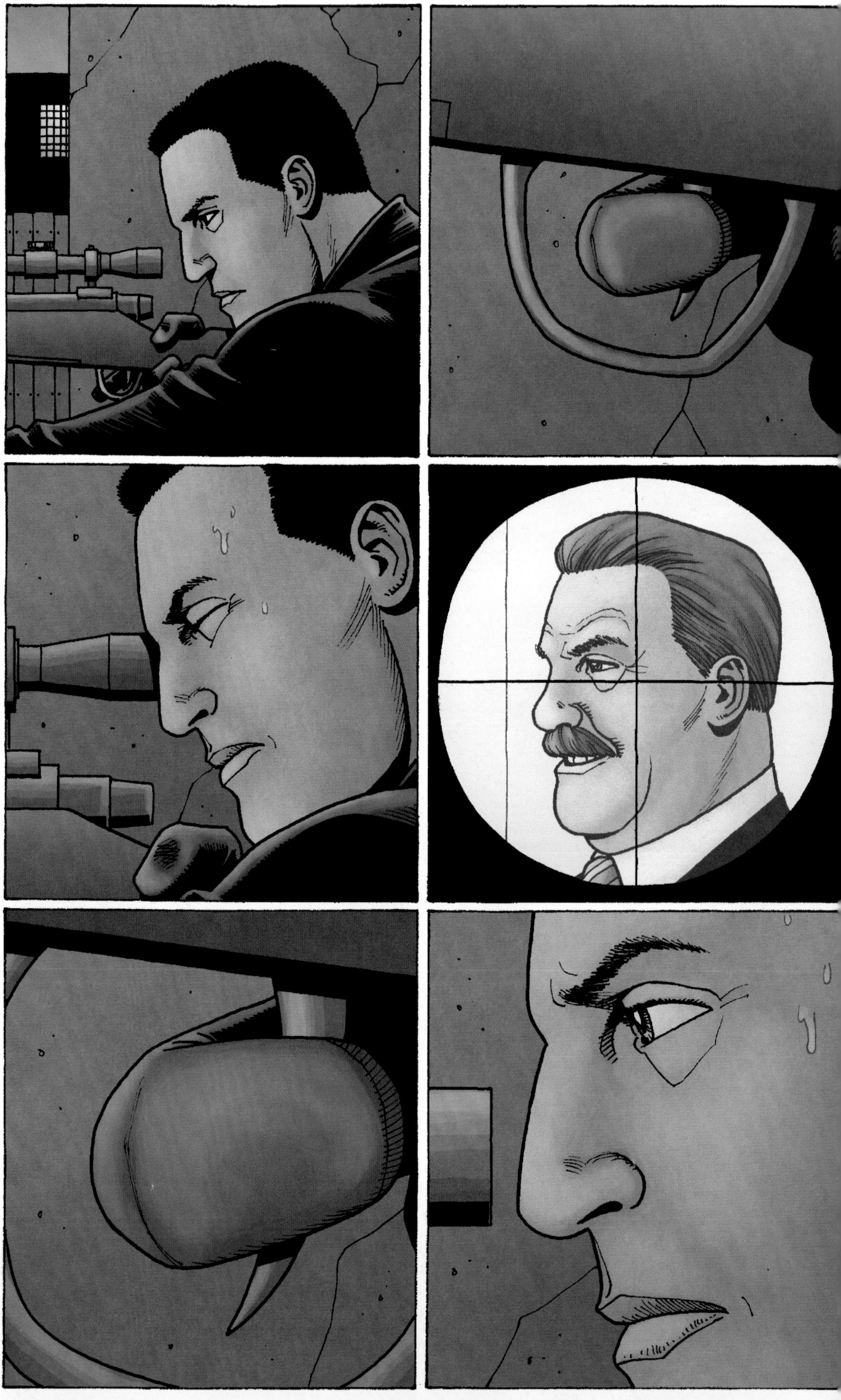

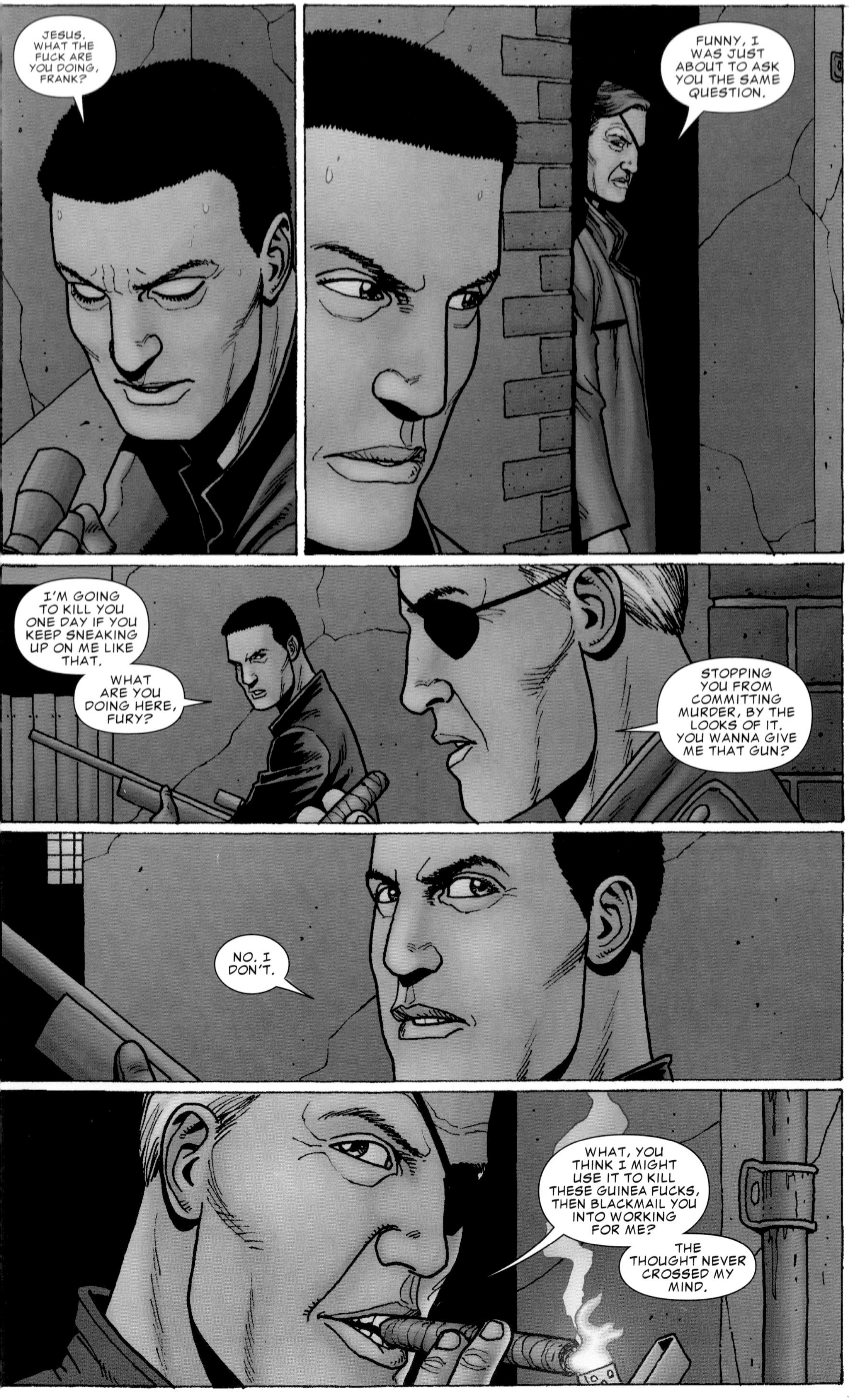
JESUS. WHAT THE FUCK ARE YOU DOING, FRANK?
FUNNY, I WAS JUST ABOUT TO ASK YOU THE SAME QUESTION.
I'M GOING TO KILL YOU ONE DAY IF YOU KEEP SNEAKING UP ON ME LIKE THAT.
WHAT ARE YOU DOING HERE, FURY?
STOPPING YOU FROM COMMITTING MURDER, BY THE LOOKS OF IT. YOU WANNA GIVE ME THAT GUN?
NO. I DON'T.
WHAT, YOU THINK I MIGHT USE IT TO KILL THESE GUINEA FUCKS, THEN BLACKMAIL YOU INTO WORKING FOR ME?
THE THOUGHT NEVER CROSSED MY MIND.

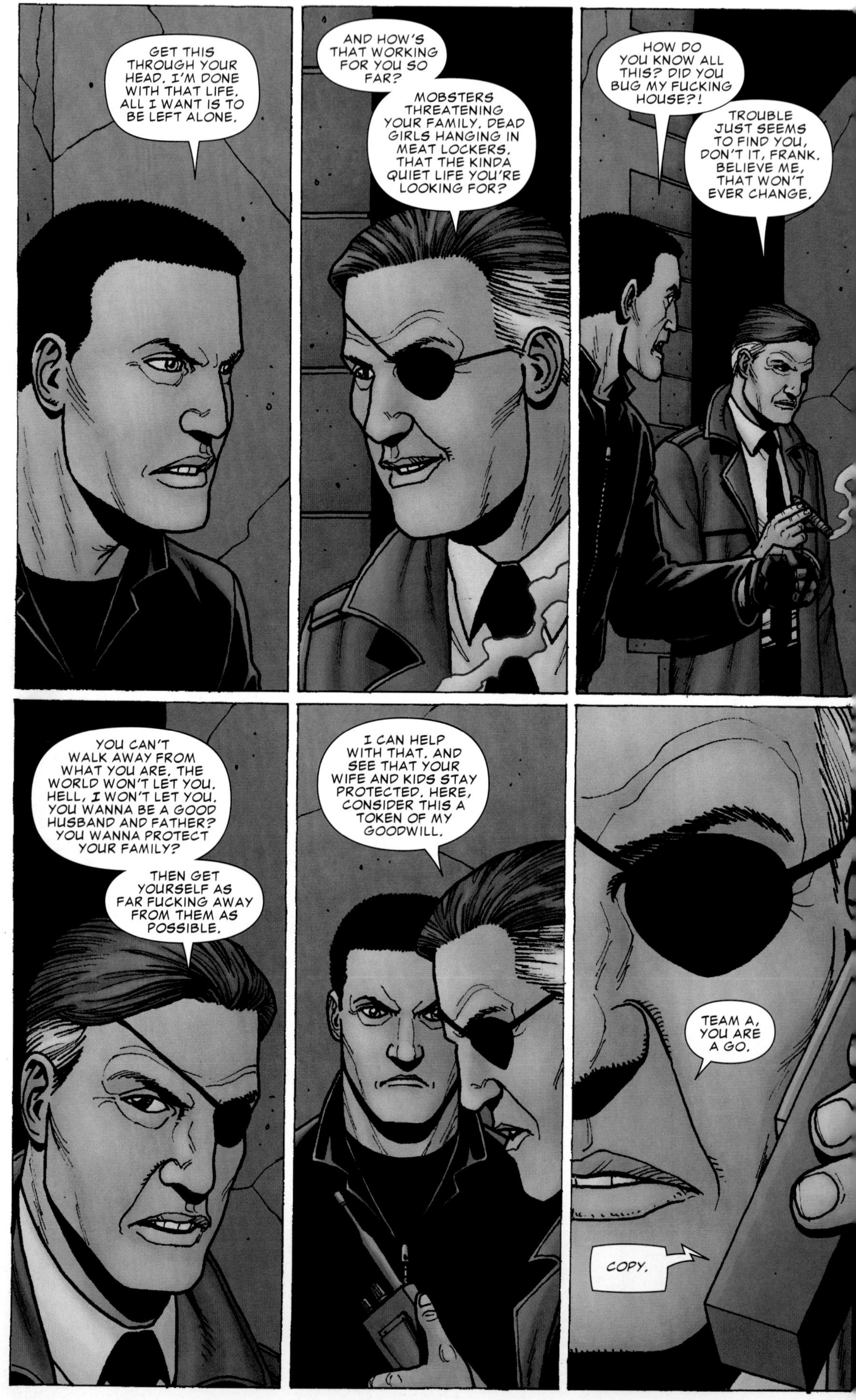
GET THIS THROUGH YOUR HEAD. I'M DONE WITH THAT LIFE. ALL I WANT IS TO BE LEFT ALONE.
AND HOW'S THAT WORKING FOR YOU SO FAR?
MOBSTERS THREATENING YOUR FAMILY. DEAD GIRLS HANGING IN MEAT LOCKERS. THAT THE KINDA QUIET LIFE YOU'RE LOOKING FOR?
HOW DO YOU KNOW ALL THIS? DID YOU BUG MY FUCKING HOUSE?!
TROUBLE JUST SEEMS TO FIND YOU, DON'T IT, FRANK. BELIEVE ME, THAT WON'T EVER CHANGE.
YOU CAN'T WALK AWAY FROM WHAT YOU ARE. THE WORLD WON'T LET YOU. HELL, I WON'T LET YOU. YOU WANNA BE A GOOD HUSBAND AND FATHER? YOU WANNA PROTECT YOUR FAMILY?
THEN GET YOURSELF AS FAR FUCKING AWAY FROM THEM AS POSSIBLE.
I CAN HELP WITH THAT, AND SEE THAT YOUR WIFE AND KIDS STAY PROTECTED. HERE, CONSIDER THIS A TOKEN OF MY GOODWILL.
TEAM A, YOU ARE A GO.
COPY.

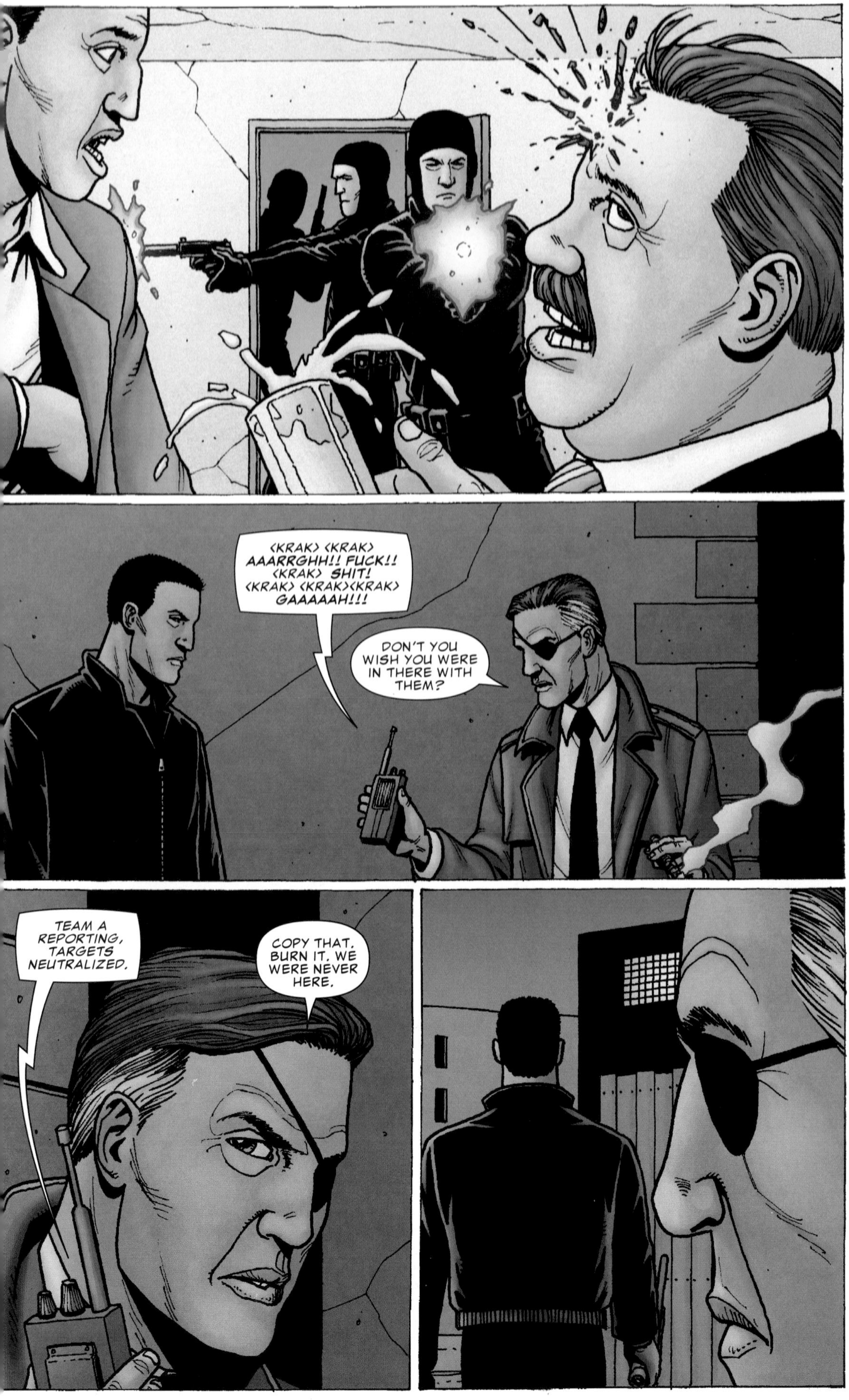
<KRAK> <KRAK> AAARRGHH!! FUCK!! <KRAK> SHIT! <KRAK> <KRAK><KRAK> GAAAAAH!!!
DON'T YOU WISH YOU WERE IN THERE WITH THEM?
TEAM A REPORTING, TARGETS NEUTRALIZED.
COPY THAT. BURN IT. WE WERE NEVER HERE.

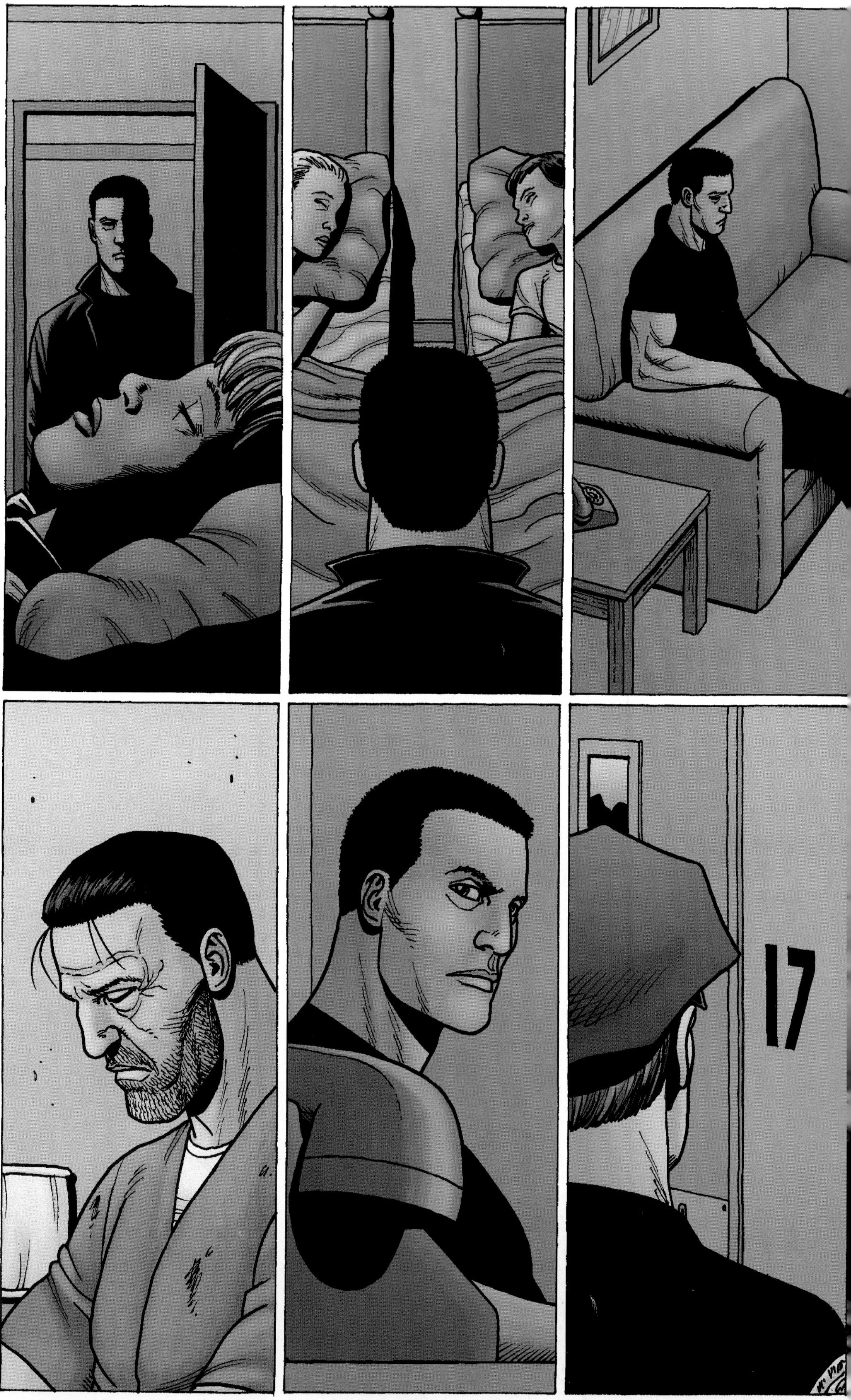
17

YEAH? HELLO?

HELLO? WHO THE FUCK IS THIS?

...

FRANK?

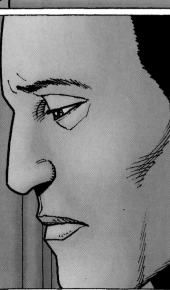

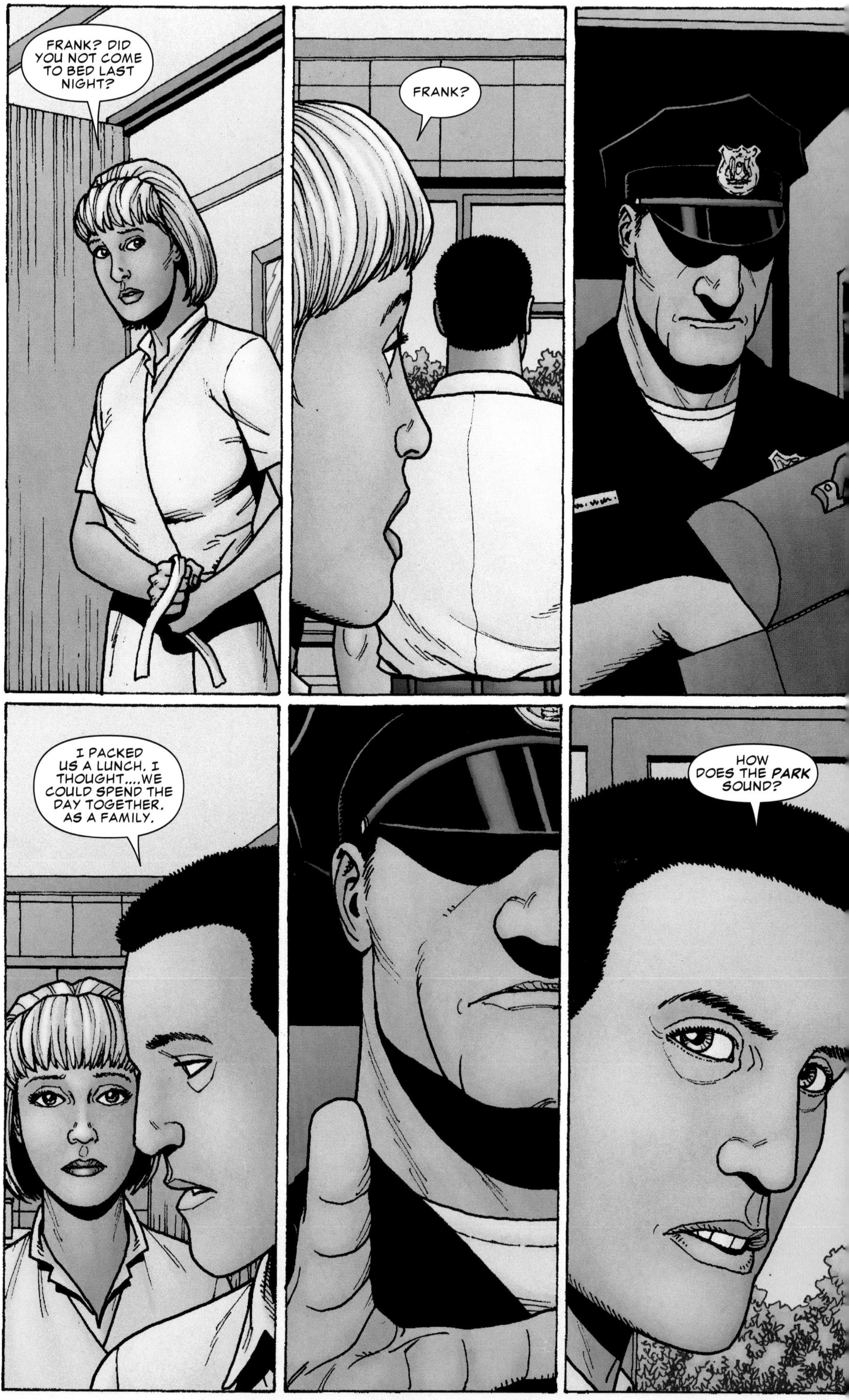
FRANK? DID YOU NOT COME TO BED LAST NIGHT?
FRANK?
I PACKED US A LUNCH. I THOUGHT....WE COULD SPEND THE DAY TOGETHER. AS A FAMILY.
HOW DOES THE *PARK* SOUND?

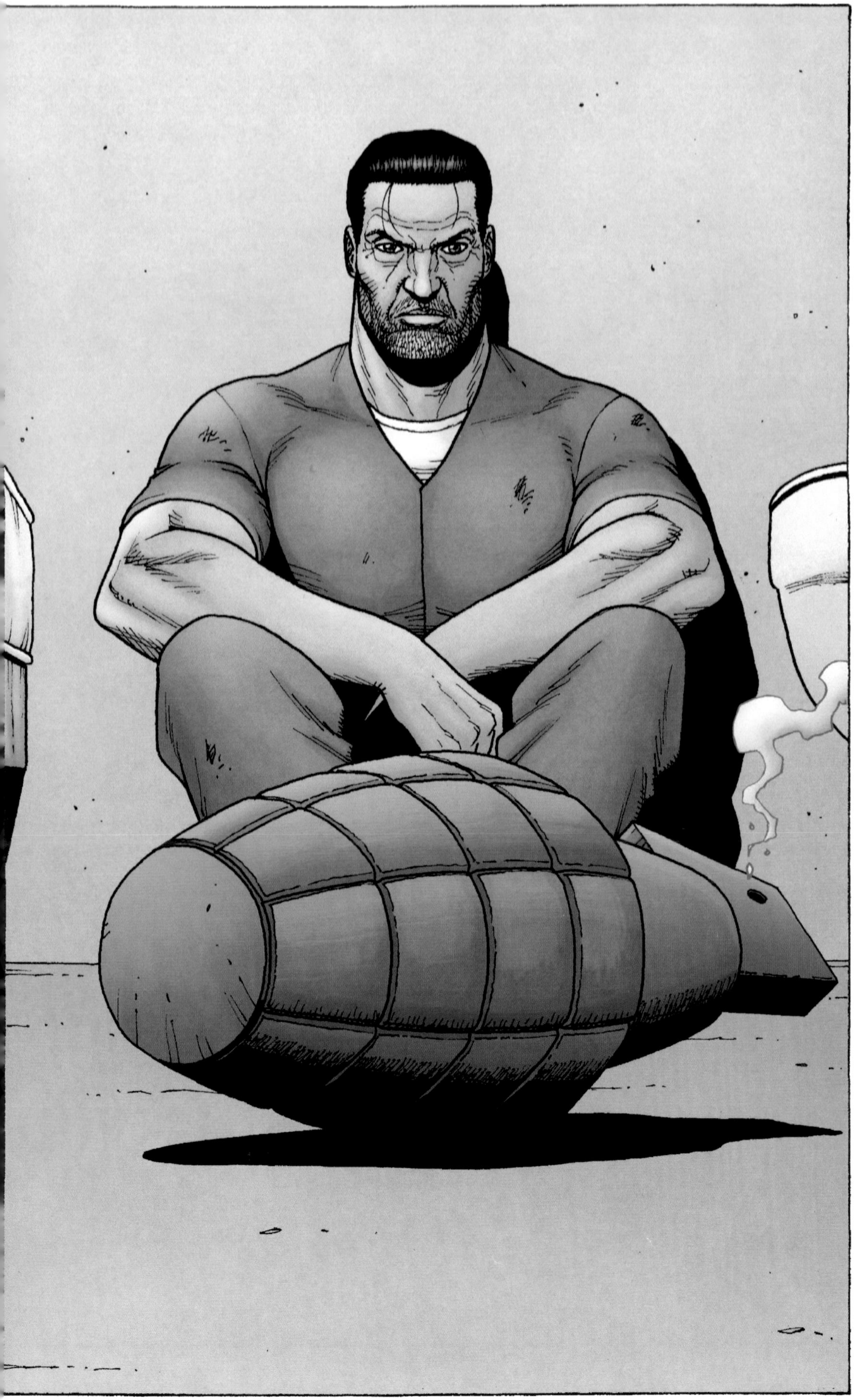

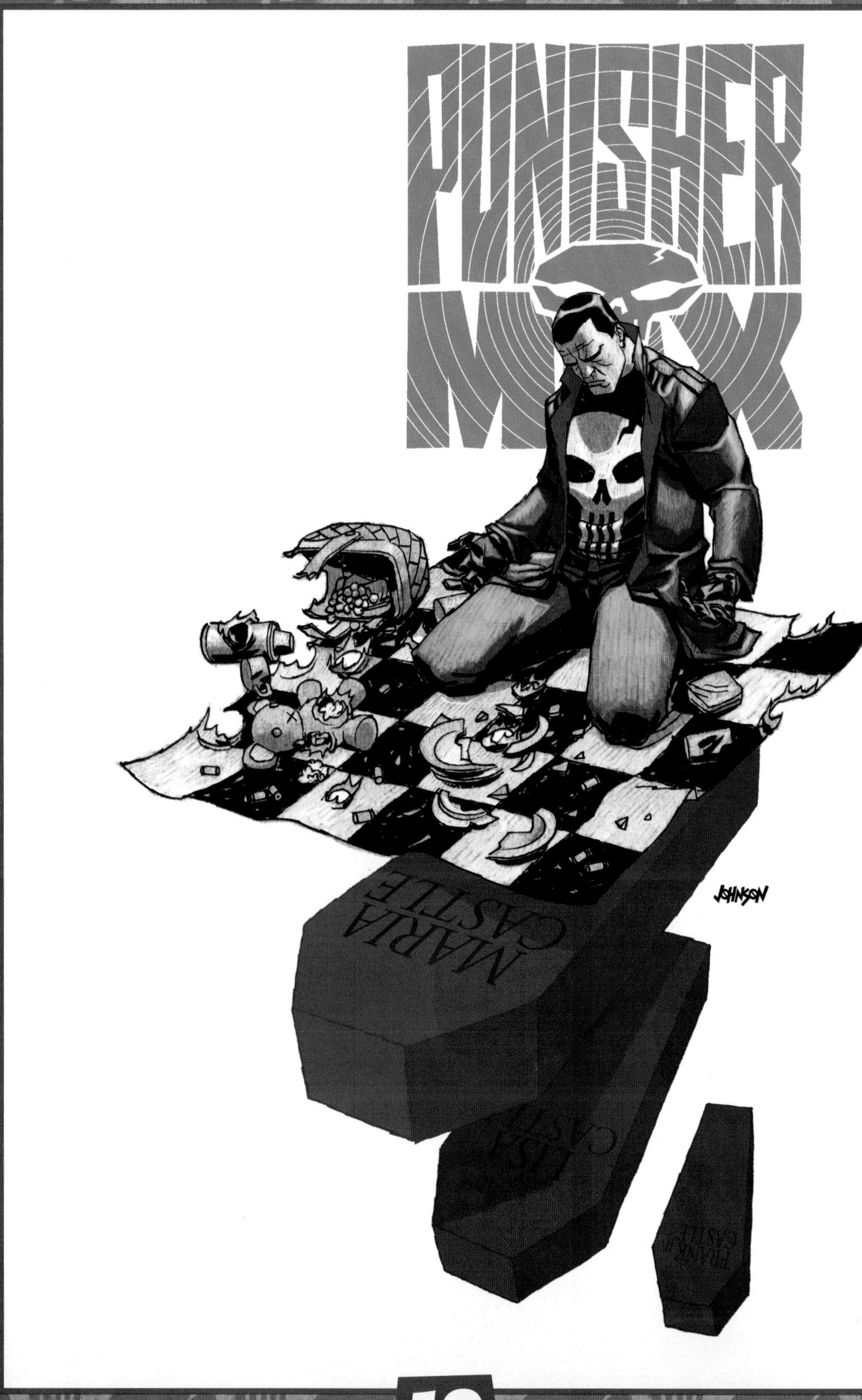
PUNISHER
MAX
JOHNSON
MARIA
CASTLE

16

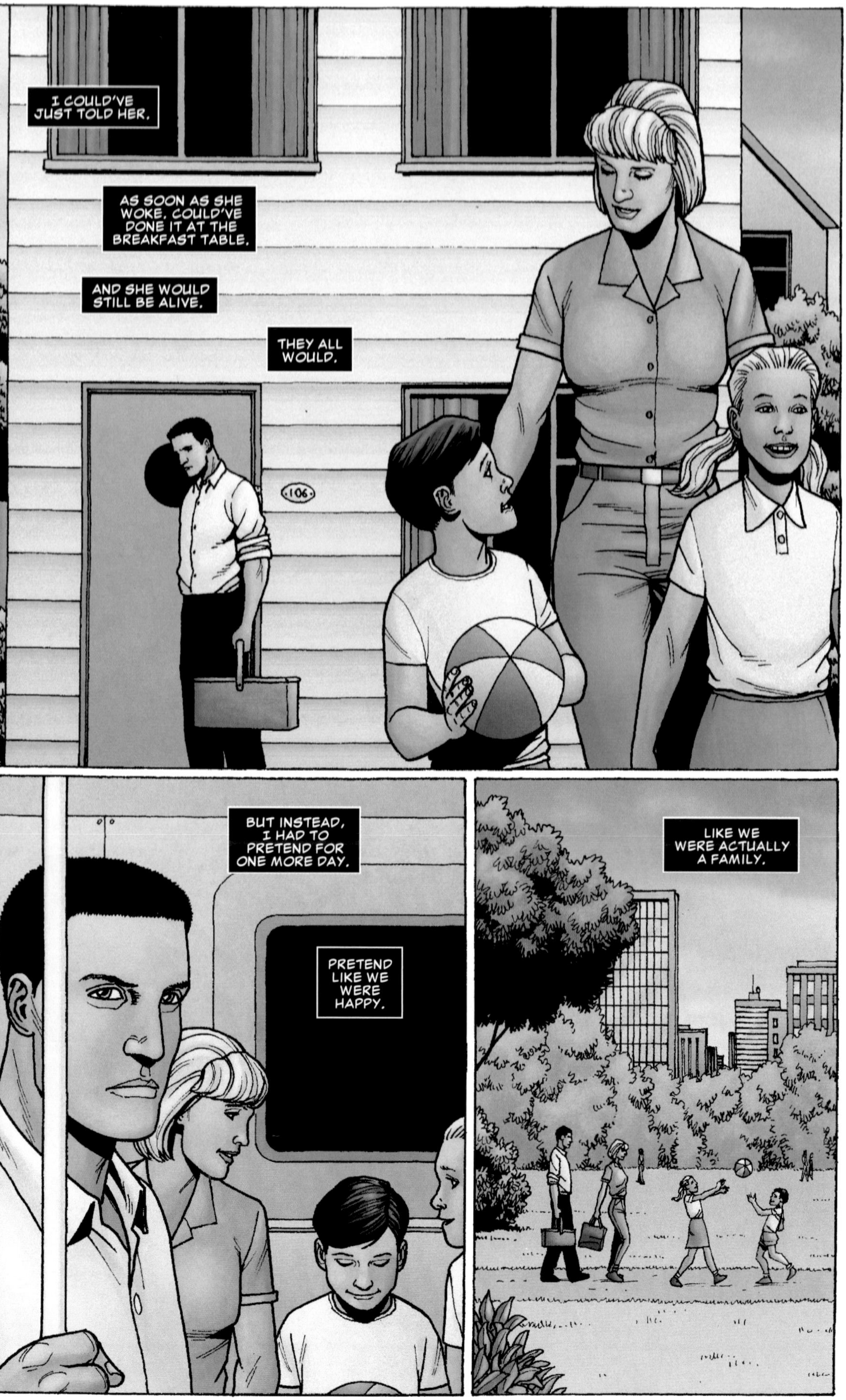
I COULD'VE JUST TOLD HER.
AS SOON AS SHE WOKE. COULD'VE DONE IT AT THE BREAKFAST TABLE.
AND SHE WOULD STILL BE ALIVE.
THEY ALL WOULD.
106
BUT INSTEAD, I HAD TO PRETEND FOR ONE MORE DAY.
PRETEND LIKE WE WERE HAPPY.
LIKE WE WERE ACTUALLY A FAMILY.

I'D STAYED UP ALL NIGHT, SEARCHING FOR THE RIGHT WORDS, BUT WHEN THE MOMENT CAME, I STILL DIDN'T HAVE THEM.

SO I JUST SAT THERE, STARING OFF INTO SPACE, TRYING TO THINK OF A WAY TO SAY IT THAT WOULDN'T MAKE HER CRY.

IF I HADN'T BEEN SO WRAPPED UP IN MY OWN HEAD, MAYBE I WOULD'VE SEEN THEM.

THOSE MEN COMING INTO THE PARK WHO OBVIOUSLY WEREN'T THERE FOR A JOG.

MAYBE I WOULD'VE SMELLED IT ON THE WIND LIKE I ALWAYS DID IN 'NAM. WOULD'VE RECOGNIZED THE AMBUSH UNFOLDING ALL AROUND US.

BUT I DIDN'T.

I DIDN'T SEE A GODDAMN THING.

MARIA...

WHATEVER YOU'VE GOT TO SAY, FRANK, I WISH YOU'D JUST SPIT IT OUT.

I CAN'T DO THIS ANYMORE.

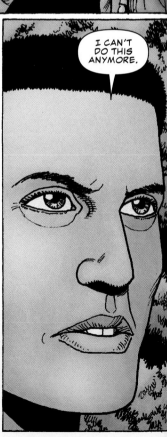

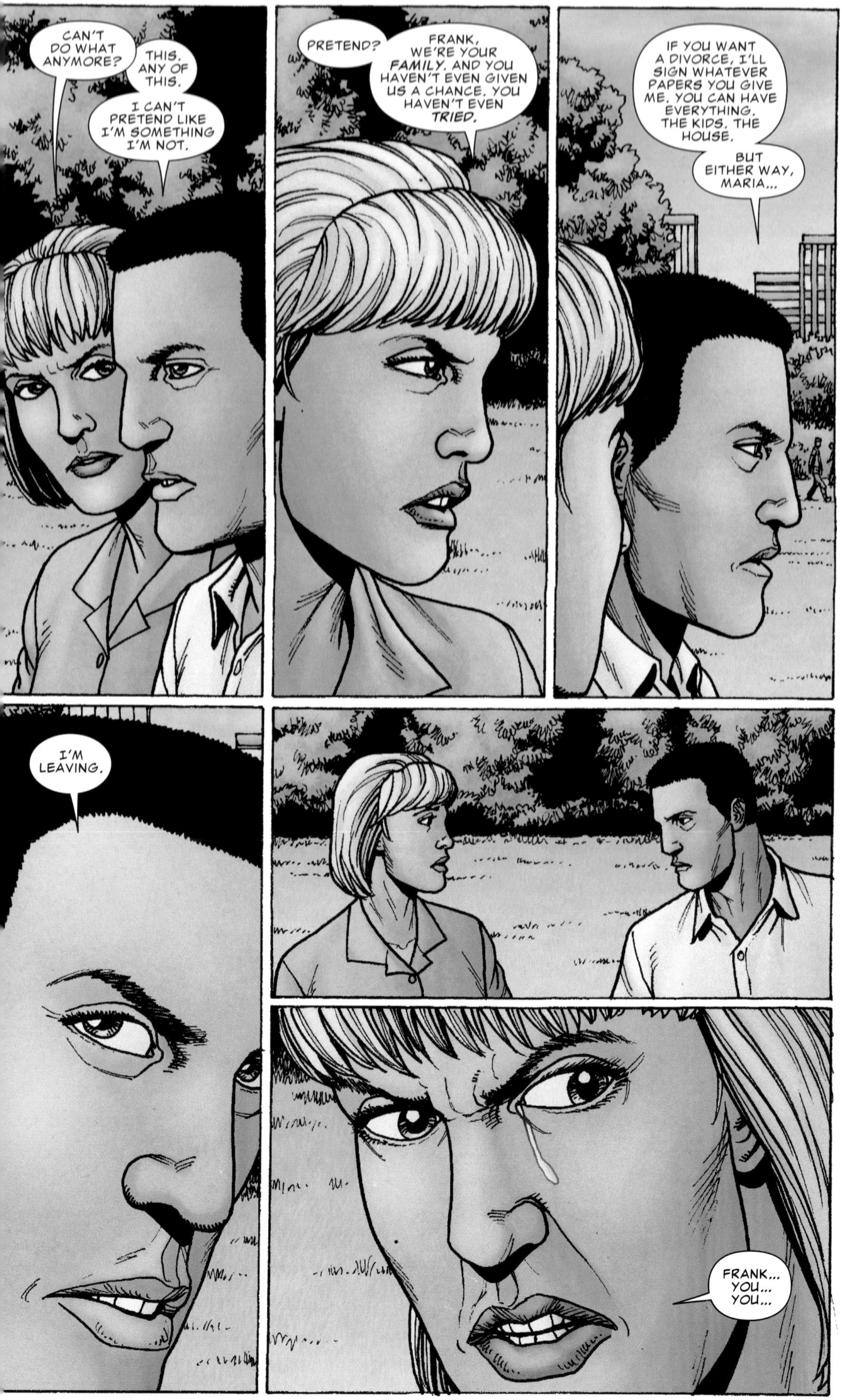

CAN'T DO WHAT ANYMORE?
THIS. ANY OF THIS.
I CAN'T PRETEND LIKE I'M SOMETHING I'M NOT.
PRETEND?
FRANK, WE'RE YOUR *FAMILY*. AND YOU HAVEN'T EVEN GIVEN US A CHANCE. YOU HAVEN'T EVEN *TRIED*.
IF YOU WANT A DIVORCE, I'LL SIGN WHATEVER PAPERS YOU GIVE ME. YOU CAN HAVE EVERYTHING. THE KIDS. THE HOUSE.
BUT EITHER WAY, MARIA...
I'M LEAVING.
FRANK... YOU... YOU...

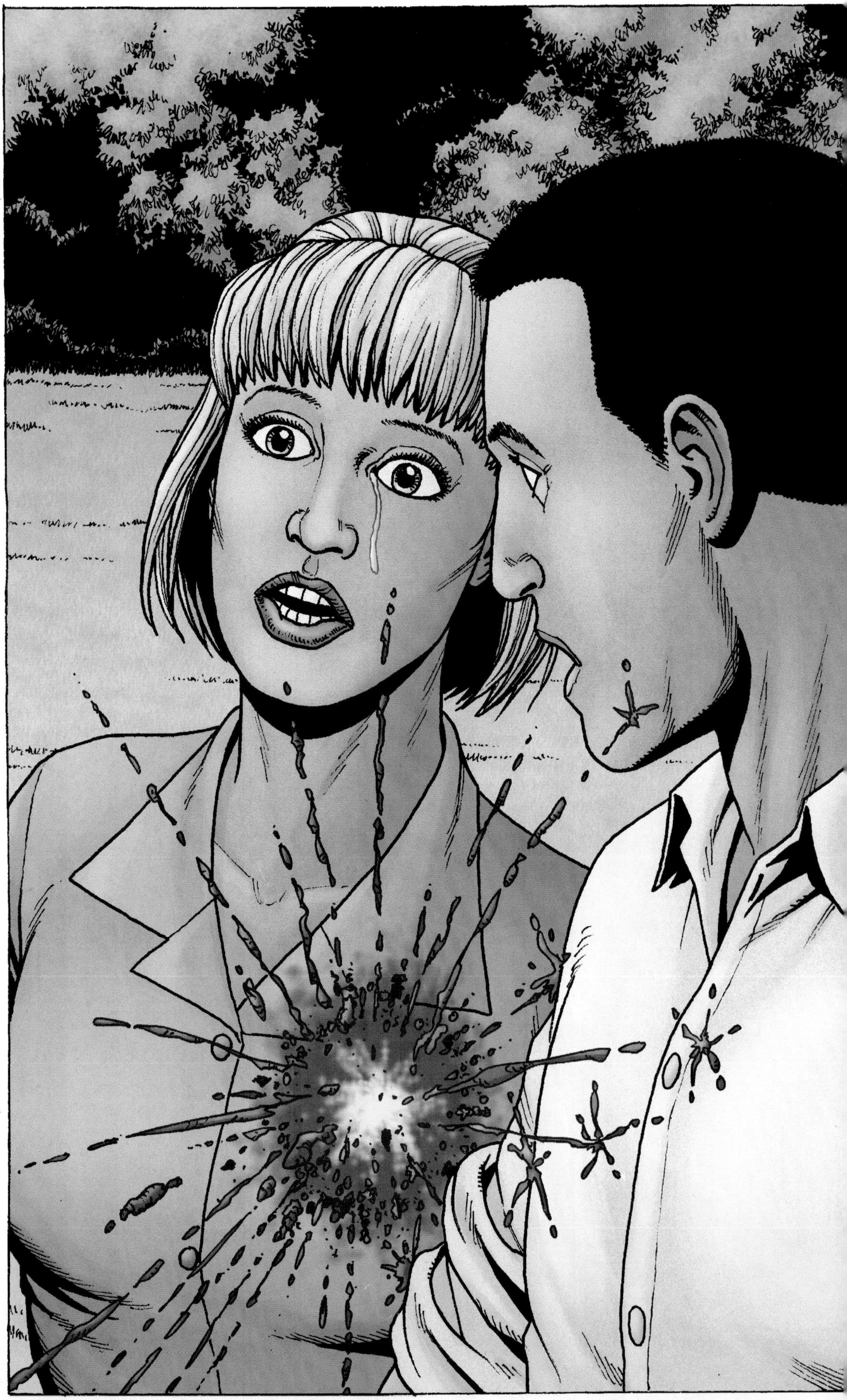

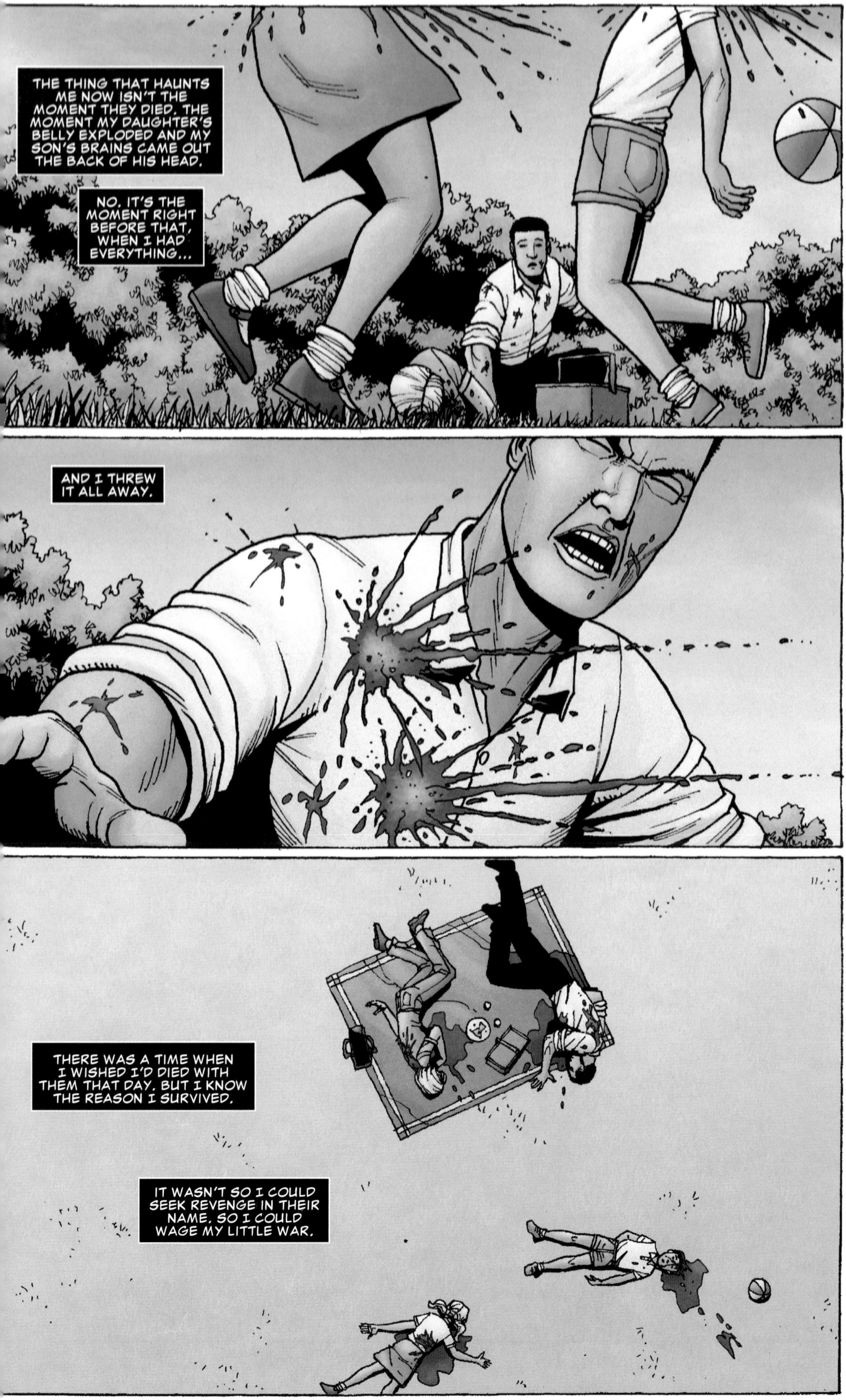
THE THING THAT HAUNTS ME NOW ISN'T THE MOMENT THEY DIED. THE MOMENT MY DAUGHTER'S BELLY EXPLODED AND MY SON'S BRAINS CAME OUT THE BACK OF HIS HEAD.
NO, IT'S THE MOMENT RIGHT BEFORE THAT, WHEN I HAD EVERYTHING...
AND I THREW IT ALL AWAY.
THERE WAS A TIME WHEN I WISHED I'D DIED WITH THEM THAT DAY. BUT I KNOW THE REASON I SURVIVED.
IT WASN'T SO I COULD SEEK REVENGE IN THEIR NAME. SO I COULD WAGE MY LITTLE WAR.

IT WAS SO I COULD SUFFER.

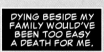

DYING BESIDE MY FAMILY WOULD'VE BEEN TOO EASY A DEATH FOR ME.

WHAT I DESERVED WAS PAIN. YEARS OF IT. I DESERVED TO BE CAST DOWN AMONG THE LOWEST OF THE LOW. SURROUNDED BY NOTHING BUT HORROR AND DEATH. NO REST. NO JOY. I DESERVED A LIFETIME OF SUFFERING.

A LIFETIME OF PUNISHMENT.

AND EVEN NOW, AFTER SO MANY YEARS, WHEN I DARE STOP AND WONDER...

HAS IT FINALLY BEEN ENOUGH?

THE ANSWER COMES FROM SOMEWHERE DEEP INSIDE...

NO.

IT WILL NEVER BE ENOUGH.

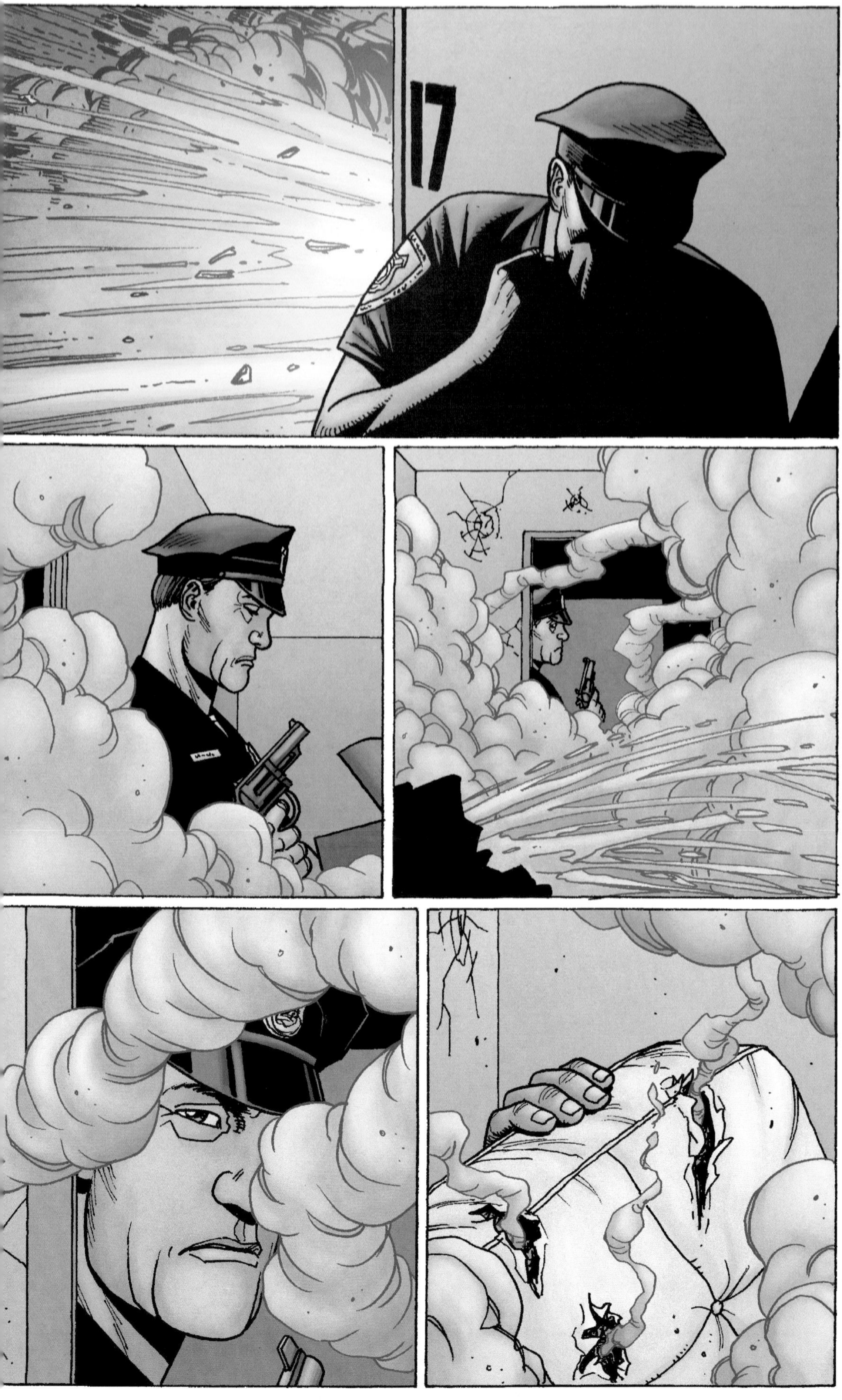
17

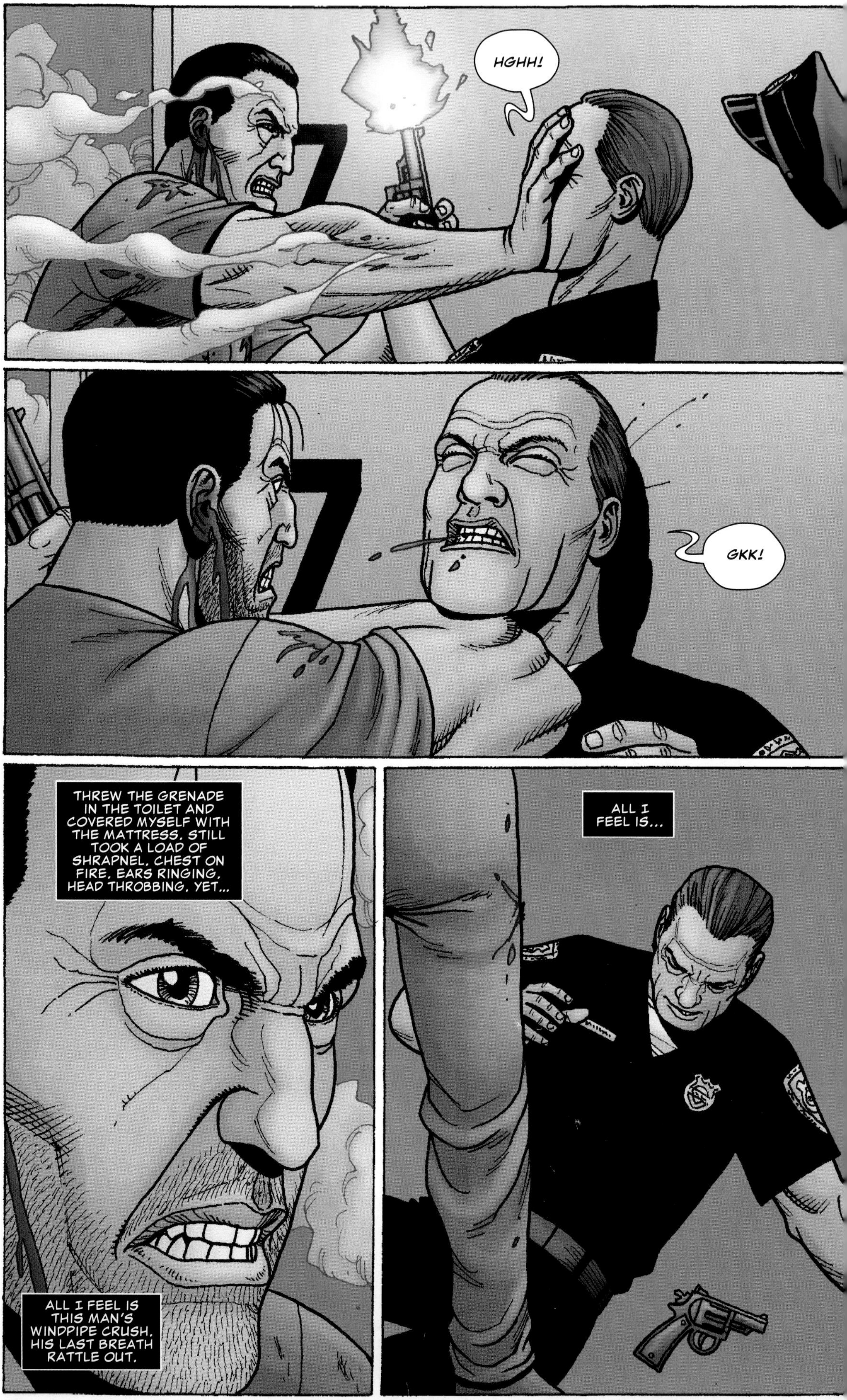
HGHH!
GKK!
THREW THE GRENADE IN THE TOILET AND COVERED MYSELF WITH THE MATTRESS. STILL TOOK A LOAD OF SHRAPNEL. CHEST ON FIRE. EARS RINGING. HEAD THROBBING. YET...
ALL I FEEL IS THIS MAN'S WINDPIPE CRUSH. HIS LAST BREATH RATTLE OUT.
ALL I FEEL IS...

GOOD.

WELL WELL WELL, HERE WE ARE...

THE PUNISHER AND THE BIG JESUS...

20

ALONE AT LAST.

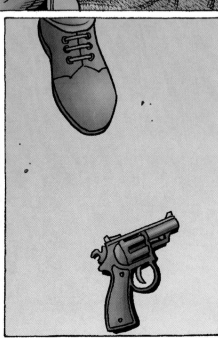

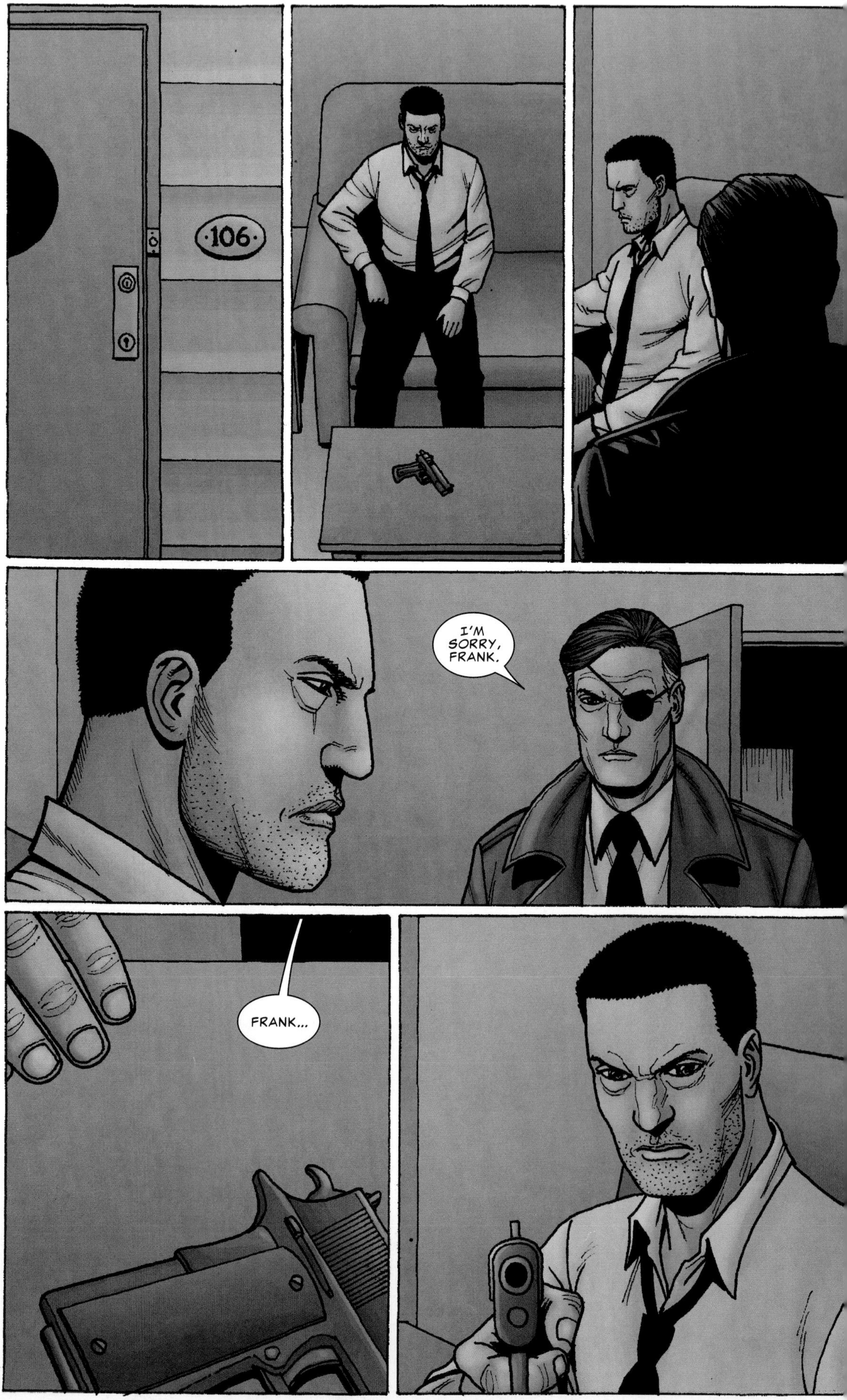
·106·
I'M SORRY, FRANK.
FRANK...

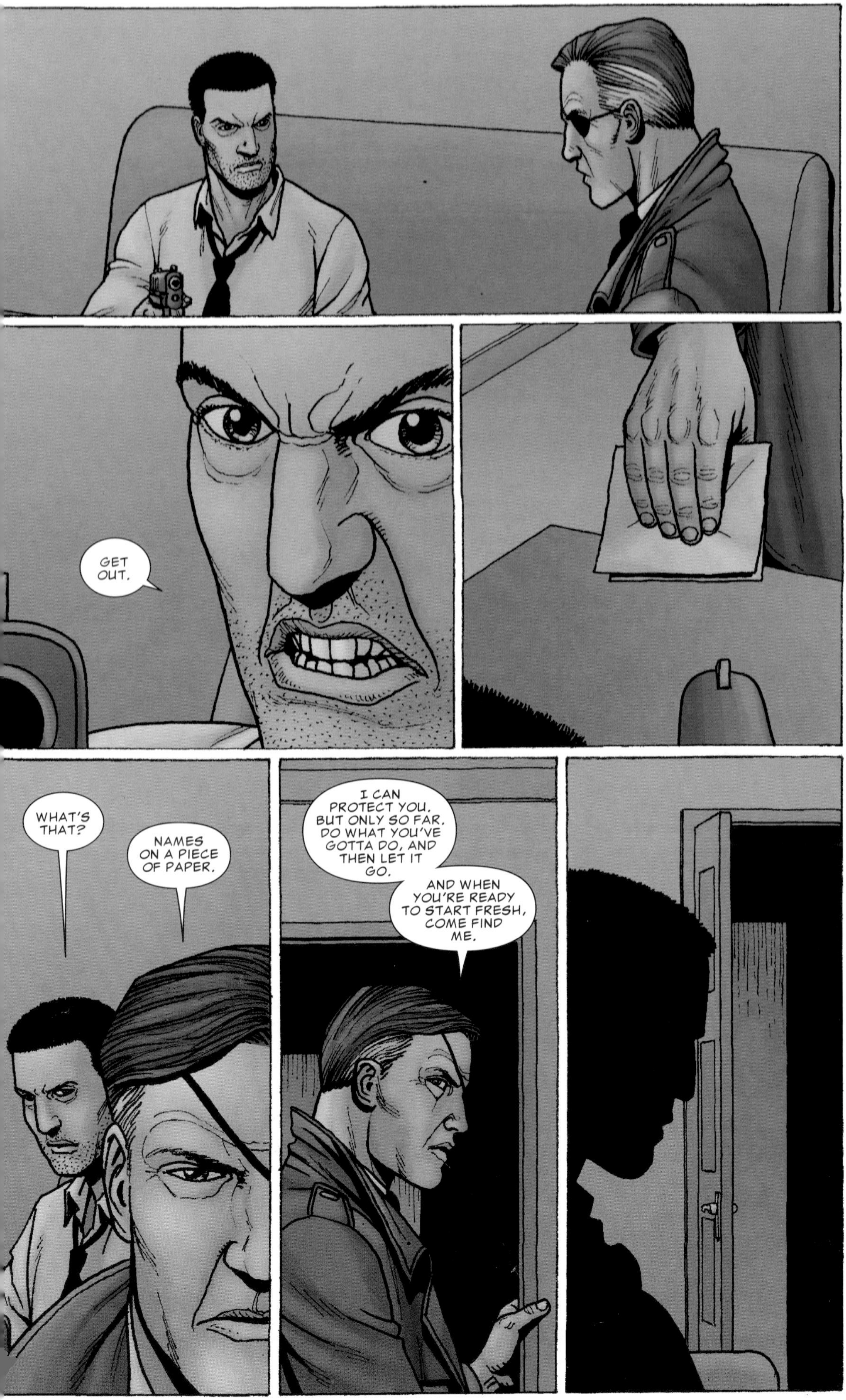
GET OUT.
WHAT'S THAT?
NAMES ON A PIECE OF PAPER.
I CAN PROTECT YOU. BUT ONLY SO FAR. DO WHAT YOU'VE GOTTA DO, AND THEN LET IT GO.
AND WHEN YOU'RE READY TO START FRESH, COME FIND ME.

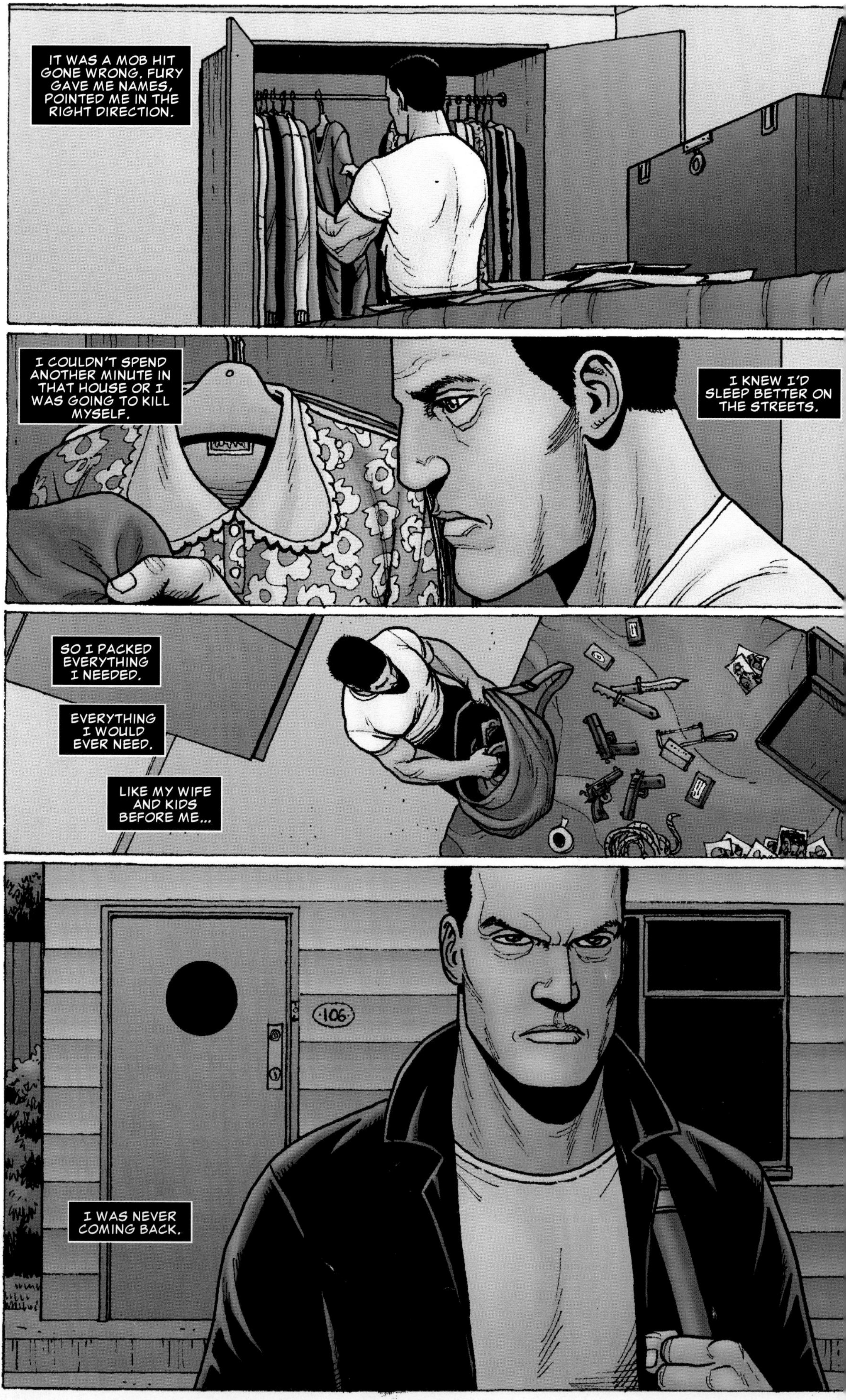
IT WAS A MOB HIT GONE WRONG. FURY GAVE ME NAMES, POINTED ME IN THE RIGHT DIRECTION.
I COULDN'T SPEND ANOTHER MINUTE IN THAT HOUSE OR I WAS GOING TO KILL MYSELF.
I KNEW I'D SLEEP BETTER ON THE STREETS.
SO I PACKED EVERYTHING I NEEDED.
EVERYTHING I WOULD EVER NEED.
LIKE MY WIFE AND KIDS BEFORE ME...
106
I WAS NEVER COMING BACK.

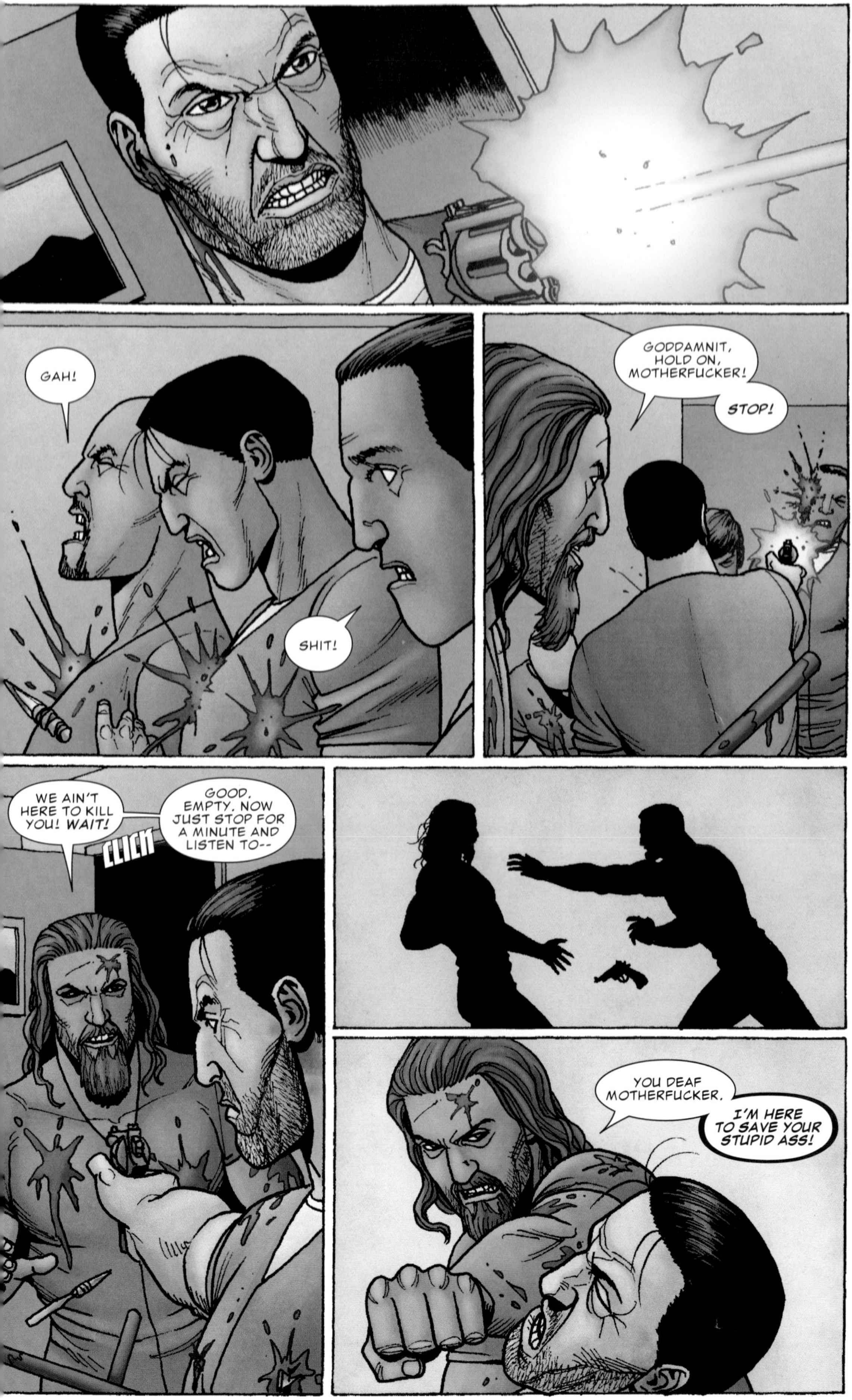
GAH!
SHIT!
GODDAMNIT, HOLD ON, MOTHERFUCKER!
STOP!
WE AIN'T HERE TO KILL YOU! *WAIT!*
CLICK
GOOD. EMPTY. NOW JUST STOP FOR A MINUTE AND LISTEN TO--
YOU DEAF MOTHERFUCKER.
I'M HERE TO SAVE YOUR STUPID ASS!

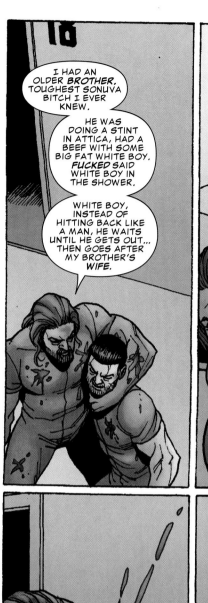

I HAD AN OLDER *BROTHER.* TOUGHEST SONUVA BITCH I EVER KNEW.

HE WAS DOING A STINT IN ATTICA, HAD A BEEF WITH SOME BIG FAT WHITE BOY. *FUCKED* SAID WHITE BOY IN THE SHOWER.

WHITE BOY, INSTEAD OF HITTING BACK LIKE A MAN, HE WAITS UNTIL HE GETS OUT... THEN GOES AFTER MY BROTHER'S *WIFE.*

WHITE BOY HAD A DOZEN CRACKHEADS RUN A TRAIN ON HER. THEN HE KILLED HER. MY BROTHER COMES AFTER HIM, WHITE BOY KILLS HIM TOO.

ME, I HEAR ABOUT ALL THIS WHILE STUCK IN HERE, SERVING CONSECUTIVE LIFE SENTENCES. I HEAR THAT BIG WHITE BOY'S COME UP IN THE WORLD A BIT SINCE THEN, BECOME A GODDAMN *KINGPIN.*

YOU HEARING ME NOW, FRANK! *WILSON FUCKING FISK* KILLED MY BROTHER!

AND CAN'T *NOBODY* FUCKING TOUCH HIM!

HEH.

NOBODY BUT *YOU.*

NOW WHAT SAY WE GET YOUR ASS OVER THAT WALL?

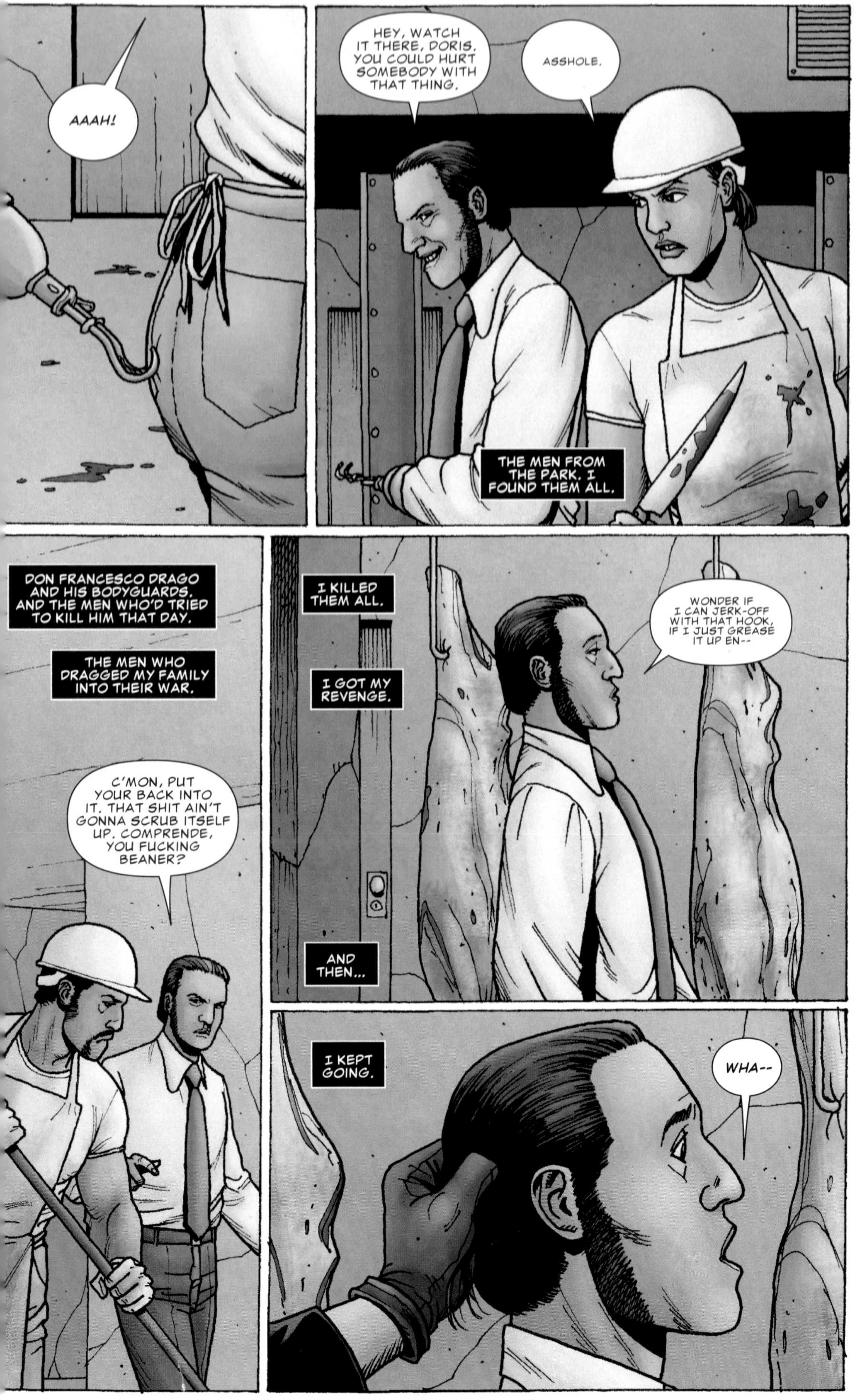
AAAH!
HEY, WATCH IT THERE, DORIS. YOU COULD HURT SOMEBODY WITH THAT THING.
ASSHOLE.
THE MEN FROM THE PARK. I FOUND THEM ALL.
DON FRANCESCO DRAGO AND HIS BODYGUARDS. AND THE MEN WHO'D TRIED TO KILL HIM THAT DAY.
THE MEN WHO DRAGGED MY FAMILY INTO THEIR WAR.
C'MON, PUT YOUR BACK INTO IT. THAT SHIT AIN'T GONNA SCRUB ITSELF UP. COMPRENDE, YOU FUCKING BEANER?
I KILLED THEM ALL.
I GOT MY REVENGE.
WONDER IF I CAN JERK-OFF WITH THAT HOOK, IF I JUST GREASE IT UP EN--
AND THEN...
I KEPT GOING.
WHA--

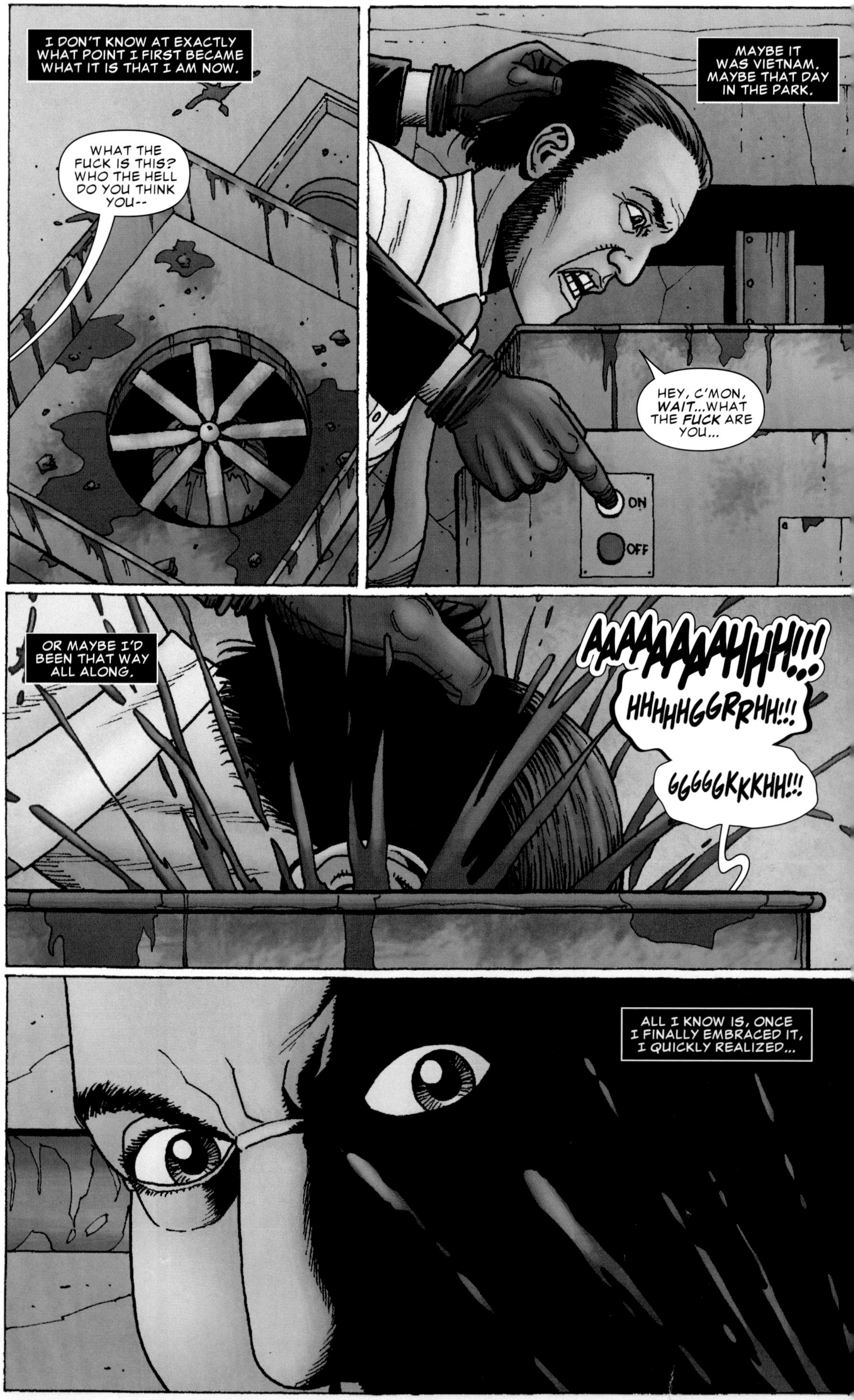

I DON'T KNOW AT EXACTLY WHAT POINT I FIRST BECAME WHAT IT IS THAT I AM NOW.
WHAT THE FUCK IS THIS? WHO THE HELL DO YOU THINK YOU--
MAYBE IT WAS VIETNAM. MAYBE THAT DAY IN THE PARK.
HEY, C'MON, WAIT...WHAT THE FUCK ARE YOU...
ON
OFF
OR MAYBE I'D BEEN THAT WAY ALL ALONG.
AAAAAAAAHHH!!!
HHHHHGGRRHH!!!
GGGGGKKHH!!!
ALL I KNOW IS, ONCE I FINALLY EMBRACED IT, I QUICKLY REALIZED...

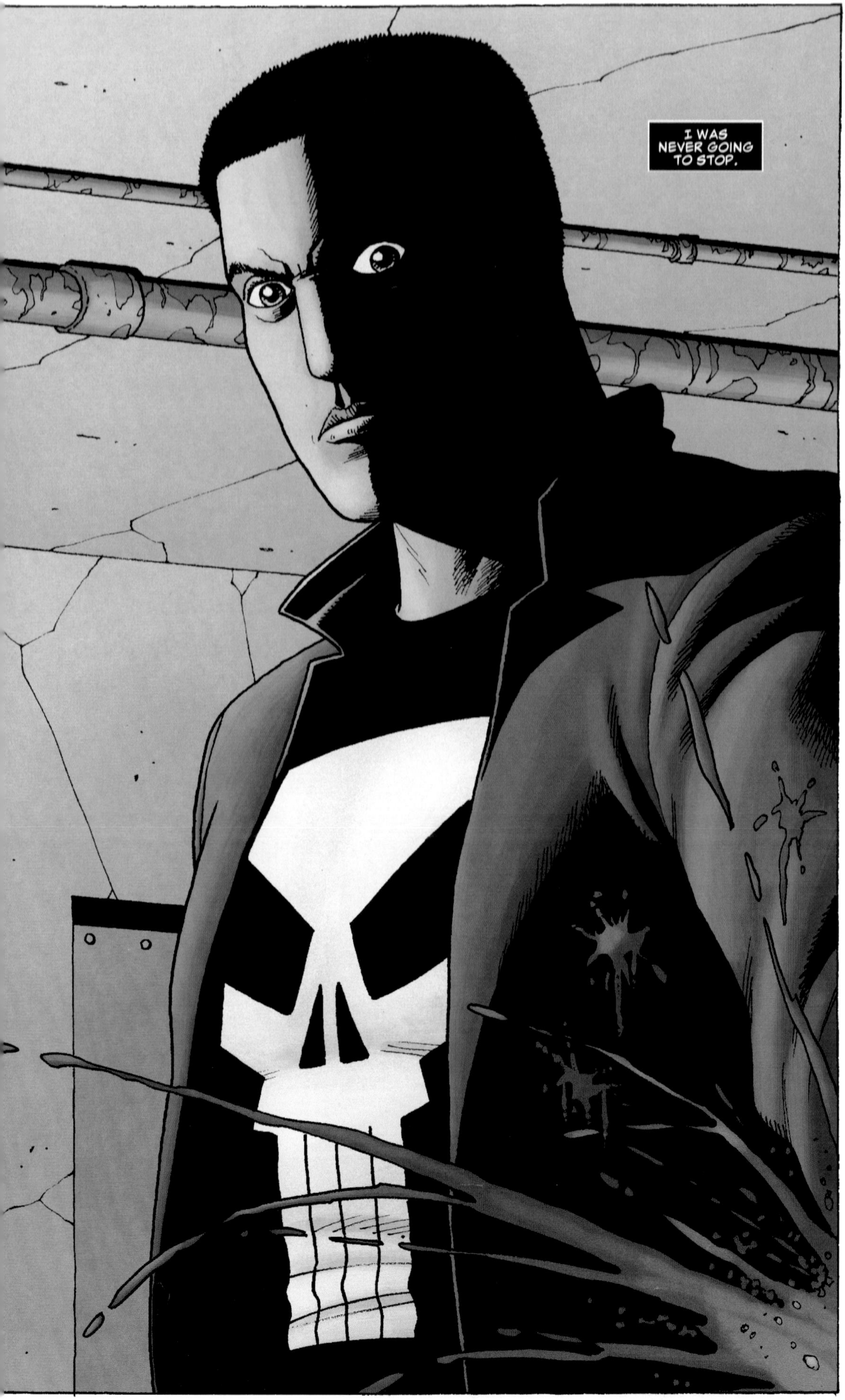
I WAS NEVER GOING TO STOP.

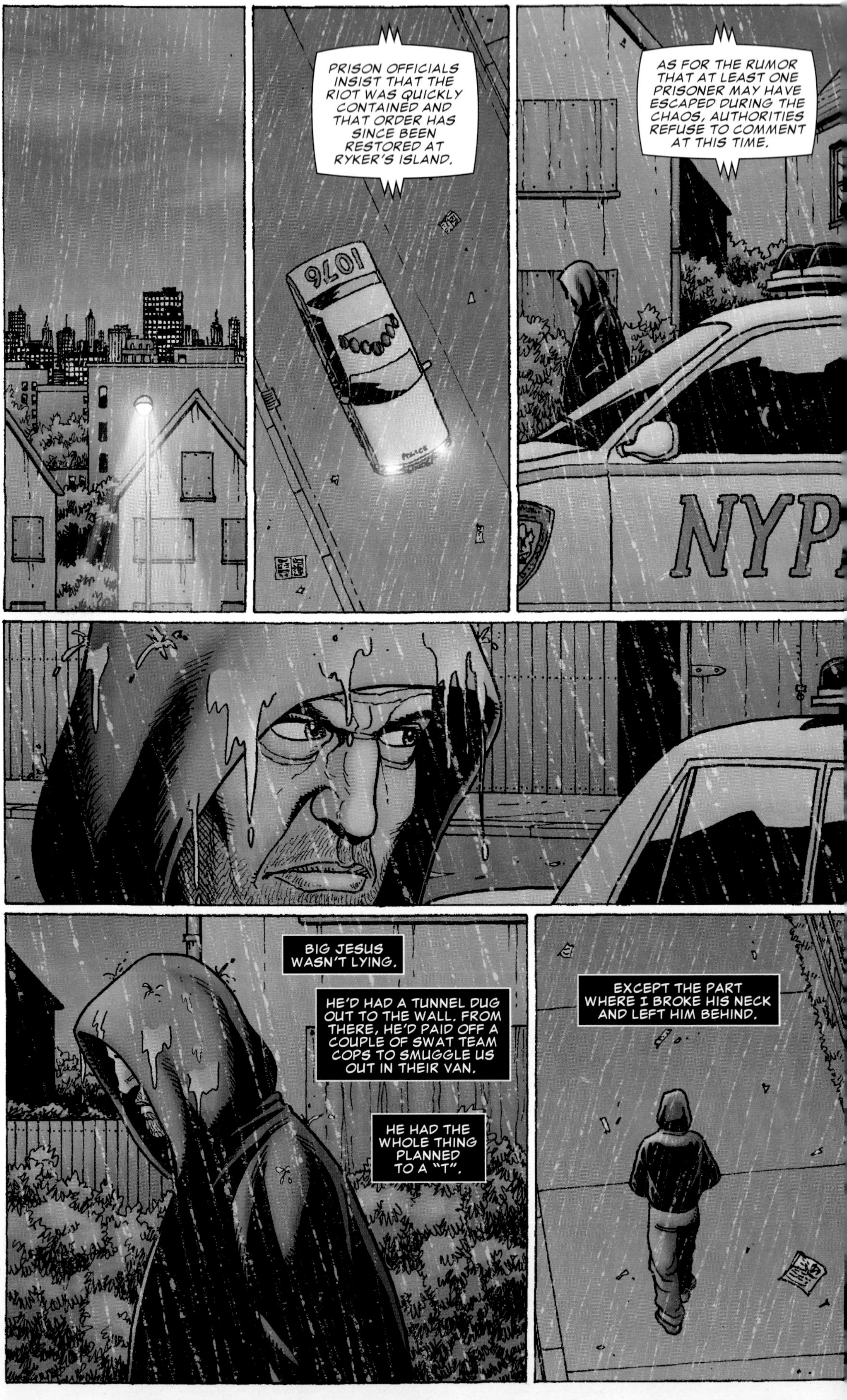
PRISON OFFICIALS INSIST THAT THE RIOT WAS QUICKLY CONTAINED AND THAT ORDER HAS SINCE BEEN RESTORED AT RYKER'S ISLAND.
1076
AS FOR THE RUMOR THAT AT LEAST ONE PRISONER MAY HAVE ESCAPED DURING THE CHAOS, AUTHORITIES REFUSE TO COMMENT AT THIS TIME.
NYP
BIG JESUS WASN'T LYING.
HE'D HAD A TUNNEL DUG OUT TO THE WALL. FROM THERE, HE'D PAID OFF A COUPLE OF SWAT TEAM COPS TO SMUGGLE US OUT IN THEIR VAN.
HE HAD THE WHOLE THING PLANNED TO A "T".
EXCEPT THE PART WHERE I BROKE HIS NECK AND LEFT HIM BEHIND.

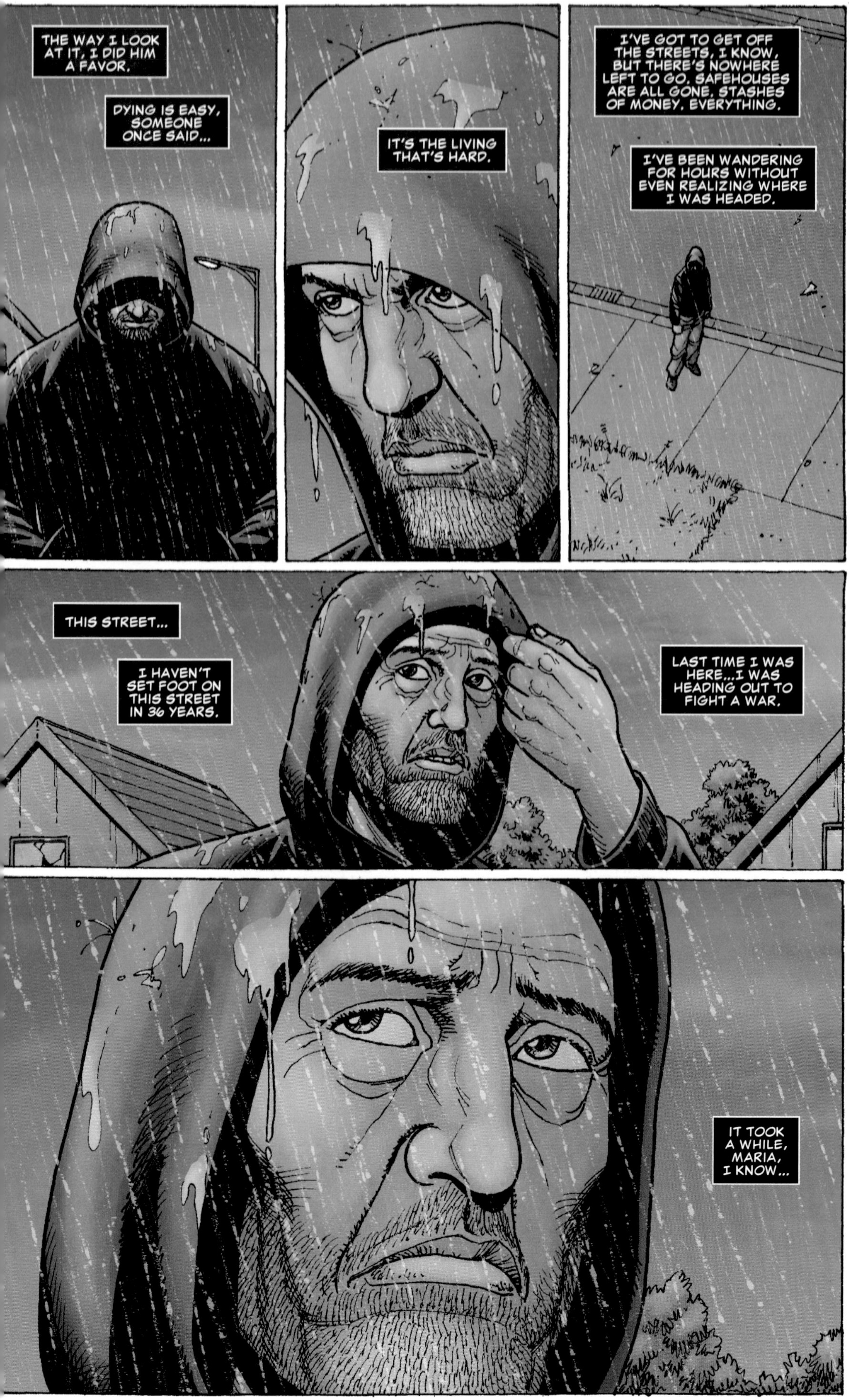
THE WAY I LOOK AT IT, I DID HIM A FAVOR.
DYING IS EASY, SOMEONE ONCE SAID...
IT'S THE LIVING THAT'S HARD.
I'VE GOT TO GET OFF THE STREETS, I KNOW, BUT THERE'S NOWHERE LEFT TO GO. SAFEHOUSES ARE ALL GONE. STASHES OF MONEY. EVERYTHING.
I'VE BEEN WANDERING FOR HOURS WITHOUT EVEN REALIZING WHERE I WAS HEADED.
THIS STREET...
I HAVEN'T SET FOOT ON THIS STREET IN 36 YEARS.
LAST TIME I WAS HERE...I WAS HEADING OUT TO FIGHT A WAR.
IT TOOK A WHILE, MARIA, I KNOW...

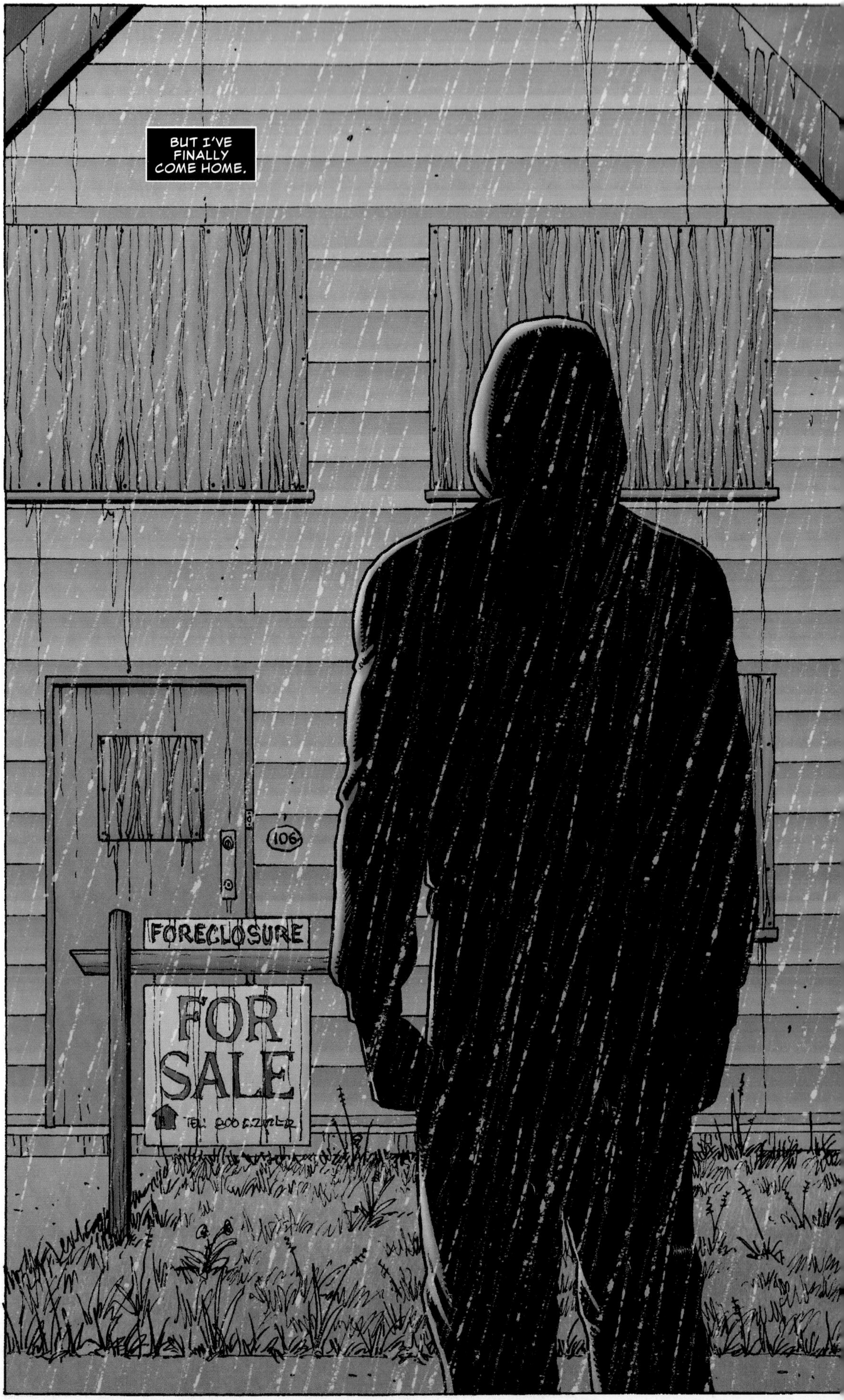
BUT I'VE FINALLY COME HOME.
106
FORECLOSURE
FOR SALE